Living (Il)legalities in Brazil

Reflecting on some of Brazil's foremost challenges, this book considers the porous relationship between legality and illegality in a country that presages political and societal changes in hitherto unprecedented dimensions.

It brings together work by established scholars from Brazil, Europe and the United States to think through how (il)legalities are produced and represented at the level of institutions, (daily) practice and culture. Through a transdisciplinary approach, the chapters cover issues including informal work practices (e.g. street vendors), urban squatter movements and migration. Alongside social practices, the volume features close analyses of cultural practices and cultural production, including migrant literature, punk music and indigenous art.

The question of (il)legalities resonates beyond Brazil's borders, as concepts such as "lawfare" have crept into vocabularies, and countries the world over grapple with issues like state interference, fake news and the definition of "illegal" migration. This is valuable reading for scholars in Brazilian and Latin American Studies, as well as those working in literary and cultural studies, anthropology, sociology, geography and political science.

Sara Brandellero is Assistant Professor in Brazilian Literature and Culture at Leiden University, the Netherlands, where she is co-Chair of the Latin American Studies programmes. Her research focuses on Brazilian literature and film, and Lusophone cultures more broadly. Her publications include the book *On a Knife-Edge: The Poetry of João Cabral de Melo Neto* (2011) and the edited volume *The Brazilian Road Movie* (2013).

Derek Pardue, PhD, is Associate Professor of Brazilian Studies within the Global Studies Department at Aarhus University in Denmark. His scholarship focuses on issues of migration, and urbanism throughout the Black Atlantic, specifically the Luso-African world of Brazil, Portugal and Cape Verde.

Georg Wink, PhD, is Associate Professor of Brazilian Studies and Director of the Centre for Latin American Studies at the University of Copenhagen. His research focuses on contemporary Brazilian society, politics and culture with special emphasis on the rise of the "new right" in Brazil.

Living (Il)legalities in Brazil

Practices, Narratives and Institutions in a Country on the Edge

Edited by
Sara Brandellero, Derek Pardue and Georg Wink

Routledge
Taylor & Francis Group
LONDON AND NEW YORK

First published 2020
by Routledge
2 Park Square, Milton Park, Abingdon, Oxon OX14 4RN

and by Routledge
52 Vanderbilt Avenue, New York, NY 10017

Routledge is an imprint of the Taylor & Francis Group, an informa business

British Library Cataloguing-in-Publication Data
A catalogue record for this book is available from the British Library

Library of Congress Cataloging-in-Publication Data
A catalog record has been requested for this book

ISBN: 978-0-367-36393-2 (hbk)
ISBN: 978-0-429-34563-0 (ebk)

Typeset in Times New Roman
by Newgen Publishing UK

We dedicate this book to the former residents of the Wilton Paes de Almeida building, featured in the introduction of this volume, a mixture of survivors and victims on many different levels. The building collapsed from a massive fire on Labor Day, May 1, 2018. Firefighters looked for 12 days to recover any buried victims under the rubble. They uncovered seven human corpses, six male and one female, including twin boys aged 10. Later the city would report that 6,000 tons of wreckage was hauled to a dump in the northern extremes of the city, an operation that would take 58 days to complete.

The building had been a squatter occupation, a social and material representation of (il)legalities. The majority of occupations in São Paulo are, in fact, "ethical". This means that they are non-profit and part of a larger socio-political movement, whose goal is to provide affordable housing to the needy, thereby giving a "social use" to empty buildings, as stipulated in the Brazilian Federal Constitution of 1988 and, more specifically, in the São Paulo City Statute of 2001. This building was not part of that movement; it was "unethical," in that a criminal organization managed it through extortion.

Contents

PART II
Representing (il)legalities 87

Figures

Contributors

Sara Brandellero is Assistant Professor in Brazilian literature and culture at Leiden University's Centre for the Arts in Society, where she is co-Chair of the BA, MA and ResMA programmes in Latin American Studies. She is co-founder and steering committee member of REBRAC (European Network of Brazilianists Working in Cultural Analysis/Rede Europeia de Brasilianistas de Análise Cultural), with Prof. Stephanie Dennison and Dr Tori Holmes. Her research engages more specifically with issues of space and mobility, migration and diaspora, in Brazilian literature and culture and transnational/Lusophone contexts. Her publications include the book *On a Knife-Edge: The Poetry of João Cabral de Melo Neto* (OUP 2011), and the edited volumes *The Brazilian Road Movie* (UWP 2013), *Graciliano Ramos and the Making of Modern Brazil: Memory, Politics and Identities* (with Lucia Villares; UWP 2017). She is Project Leader of the HERA-funded collaborative research project "Night Spaces: Migration, Culture and Integration in Europe" (NITE), 2019–2022.

Stephanie Dennison holds a Chair in Brazilian Studies at the University of Leeds, UK, where directs the Centre for World Cinemas and Digital Cultures. She has published widely on World Cinema, Latin American cinema and Brazilian film culture. Her latest monograph, *Remapping Brazilian Film Culture in the 21st Century*, was published by Routledge in 2019.

Alexander S. Dent is a linguistic and cultural anthropologist who has taught at the George Washington University for 14 years. His work analyzes media, language, piracy and intellectual property. His first book, on Brazilian "country" music, was published by Duke University Press in 2009. His second book is *Digital Pirates: Policing Intellectual Property in Brazil* (2020). He lived in Brazil during the late 1990s, and returns annually for research. He plays guitar for Washington, DC, punk band Weird Babies.

Gabriel Feltran is Professor of Sociology at the Federal University of São Carlos (UFSCar) and researcher at the CEBRAP (Brazilian Center of Analysis and Planning). He is also an Invited Scholar and Visiting

Professor at Humboldt University (Berlin, 2018), CIESAS (México, 2017), Sciences Po (Paris, 2013), Goldsmiths College (Londres, 2019) and Oxford University (Oxford, 2019). Gabriel holds a PhD in Social Sciences (2008) at the State University of Campinas (UNICAMP), with a collaborative period at the Ecole des Hautes Etudes en Sciences Sociales (EHESS). He currently researches the illegal markets in Brazil, based on previous work with the everyday social/political dynamics of urban outskirts, focusing on collective action, marginalized groups and "the criminal world" in São Paulo.

Daniel Hirata is professor of sociology at Federal University Fluminense, researcher in the Center of Conflict, Citizenship and Urban Violence Studies (Núcleo de Estudos em Conflito, Cidadania e Violência Urbana-Necvu/UFRJ) and coordinator of the Center of Studies of the New Illegalisms (Núcleo de Estudos dos Novos Ilegalismos-GENI/UFF).

Igor Machado is a Professor of Anthropology at the Federal University of São Carlos. He is specialized in the topic of anthropology of migration and kinship. His publications include: *Cárcere Público*: *Processos de exotização entre brasileiros no Porto* (ICS, Lisbon 2009); *Japonesidades multiplicadas*: *Novos estudos sobre a presença japonesa no Brasil* (EdUFSCar 2011); *Deslocamentos e parentesco* EdUFSCar 2016; and *Antropologia do Refúgio no Brasil* (EdUFSCar 2020). More details can be found at: www.ufscar.br/~igor.

Felipe Milanez Pereira is an Associate Professor at the Professor Milton Santos Institute of Humanities, Arts and Sciences (IHAC), Federal University of Bahia. PhD in Social Studies at the University of Coimbra. His publications include *Memórias Sertanistas: Cem Anos de Indigenismo no Brasil.* 1. ed. São Paulo: Sesc, 2015. He is also a co-author of "Existência e diferença: o racismo contra os povos indígenas" in *Revista Direito e Práxis* (2019).

Derek Pardue, PhD, is Associate Professor of Brazilian Studies inside the Global Studies Department at Aarhus University in Denmark. He is a trained cultural anthropologist, who has focused on issues of migration, urbanism and identity politics throughout the Black Atlantic, specifically the Luso-African world of Brazil, Portugal and Cape Verde. He recently finished his tenure as a Senior Fellow at the Hanse-Wissenschaftskolleg Institute in Germany (www.h-w-k.de/en/hwk-overview.html), where he wrote ethnographic fiction featuring newly arrived West African and Haitian migrants in São Paulo, Brazil. Publications include: *Cape Verde, Let's Go: Creole Rappers and Citizenship in Portugal* (2015), *Brazilian Hip-Hoppers Speak from the Margin: We's on Tape* (2011) and the edited volume *Ruminations on Violence* (2008).

Lúcia Sá is Professor of Brazilian Studies at the University of Manchester. She is the author of *Rainforest Literatures, Amazonian Texts and Latin*

American Culture (Minnesota, 2004); *Life in the Megalopolis: Mexico City and São Paulo* (Routledge, 2007), and various articles on Brazilian and Spanish American culture. She is Principle Investigator in the AHRC/GCRF Project "Racism and Anti-Racism in Brazil: the Case of Indigenous Peoples" (2017–2019), and co-investigator, with Peter Wade and Ignacio Aguiló in the AHRC project "Cultures of Anti-Racism in Brazil".

Marcia Tiburi holds a Master's and PhD in Philosophy. Her main publications include: *As Mulheres e a Filosofia* (Women and Philosophy, 2002), *Filosofia em Comum* (Philosophy in Common, Ed. Record, 2008), *Olho de Vidro* (Glass Eye: Television and the State of Exception of the Image, 2011), *Sociedade Fissurada* (Cracked Society, 2013), *Filosofia Prática* (2014), *Como Conversar com um Fascista* (How to Talk to a Fascist, 2015), *Ridículo Político* (2017), *Delírio do Poder* (2019) and six novels. She is currently a visiting professor at University Paris 8.

Claire Williams is Associate Professor of Brazilian Literature and Culture at the University of Oxford. Her research focuses on women's writing, minority writing and life-writing from the Lusophone world. Publications include the monograph *The Encounter Between Opposites in the Works of Clarice Lispector* (HiPLA, 2006), and the co-edited volumes *Feminine Singular: Life Writing in the Luso-Hispanic World* (Peter Lang, 2017), with Maria-José Blanco, the forthcoming *Transnational Portuguese Studies* (LUP, 2020), with Hilary Owen, and *After Clarice: Reading Lispector's Legacy in the Twenty-First Century* (Legenda, 2020), with Adriana Jacobs. She co-ordinated a selection of Lispector's interviews for Editora Rocco in *Entrevistas* (2007). She is also a member of the Grupo de Estudos em Literatura Brasileira Contemporânea (Brasília) and sits on the Editorial Board of Portuguese Studies.

Georg Wink is Associate Professor of Portuguese and Brazilian Studies as well as Director of the Centre for Latin American Studies at the University of Copenhagen. With an interdisciplinary education in Latin American and Brazilian Studies, he held previous positions at Freie University Berlin, Technical University Dresden and Federal University of Minas Gerais in Brazil. His research focuses on the cultural and social history of Brazil in texts and contexts, in an interdisciplinary approach that integrates history, social studies, cultural studies and literary studies. Beyond numerous articles, he has published monographs on the alternative press during the Brazilian military dictatorship and on the discursive constructions of collective identity in Brazil. Currently, he is active in several joint research collaborations on the rise of the "new right" in Brazil.

Jean Wyllys holds a Master's in Literature and Linguistics from the Institute of Literature and Linguistics of the Federal University of Bahia (Brazil). He is visiting professor of the Afro-Latin American Research Institute, Hutchins Center at Harvard University. He is the author of the books

Tempo bom, tempo ruim – identidades, políticas e afetos (Paralela, 2014) and *O que será – a história de um defensor de direitos humanos no Brasil* (Objetiva, 2019). Three-time elected federal deputy, he held his seat in the Brazilian Chamber of Deputies between the years of 2011 and 2018, when he was forced to resign and go into exile citing continued death threats. These threats were recognized by the Inter-American Commission on Human Rights of the Organization of American States. He has been a high-profile campaigner for gay rights and human rights more broadly.

Acknowledgements

We would like to thank our contributors for collaborating on this project and for the collegiality throughout the different stages of preparation of this book. We acknowledge our debt of gratitude to our colleagues at the Universities of Leiden, Aarhus and Copenhagen and to our respective institutions for supporting research that led this book to fruition. A special thank you to those whose work is the subject of the chapters here, for their generosity in sharing their work and experience. We thank the commissioning and editorial team at Routledge for their guidance and assistance throughout the process of publication. The chapter by Jean Wyllys was translated by Sara Brandellero. Márcia Tiburi's chapter was translated by Derek Pardue. Gabriel Feltran's chapter was translated by Juliana Valente. All translations are theirs unless otherwise stated. A special mention goes to REBRAC, the European Network of Brazilianists Working in Cultural Analysis, whose third international conference, in 2018, was the original inspiration for this edited volume. Last but not least we thank our families and friends for their support.

Introduction

Living (il)legalities in Brazil

Sara Brandellero, Derek Pardue and Georg Wink

What on earth is happening to Brazil? Perhaps the tragic collapse on May 1, 2018, of the Paes de Almeida skyscraper, a building designed in brutal modernism, located in the once posh downtown São Paulo and a former "illegal" squatter residence, provides a more profound foreshadowing than originally thought. In fact, the urban edifice featured below (Figure 0.1) seems metonymic of the current state of affairs affecting the country. This is because this emergent Global Player, advocate of BRICS and the Global South, and not to put too fine a point on it, the world's fourth largest liberal democracy, fifth largest and most populous country, with the eighth largest economy is currently undergoing unexpected political and societal transformations, the development of which is being followed keenly the world over. Views on these transformations have reflected differing perspectives across the political spectrum, but a striking commonality of these often heated debates is that they have tended to gravitate heavily around the legal or illegal merits underpinning the changes Brazil as a country is undergoing.

Brazilianist scholars and Brazilians alike often begin a conversation about local politics with a caveat – "Brazil is such a young country". What is meant by this is that Brazil's relationship with representational democracy has been intermittent and perhaps might only be effectively assessed since the formal transition from a military dictatorship to a popularly elected president in 1989. And, yet, the government under Fernando Collor did little to assure Brazilians that the massive structural problems of inequality, state repression such as that played out in Brazilians' daily lives, especially the poor, through actions of police violence, and large-scale corruption were even being addressed. Indeed, it is significant how the banner of the "fight against corruption" has been used and abused to put a break on policies for social change and equality, with evidence of the systematic appropriation and plundering of the State by the economic elite through means of corruption. In September of 1992, the Chamber of Deputies voted to impeach Collor (who had campaigned as the "squeaky clean", anti-corruption candidate) on grounds of "crimes of responsibility," better known as passive corruption.

Figure 0.1 A view of the bottom floors of the Wilton Paes de Almeida Building, São Paulo, Brazil. Photo by Derek Pardue, June of 2017.

Subsequent governments representing the centre-right party of the PSDB (nominally "Social Democrats") and the centre-left party of the PT (Partido dos Trabalhadores, i.e. Labour Party) also struggled with institutional breaches of legality. However, albeit in an arguably timid fashion, it is the PT under the charismatic leadership of Luiz Inácio Lula da Silva ("Lula") that made the most marked strides in addressing the three basic issues cited earlier. Most visible were the debated cash-transfer programmes of *Bolsa Família* and home ownership credit programmes such as *Minha Casa Minha Vida*. The result of these programmes and other redistributive policies was the uplift of 30 million Brazilian, as a conservative estimate, from a category of "poverty" to a "low middle class" (so-called "Class C") that contributed significantly to domestic consumption and helps explain the Brazil's healthy economy during the first 15 years of the 21st century.

Coincidence or not, it was mainly after the government change in 2003 that practices of good governance (and the respective checks and balances) were implemented in an attempt of State-building and human rights empowerment that had already began in the 1990s. Among these measures are, to cite just a few, the Law of Fiscal Responsibility (2000), the creation of a Comptroller General of the Union (2003), the strengthening of the Federal Police and Federal Judiciary (2003), the creation of the Portal of Transparency for all public bodies (2004), the Law of Clean Record for Candidates (2010), the Law of Access to Information (2011) and against Money Laundering (2012), the Anticorruption Law (2013), the Plea Bargain Law (2013) and, finally, the Supreme Court's decision to prohibit business financing of Campaigns (2015).

Moreover, under Dilma Rousseff, Lula's successor as president (2011–2016), the state facilitated the legal machinations to investigate corruption as part of the *Lava Jato* or "Car Wash" financial scandal. The insistence on transparency under Dilma would ultimately be distorted and be used remarkably to impeach her and imprison Lula. Despite the lack of evidence (Lula) and post-impeachment acknowledgement that Dilma, in fact, had not committed an impeachable offence, the judicial coup and lawfare remained intact. In other words, these ambitious good governance and accountability policies, implemented without changing the unequal distribution of power within the social hierarchy, turned out to be political suicide for these progressive governments.

The recent election of the extreme far-right candidate Jair Bolsonaro to the country's presidency, together with a considerable shift from the centre-right to the right in the congress, was met with considerable dismay by those fearful for Brazil's young democracy. Bolsonaro's project, economically ultraliberal and die-hard conservative with regard to customs and values, is fervently supported by a sizeable number of voters (39%). Others voted for Fernando Haddad, at least abhorred by Bolsonaro's violent, racist, misogynistic views, even though not necessarily aware of the serious socio-political and economic implications of his agenda (32%). Others still others, disengaged from a largely discredited political system, negated their vote to both candidates (29%). Given this scenario, there is no doubt that the country is on the eve of a change so far unparalleled in Brazil.

The centrality of the legal system (politicised judiciary, or "lawfare"), the stretching of the limits of legitimate means in Brazilian far-right politics (such as in public relations but also intimidation and tampering), and the fostering of disreputable political communication styles (hate speech, fake news and defamation) provide much food for debate and controversy both within academic and non-academic circles, in and outside of Brazil. Bolsonaro's ultraliberal legislative action plan (most recently with the Law of Economic Liberty) in order to move the already flexibilised Labour Laws towards "informality,"[1] in a country were half of all occupations already are in the informal sector, raises important questions. Moreover, the appointment of Sérgio Moro as Minister of Justice in Bolsonaro's government threw into sharp focus the contentious nature of the situation. After all, Moro had been the secret prosecutor, disguised as judge, of former president Lula, who was leading the polls before and even after his imprisonment earlier in 2018, until his candidature was suspended by the Superior Electoral Court through the Clean Record Law –while other 1200 candidates in similar juridical circumstances were allowed to run. As Minister of Justice in Bolsonaro's government, and the declaration of a "culture war" to reestablish nostalgic forms of "social normality" throw into sharp focus the contentious nature of the situation. While at this moment the effects of the government change on legality/illegality can only be assessed in a preliminary way, it is crucial to approach a more comprehensive understanding of the slanted idiosyncrasies the current and upcoming government policies represent. Discussions surrounding legality and illegalities are central and therefore closely connected to the scope of this volume.

Through a transdisciplinary approach, the book assesses the relation between legality and illegality at institutional levels, (daily) practice and cultural representation. (Il)legalities, we argue, are not only relevant in understanding Brazil's current political situation, but have relevance for established Brazilian cultural and societal practices, as we elaborate below. They are even enshrined as doxa in the country's national identity; at least this is what notions such as "jeitinho," "malandragem" and "cordiality" suggest. But the question of the disputed borders of what is considered legal also resonates beyond Brazil, as concepts such as "lawfare" have crept into vocabularies, and countries the world over grapple with issues of state interference, fake news, the definition of "illegal" migration, and so on.

The chapters included in this volume contribute with different methodological and theoretical approaches and case studies, but are driven by the unifying understanding of (il)legalities as socio-political *productions*. The authors explore the limits of legality, including spatial, discursive, creative, aesthetic, political, economic and theoretical, as contested and confrontational. Hard, violent lines are drawn; creative and risky transgressions occur – the manifestations of which are considered through the varied selection of case studies and the transdisciplinary approach brought together here.

Recent anthropological scholarship on trust is worth noting at this point. In particular, the work of Florian Mühlfried (2018) and Matthew Carey (2017) has been refreshing by steering the inquisitive reader back to rethink trust as central to social ideals and mistrust (as well as distrust) as inherently disengaged, detached and epiphenomenal to producing a healthy society. Just as both trust and mistrust require "attitudes of engagement," so too do legality and illegality often suggest or even require contingent social relations. The upshot is that such relationships are not oppositional or negative. Rather, in a gesture to Emile Durkheim, it might be more accurate to state that crime and other forms of illegality are fundamental to society, not as a necessary evil but as a mirroring measure.

For millions of Brazilians modern "normal" life is just a step away from illegality. People are forced into unlawful or socially sanctioned practices and, sometimes, are actively seeking them. The (il)legal practices we focus on are not simply illicit transgressions such as criminal offence or State violence. We explore phenomena of a vast grey area between the legitimate and the illegitimate: a more or less hidden field of (day-to-day) practices that might be not legal any more, or not yet legalised, legal but socially not accepted, or just deemed beyond any legal normalisation. Some of the questions posed by the chapters in this book are: How does the fluid boundary between legality and illegality manifest itself in Brazil and how can we productively understand this relationship in a contemporary context? And following on from this: How are informal, illegal practices, in fact, institutionalised in Brazil? How is a fluid boundary between legality and illegality spatialised in the city? Which narratives emerge from these life experiences? What moral or ethical values are at stake?

Reflecting the broad range of expertise of scholars included in this volume, spanning the Humanities and Social Sciences, the book addresses some of Brazil's foremost societal challenges in 11 chapters clustered around two main themes: the production of (il)legalities and the representation of (il)legalities. The first section centres on studies that adopt ethnographic and sociological/historical approaches. Section 2 brings together chapters focused on instances of cultural representation of the complex boundary of legality/illegality as created in social contexts today.

Producing (il)legalities

This section opens with a chapter by Jean Wyllys, three-time elected Federal Deputy to the Brazilian parliament and prominent human rights activist. Forced to leave his post and go into self-exile since early 2019 due to repeated death threats, in "Borders of (Il)legality" Wyllys questions the issue of how justice is dispensed in Brazil and how those historically excluded from the democratic process cannot claim to have ever had justice. Wyllys's chapter considers new forms of political propaganda delivered through new social media platforms in the context of "lawfare," seen not as a new phenomenon but as a historic model that has ensured the continued disenfranchisement of certain sections of society.

Homing in on some of the social groups to which Wyllys refers, Daniel Hirata's chapter, entitled "The Government of Street Vending: Formalizations of Informality and use of Force," analyses the precarious condition and ongoing struggles of street vendors, with particular attention to the transversalities, that is, points of potential policy connection, present in Rio de Janeiro and São Paulo during the decades 1980–1990 and 2000–2010, when major changes emerged in the government of street vending. Hirata focuses on the dynamic use of force to regulate the (il)legalities and (in)formalities of commerce in urban public spaces.

Connecting with Hirata's discussion on policing, labour and social dynamic in the public spaces of urban thoroughfares, Derek Pardue and Igor

Machado's "Migrant Refugee Spatialities Lived and Legislated in São Paulo" investigates the intersections of the new Immigration Law (2017) and lived realities among newly arrived African migrants in a range of cities in the state of São Paulo. Ultimately, the authors assess the fact that "black" migrants are both hyper-visible and invisible. Migrants create presence through a myriad of occupations on the one hand, via precarious employment and orientalised ethnicity, and are written off of the social map of the city through personal and institutional racism, on the other hand.

Such discussion hinges on questions of power and inequality that are explored from a cultural history and theoretical perspective in Georg Wink's "*Jeitinho* revisited," a chapter that focuses on what is without doubt the most famous umbrella term used to describe social practices existing in the grey zone between legality and illegality in Brazil. Understood as "typically Brazilian," the *jeitinho* is seen as creative problem-solving strategy to circumvent norms and rules with the purpose of attaining personal objectives. The legitimacy of this concept and its limitations as a useful label for Brazilianness is questioned here in Wink's critical literature review, considering how the term has been deployed to veil and preserve asymmetric power relations and the status quo of social inequality.

Closing the first section of the book, Márcia Tiburi's chapter "Political Sexology" addresses this same question of social inequality from an avowedly gendered perspective. In considering an issue described as relevant to authoritarian regimes around the world, Tiburi argues that sex is deployed as a weapon of combat – in the form of discourses, practices, performances and even production of artefacts – used by the extreme right to reach power. Indeed, sex, Tiburi argues, becomes part of a complex political strategy made up of discourses and practices that go far beyond moralism, but aim to dismantle the serious work carried out by those involved in the field of gender studies and, finally, reach the core of democracy.

Representing (il)legalities

This section turns the reader's attention to cultural representations and opens with a chapter on Brazil's musical production, in an acknowledgement that music is one of the cultural manifestations, and an often politicised one, for which Brazil is often most widely known internationally. Moving beyond common perceptions of Brazil as the land of the feel-good rhythms of *Bossa Nova*, Alexander Dent adopts an innovative take on the issue by considering the lesser-known counter-cultural punk movement and its run-ins with the "law" in his chapter "Using Lime Juice to Make Yourself Puke, and the Correct Way to Beat an Old Lady: Policing Early Punk Rock in São Paulo." In the early development of punk rock in 1980s São Paulo, conflicts with the police were frequent. Sometimes, police were called upon to break up fights, or because of noise complaints. However, at other times, police simply knew that punk events were taking place and showed up ready to make arrests;

this was the case for the largest early punk event, "The Beginning of the End of the World" – held at SESC Pompeia and designed to unite Brazil's two warring punk factions from the city of São Paulo itself and the satellite cities known as *ABC* (Santo André, São Bernardo do Campo, São Caetano do Sul). This chapter provides a historical perspective that will shed light on similarly illegalised contemporary music styles such as funk, by investigating the relationship between policing of punk in the late seventies and early eighties, and the social critique that punks were carrying out, focusing on the co-constitutive relationship between the two.

Following Dent's discussion of the relations between cultural production and the politics of law and order, Gabriel Feltran's chapter *Illegal realities in the lyrics by Racionais MC's* provides a complementary perspective on the relationship between popular music and legalities. His text discusses the distinct *realities* produced by illegalities in contemporary urban Brazil. The essay departs from the lyrics to the song "I can hear someone calling me" (original: *Tô ouvindo alguém me chamar*), performed by the group Racionais MC's, which was released in the acclaimed album *Sobrevivendo no Inferno* (Surviving in Hell) in 1997. Its lyrics tell the story of a typical trajectory of life in crime in São Paulo, and are narrated by a man who is in between life and death. The real consequences of real stories, similar to the ones that inspire the song's plot, are discussed in this essay, which is also based on the ethnographic work Feltran carried out in São Paulo's periphery neighbourhoods (1997–2017). In the conclusion, he argues that there is a reality to the illegal, which is recurringly fictionalised as a cultural product and serves to hold up the official as an ideal.

Building on Dent's earlier discussion on politics of law and order, Stephanie Dennison brings the issue of the Law centre stage in "Kafka and Lawfare in Maria Ramos's *The Trial*." Dennison discusses the issue of lawfare, defined as the improper use of legal mechanisms as a means for political persecution, as it transpires in Maria Augusta Ramos's 2018 documentary *O Processo* (*The Trial*). The film follows the work of the defence team during the final months of the impeachment of Brazilian president Dilma Rousseff in 2016, and Dennison discussion of the film illustrates how *lawfare* has manifested itself in contemporary Brazilian politics and of how a cultural studies perspective can provide valuable support for understanding Brazil's far-reaching contemporary legal questions.

The significance of Brazilian cinema in recording the negotiation of the borders between legality and illegality is addressed from the point of view of its fictional production in the chapter by Sara Brandellero – "Night Trespassing in Contemporary Brazilian Cinema: Unveiling (Il)legalities in *Neighbouring Sounds*." Focused on urban Brazil, a topic widely discussed in contemporary scholarship, the chapter in fact zooms in on the city at nighttime, addressing the fact that little attention has been given so far to the daily temporal shifts that affect how spaces are shaped and experienced. Thus, the chapter argues that the nightscapes in the film are where the limitations of contemporary urban living in Brazil are exposed and when the slippages between legality and illegality are most eloquently revealed. Focusing specifically on Kleber Mendonça Filho's *O som ao redor* (*Neighbouring Sounds*) (2012), this chapter takes its cue from Matthew Beaumont's (2015) discussions on the historical figure of the nightwalker as one who "embraces the outlaw status," to consider how nighttime mobilities in the film appear as acts of trespassing, dramatising the tension between guilt and retribution. What happens while the city "sleeps," Brandellero argues, provides a foray into the complex web of social relations that determine who can be where and when and how guilt and responsibility are apportioned.

Moving from film to literature, Claire Williams's "Something to Declare: Illegal Immigrants in Contemporary Brazilian Literature" connects with Pardue and Machado under the rubric of (il)legal migration, from a cultural analysis perspective. Despite the trend, particularly since the new millennium, of novels describing Brazilians travelling abroad or even set outside the country's borders (e.g. Bernardo Carvalho's *Mongolia*, Adriana Lisboa's *Hanoi*, the ten "Amores Expressos" novels), there is a distinct lack of representation of illegal migrants to other countries in contemporary Brazilian literature. Williams addresses this gap and homes in on works by Luiz Ruffato, Regina Rheda and Claudia Canto, which do articulate the undocumented Brazilian migrant's experience of bureaucracy, working conditions, survival and acculturation.

The final chapter of this volume develops on the question of prejudice discussed in Williams's chapter by focusing on the issue of racism in relation to indigenous people within Brazil's borders. In their chapter, "Painting Racism: Protest art by Contemporary Indigenous Artists," Lúcia Sá and Felipe Milanez Pereira take on one of the most foundational and persistent ideological practices of Brazilian (il)legalities. Racism is a non-bailable offence in Brazil, a crime punishable with one to five years in prison. Yet, in contradiction to the far right's trivialisation of racism as huffiness of hypersensitive minorities, racism is pervasive in Brazilian society, in practices that range from the direct violence of police targeting of black youth in favelas and the extermination of indigenous populations by land grabbers, to insidious, generally accepted everyday attitudes, such as the telling of racist jokes or the denial of indigenous people's right to their identity, once they have adopted the use of modern gadgets. Sá and Milanez Pereira focus on the work of two contemporary indigenous artists, Denilson Baniwa and Jaider Esbell, and their depiction of racism and the persistence of colonialist practices against indigenous populations in modern Brazil. Both artists have adopted Western media, such as painting, video, graffiti, social networks, and engage critically with Western/Brazilian art movements. Their work highlights particular characteristics of racism against indigenous populations in Brazil, such as the invisibility of indigeneity (particularly urban), the expectation that indigenous persons should look like and behave as stereotypical images of "o índio," and the attacks on traditional knowledge and religions by religious and academic institutions. Their works often question the colonialist roots of Brazil's legal system and its blindness to the violence committed against Indigenous populations. At the same time, they call attention to practices that, although perhaps not illegal, are definitely racist and have a devastating effect on the sense of identity of Indigenous populations.

Note

1 www.planalto.gov.br/ccivil_03/_ato2019-2022/2019/lei/L13874.htm.

References

Beaumont, Matthew. *Nightwalking: A Nocturnal History of London Chaucer to Dickens*. London: Verso, 2015.

Carey, Matthew. *Mistrust: An Ethnographic Theory*. Chicago: HAU Books, 2017.

Mühlfried, Florian. "Introduction". In *Mistrust – Ethnographic Approximations*, edited by Florian Mühlfried, 7–22. Bielefeld: transcript, 2018.

Part I

Producing (il)legalities

1 Borders of (il)legality

Jean Wyllys

Two works of fiction – one a film, the other a play – will provide my starting point for thinking through the relationship between issues of (il)legalities and "post-democracy" (Casara 2017), from a Cultural Studies perspective; this productive and unruly "theoretical uproar" (Hall 2000).[1] The film I wish to reference is *Cronicamente inviável* [Chronically Unfeasible] (2000), directed by Sérgio Bianchi. In one of the film's most disturbing scenes, a São Paulo high-middle-class woman – played by Maria Alice Vergueiro – runs over a homeless teenage boy who was crossing the road outside of the pedestrian crossing. While the victim agonizes on the blood-soaked ground, the driver steps out of her car and without checking whether the boy is dead or alive and without bothering to provide any assistance, simply tells bystanders, who look on impassively, that she was not at fault, did not break the law, and that she is a "legalista".

Turning our attention to the second work of fiction, the play entitled *Rose*, by Cecília Ripoll (2018, first staged in 2017), tells the story of an employee at a local state school who at weekends works as a maid in a rich family home where the patriarch belongs to the local political oligarchy and is a member of the municipal government. Taking advantage of the fact that she is in charge of doing the weekly household shopping and having noticed the amount of food wasted by the family, Rose buys extra food, which she uses to make pies to take to school on a weekly basis in order to feed the children – who have gone without school-provided snacks for months due to a political corruption scheme involving education budgets. One important detail only becomes apparent later on in the play: the politician for whom Rose works at weekends as a cleaner is implicated in the siphoning-off of funds that should be destined for the same schoolchildren's snacks. The play centres on the dialogue between Rose and the school principal, who discovers her "illegal" stratagem to keep the children fed. What the maid does is rebuked as "illegal", and she is punished for it. The illegality surrounding her boss and local politician's behaviour goes unfettered.

Mindful of what the two fictional narratives outlined here tell us, we can say that not all illegality is immoral, and there are legalists who are unethical and immoral. As the foundation for the modern nation-state, the realm of legalities (stipulating what is permitted and what is not, subject to the rule of law and the right to defense) changes over time and in space (i.e. what is deemed legal in Brazil today is not the same as what was considered legal at the time of the proclamation of the republic, in 1889, nor is it the same as what applies in the United States, for example). The realm of the law is defined by the Federal Constitution and by infra-constitutional legislation.

We know that in republican democracies the constitutional assemblies draw up the Constitution and then the legislature – supposedly the most democratic of the three powers of the republic – elaborates the mesh of infra-constitutional laws that must safeguard the rights enshrined in the country's Magna Carta. But, we also know to which class the members of these assemblies and of the legislature have historically almost entirely belonged (and still largely belong).

In a republic such as Brazil, born from a military coup against a monarchy that had emerged from a history of European genocidal colonialism, a year after the formal abolition of slavery that had lasted 350 years and that came to an end thanks to pressures from the nascent industrial capitalism in England (Schwarcz and Starling 2015), is it even possible to speak of "democracy"? It is possible only if we consider democracy as a domain the frontiers of which are shifting and moveable and that, since its beginning until today, in Brazil, has fully protected only those belonging to certain origins and ethnicities, social classes and religions (not by pure coincidence those of the colonizers), and only partially protect those who managed and manage to achieve some representation in the legislature, despite all of the obstacles that have been imposed by those who enjoy democracy to the full. But who succeeds in achieving representation in the legislature?

As sociologist Jessé de Souza (2017) explains, the slave-owning elites, descendent from the original colonizers endowed by the Portuguese Crown with hereditary land strips of empire, known as *Capitanias hereditárias* [hereditary captaincies], have maligned popular sovereignty since the proclamation of the republic – by denouncing the supposed corruption of public office, by arguing that what is public is not good – at the same time as they were finding ways of taking private ownership of public wealth by controlling the political system, taking advantage of all the privileges that they enjoyed: from ensuring food on the table for them and theirs, to entertainment, access to weapons, and the possibility to co-op allies amongst those who have exploited them. This has meant that democracy has been enjoyed by the few rather than the many, and when its reach has extended a little this has been the result of bloody struggles, such as the one fought during Brazil's last period under dictatorial rule (1964–1985), which resulted in the campaign for direct elections for president and the instalment of what then became known as the New Republic (1985).

During the democratic intervals within the history of authoritarian rule on which Brazil was built, as Lília Schwarcz (2019) shows, the chances of the excluded from democracy to win elections and be represented in parliament, thereby interfering in the fabric of legality and attempting to address historic injustices or simply preventing their perpetuation, appeared undermined by obstacles created by economic inequality (private and business funding of electoral campaigns that only benefit candidates from the elites) and by the control of electoral tribunals and the remainder of the judiciary on the part of these same elites since the establishment of these same institutions. This has resulted in the recurring criminalization of candidates and/or political parties whose interests are at odds with maintaining the privileges of the elites and who have interfered, or may come to interfere (through their life stories, discourses, and actions) in the representations which reproduce and make up subjectivities and social imaginaries in the sense of Lacan (1998) as well as Horkheimer and Adorno (1985). These have sustained such status quo; above all, through representations of the subaltern that support hegemonic world views and an array of prejudices that have been historically and socially shared. Not without some resistance from individuals and groups here and there, such (re)configured collective imaginaries have been articulated mainly by mass media outlets, property of the elites, and more recently also by new communication technologies, also impacted by their economic power, which have propagated *fake news* against those who wish to extend the limits of democracy and, as a result, also the limits of full citizenship to more people. This contemporary development forms part of age-old tactics of the elites to manipulate the majority of the electorate in favour of maintaining their hegemony and privileges.

Now widespread, the novelty of the phenomenon of *fake news* has to do with the new communication and information technologies that allow (1) the clearer identification of users who may potentially be manipulated through data provided to online communication platforms such as Google, YouTube, and Facebook, when posting and "liking" online content and/or when making online purchases, and (2) to limit the resistance that these same individuals may pose to such manipulation. In this new communication landscape, where the identification of subjects who can be manipulated and who may decide an election result requires users' data collection on which online platforms place a high market value, *fake news* and conspiracy theories are key to maintaining the hegemony that the elites enjoy, even though, by abusing these communication strategies, these same elites have unleashed the sanitary belt that prevented the fascist infection that now threatens them as well.

The fact that the illegalities practised by those who are wholly or partly outside the realm of democracy – and, consequently, that of legality – are mostly perceived as such and punished more often and with harsher penalties depends on these constructed imaginaries, as does the actual acceptance of this unjust state of affairs. For this reason, too, the struggle for equality of rights and justice is, above all, a dispute of these imaginaries. Such struggle is the means by which so-called identity-driven social movements – in the case of Brazil, mainly feminist groups, LGBTQ (lesbian, gay, bisexual, transgender, and queer) groups, and Afro-Brazilian religious groups (practitioners and followers of religions of African origin such as candomblé, umbanda, batuque, xangô, and terecô) – unmask the campaign of defamation levelled against them by leaders of fundamentalist Christian neo-Pentecostal churches. These campaigns emanate mainly from the pulpit and from TV programmes (a large part of non-subscription television programming in Brazil is, today, with the exception of TV Globo, made up of faith services and other fundamentalist evangelical religious content, concentrated, in particular, in the TV Record channel) as well as from social media. Traditionally discriminated-against groups strive to change definitions of legality by proposing legislative action through bills and amendments or lobbying the judiciary in order to ensure punishment for discriminatory behaviour and violence motivated by prejudice and hate (be it conscious or not) against people for their sexual orientation, gender identity, religion, origin and race, as well as to guarantee access to rights currently denied because of institutionalized discrimination.[2]

Fundamentalist religious leaders and their churches have enormous advantages in their approach to minority movements. Tax exemptions and immunities they enjoy (a result of the flagrant disregard for the principle of the secular state enshrined in Brazil's Federal Constitution which undermines the notion that we live in a republic) allow them not only to invest in legal undertakings but also to also turn their churches into "laundries" for illegal businesses such as illicit drug trafficking, weapons, and people trafficking, which results in increased capital accumulation and campaign funding for legislative candidates. In addition to these advantages, neo-Pentecostal churches and far-right Catholic clergy have on their side millennia of patriarcal Judeo-Christian culture, which shaped our nation and the values of which are more than deeply inscribed in our subjectivities: they are the very foundations of the Brazilian "subjected" subjects, in line with Michel Foucault's considerations on the genealogy of power (Foucault 1999).[3]

Leaders of Christian churches tend to be part of or manage to gain access to the elite thanks to their accumulation of capital, thus also controlling the boundaries of legality, consequently also being able to determine what lies outside of the law. By this I mean the "foreign land" of illegality (always identified with the notion of sinfulness, and hell, shared by the community of "believers" who belong to hegemonic religions), inhabited by those considered – and portrayed as – outcasts and/or "enemies" to be hated, fought, and punished. It is these leaders, therefore, who also decide who deserves a place in "paradise" and who does not, who lives or not under a democracy.

It is no coincidence that the term "illegal" has been linked so strongly to the word "immigrant" to refer to undocumented people originally from outside the territorial boundaries of the nation-states in which they live, and even less surprising that these people are held responsible by right-wing politicians who are members of the elites of these nation-states (1) for the high rates of unemployment among members of the higher classes (although immigrants occupy positions in the labour market that they would never be inclined to take on, such as cleaning services, for example) and (2) the rise in urban crime, which actually has multiple and complex causes, one of these – if not the main one – social inequality.

Even an institution such as the public prosecution service – created to defend the democratic rule of law – ends up operating in practice, save the exceptions, so that this rule does not apply to all Brazilians, either (1) by omission (until now, for example, there has been no prosecution of police extrajudicial summary executions against the poor – and specifically the black poor – that the police accuse of involvement in crimes against private property and illicit drug trafficking, disguising as "self-defense acts" [*autos de resistência*] the imposition of a completely illegal and immoral death penalty since Brazil formally abolished capital punishment even before the proclamation of the republic, and since those sentenced to this death penalty are not entitled to a fair trial). Or (2) this is done by prevarication on the part of members of the public prosecution or attorneys with respect to the rights of those who do not belong to their social class or share their political ideology. Such has been the case of Operation Lava Jato [Operation Car Wash], in which, according to allegations published by *The Intercept*, supported by abundant and robust evidence, prosecutors pressed ahead with an unproven accusation against former President Lula and sabotaged his defense attorneys by agreeing the sentence to be passed down in advance with the judge who sentenced Lula to prison, Judge Sérgio Moro.

The legal head and the de facto head of Operation Car Wash – prosecutor Deltan Dallagnol and ex–federal judge Sérgio Moro, as he was known before his appointment as justice minister of the Jair Bolsonaro government – are white, wealthy, Christian men, who harboured a badly disguised hatred for Lula. The life story of Lula, a poor mixed race metal worker who led the great workers strikes that shook the military dictatorship in the late 1970s and early 1980s, founding member of the Workers' Party [Partido dos Trabalhadores (PT)], twice consecutively and democratically elected president of the republic, who implemented policies that eradicated hunger and unemployment and guaranteed access to education, especially to higher education (until then a privilege of the elites and the traditional middle class), to segments of the population historically excluded from this right produces a powerful fissure in the imagination that upholds and reproduces the hegemony and privilege of elites as it serves as an example to others of its class. Therefore, at the very least, the elites consider individuals such as Lula an inconvenience for their potential to impact on and undermine this imaginary and because they can interfere and indeed do interfere in the legislative fabric in order to extend democracy and citizenship to more people.

Hence the reason why spokesmen and representatives of these elites strive to publicly destroy the reputations of those who pose a potential threat by way of fake news, whether these (1) contain explicit lies – those that can now be spread by newer communication and information technologies, or (2) dilute the truth of the facts in stages and transpose statements to contexts different from those in which they were originally issued in order to produce, at the moment of reception, meanings that harm those who originally issued them: that is, fake news produced and aired almost exclusively by news broadcasts owned by private mass media companies that have the "public concession" to commercially exploit radio and TV signals. These are private companies belonging to the same elites that endorse the politicians who award them these same "public concessions". Both types of fake news contribute to the destruction of the people's reputation in the eyes of public opinion and the public sphere. While the two types of fake news exist between different media (see, for example, OI 2009),[4] and the second type of fake news usually serves to fabricate the fake news of the first kind I mentioned, the difference between them lies in the medium in which they originated and were initially circulated, and the fact that fake news of the second type may be challenged in the field of legality (such as the right of reply granted by judges to people who have sued newspapers, TV news and news sites for defamation). Fake news of the second type can only be legally challenged when their propagators are identified.

When one considers the victims of fake news who participate in the Brazilian political scene (including Lula, Manuela D'Ávila, and Marielle Franco, even after her murder, as well as myself), we will find that the most targeted are those who have managed to negotiate or have the potential to circumvent obstacles imposed on their election and/or who intervened or may intervene in the social imaginary that upholds the hegemony and privileges of the elites. They are those that have erased or can erase stereotypes related to the sections of the population that they represent and/or those who have enabled or may enable new representations of the sections to which they belong.

It is important to highlight that the elites finance the production and circulation of fake news of both types also to strengthen their own reputation before public opinion and in the public domain. In this sense, we can say, for example that the entire reputation of Operation Car Wash and its protagonists – especially the reputations of then judge Sérgio Moro and prosecutor Deltan Dallagnol – were built on fake news. These also supported the fascist identification of most voters with Jair Bolsonaro. Although Workers' Party activists resorted to fake news of the first kind in favour of Lula's reputation as it was being destroyed by fake news from both kinds propagated by sections of the elite, the use of fake news in decision making is typical of these elites.

Thus, despite it being increasingly used in legal and political contexts, due to the new forms of political coups perpetrated against leaders and popular governments in Latin America in the past decade, the term *lawfare* – the use of laws and legal procedures by those who have historically produced and controlled them against political agents that undermine their interests or threaten their privileges, that is, the practice of illegality in (and stemming from) the domain of legality itself – has in fact been applicable in Brazil at least since the proclamation of the republic in 1889.

The illegality of Operation Car Wash and the view of its members that only the illegalities practiced by members of the Workers' Party and the left can be treated as such and are punishable (a view that became clear in the Telegram group exchanges leaked by *The Intercept* in 2019) are just the latest manifestation of the lawfare practiced for over a century by Brazilian elites. Another example of this lawfare is the parliamentary coup, maskeraded as impeachment, perpetrated against President Dilma Rousseff by the majority of congressmen and backed by the public prosecution service and the judiciary, whose members – high-wage public servants whose generous salaries allowed them to become entrepreneurs and/or rentiers – had every interest in overthrowing a government and electorally sabotaging an entire political field that was trying to impose some legal limits on their profits and their exploitation of workers.

The concept of "post-democracy" presupposes the replacement of a democracy with strong, fully functioning institutions. Thus, and at the end of these considerations on the issue of (il)legality from the perspective of Cultural Studies, we can say that the "democracy stage design" to which Rubens Casara refers – with institutions that are nothing but hollow façades for institutions that functioned well in the past – is only a problem for those who have always (the elites) or partly (the segments of the population that succeded in gaining representation in the legislature and therefore some voice, thereby leaving their place of subalternity)[5] moved with within the circles of democracy. For the rest of the population, there has never been democracy – or, to put it another way, "the rule of law has not reached the heart of Pará", as the songwriter Caetano Veloso (2014) sings, nor has it reached the slums and pockets of poverty throughout the country. Thus, for those who live and have always lived beyond the borders of the democratic rule of law, there can be no post-democracy – or in any case such a thing makes no sense to them – since they have not experienced democracy.

The character of Rose in Ripoll's play is an allegory of Lula and the PT, when they were in government, and illustrates their relationship with the Brazilian elites, which in the play are represented by the character of Rose's boss. In the real-life episode that inspired the play, the party of politicians involved in stealing the schoolchildren's meals was the Brazilian Social Democracy Party [Partido da Social Democracia Brasileira (PSDB)], a plutocratic club whose corrupt members have never been exposed or punished in the same way as members of the PT accused of amassing illicit wealth or illegal financing of election campaigns were. The school principal, on the other hand, represents members of the middle class operating in the judiciary and the mass media, always complicit with the crimes of the elites, but relentless towards the illegalities in which the Workers' Party had to get involved – imperative for the very functioning of the political system since the abolition of slavery and the proclamation of the republic – to implement policies to combat hunger and income distribution. The school principal represents the hypocritical middle class that is resentful and hateful of the social mobility of the poor – Sérgio Moro and Deltan Dallagnol being its most notable examples.

Sérgio Moro is also embodied in the character of Maria Alice Vergueiro in *Chronically Unfeasible*: despite knowing that he has committed an immoral and atrocious act that has claimed and still claims lives – and we can think of all the lives lost because of the fascism that took a hold in Brazil as a result of Operation Car Wash: losses symbolized in the murders of the politician and human rights activist Marielle Franco, of the capoeira master Moa do Catendê and of little Agata, recently murdered in a police operation (not by chance three black Brazilians, two of female gender, and one a child), – he insists on proclaiming that he stands within the bounds of legality.

Which legality?

Notes

1 Hall refers to the field of *unruly knowledge* to the extent that it is not linked to any specific disciplines or sciences but can draw on all of them in interpreting cultural phenomena and products. The field of Cultural Studies is still relatively *unruly* in Brazil, given that it exists in individual research projects and in university departments in the fields of Journalism and Literary Studies, whereas in the United Kingdom and the United States, Cultural Studies has established itself as a distinguishable disciplinary field for some time.

2 For example, when in June 2019 the federal Supreme Court decided to criminalize homophobia and transphobia.

3 See also *Historia de la sexualidad IV: Las confesiones de la carne*. Trans. Horacio Pons. España: Siglo XXI España, 2019.

4 The publication of the false criminal record attributed to Dilma Rousseff (then head of staff for President Lula) in 2009 originally appeared in blogs and fake websites, later appearing in the pages of the printed press, which made the news go viral on social media.

5 For Spivak, those who find a way to speak or to be listened to in the public sphere cease to be subaltern.

References

Casara, Rubens. *Estado pós-democrático de Direito – Neo-obscurantismo e gestão dos indesejáveis*. Rio de Janeiro: Civilização Brasileira, 2017.

Foucault, Michel. *História da Sexualidade I: A vontade de saber; História da sexualidade 2: O uso dos prazeres; História da sexualidade 3: O cuidado de si*. Translated by Maria Thereza da Costa Albuquerque. Rio de Janeiro: Edições Graal, 1999.

Hall, Stuart. *A identidade cultural na pós-modernidade*. 4th ed. Translated by Tomaz Tadeu Silva and Guaciara Lopes Louro. Rio de Janeiro: DP&A, 2000.

Horkheimer, Max, and Theodor W. Adorno. *Dialética do esclarecimento: Fragmentos filosóficos*. Translated by Guido Antônio de Almeida. Rio de Janeiro: Zahar, 1985.

Lacan, Jacques. *Escritos*. Rio de Janeiro: Zahar, 1998.

OI – Observatório da Imprensa. "Folha publicou ficha falsa de Dilma." April 25, 2009. http://observatoriodaimprensa.com.br/imprensa-em-questao/folha-publicou-ficha-falsa-de-dilma. Accessed on November 2, 2019.

Ripoll, Cecília. *Rose* [play]. Rio de Janeiro: Cobogó, 2018.

Schwarcz, Lilia Moritz. *Sobre o autoritarismo brasileiro*. São Paulo: Companhia das Letras, 2019.

Schwarcz, Lilia Moritz, and Heloisa Murgel Starling. *Brasil: Uma biografia*. 1st ed. São Paulo: Companhia das Letras, 2015.

Souza, Jessé. *A elite do atraso: Da escravidão à Lava Jato*. Rio de Janeiro: Leya, 2017.

Spivak, Gayatry Chakravorty. *Pode o subalterno falar?* Translated by Sandra Regina Goulart Almeida, Marcos Pereira Feitosa, and André Pereira Feitosa. Belo Horizonte: Editora UFMG, 2010.

Veloso, Caetano. 2012. "O império da Lei" [song]. Album *Abraçaço*. Nonesuch Records Inc. 2014. www.youtube.com/watch?v=Dhn0XsLcCPI. Accessed on November 2, 2019.

2 The government of street vending

Formalizations of informality and use of force

Daniel Hirata

This chapter is a critical reflection on the "government" of street vending in the cities of São Paulo and Rio de Janeiro, based on research undertaken jointly with street vendors and their political leaders, public administrators, consultants and police. The term "government" here denotes a set of relations between those involved in the following activities: buying and selling goods; creating, extending or participating in channels of political dialogue in negotiations and disputes; enforcing legal or infra legal rules in those markets; wielding repressive or educational controls on street activities, and quantifying or qualifying "streets markets." Considering these various aspects and the historic particularities of the cities, the article summarizes some of the transversalities, that is, points of potential policy connection, present in both cities between the decades 1980–1990 and 2000–2010, when major changes emerged as "problematizations" in the government of street vending.[1]

Such changes point to relations of force and agencies that allow the existence of these markets, demarcate volatile frontiers between what is deemed "in" and "out" of the legal order and position how such markets are contentiously regulated. More precisely, this chapter investigates informality, not only as an exercise of the stated changes that seek to define it as a noun and adjective ("informality" or "informal" economy), but especially the "informal" and "illegal" shape the government of such ordinary economic practices and their forms of subjectivization. The research strategy and the exposition of this article involve not so much the definition of "informality" but rather discuss the disputes and controversies of "formalization" processes. One could say that formalizations are modalities of conversion (Guyer 2004), where different attempts to set the "game of exchange" (Braudel 1979) are made by investing in forms (Thèvenot 1986) and the document agency (Hull 2012). Formalizations look to stabilize the reticular circulation of people and merchandise and create conventions of equivalence (Desrosières 1993) that enable particular forms of government. From this viewpoint, it is very difficult to separate something like a "spontaneous economy" from a "formalized economy" (Vatin 2013), and therefore think that the boundaries between the State, society and market are preceded by the existence of such entities (Mitchell 2005).

This means that formalizations are inseparable from informality. They are relational socio-technical constructions that do not imply that something previously identifiable (such as "the informal") already exists. In fact, when informality is always "the other" of formality, the formal is established and, as a result and by contrast, the informal is identified. Informal economic practices are defined by what they "are not," by what "is lacking in them" or by what "they could potentially be," such as "something incomplete, outdated, archaic, not modern," or inversely "as a potency, a possibility, a way of overcoming obstacles." One must examine the openness to "what is debatable" (Latour 1988) in order to understand the formalizations; that is, what is debatable lies not only in building common parameters of cognitive and political representations, but also in the possibility of undoing the conventions of established equivalences, of questioning their references that build the relevance of the debate. I term this heterogeneous set of socio-technical inscriptions *reference*. Through this terminology I try to better describe the inflections in the relationship among informalities and formalizations between the decades of 1980–1990 and 2000–2010.

Scholarship on informality has traditionally focused on countries in Africa and Latin America, where the labor norm created in European countries seemed but a distant horizon (Hart 1973; Rabossi 2006). In Latin America, "informality" is a controversial topic relate to the productive and occupational structure of cities (Kowarick 1975; Nun 1969; Quijano 1971). It is precisely in the contrasting horizon between the experiences of these different countries that informality becomes a transitory activity as part of the modernization of labor. At first, in the period 1970–1980, the critique of marginality theories refuted the transitory nature of the informal, identifying the latter as a condition of peripheral modernization or underdevelopment (Kowarick 1975; Oliveira 1972). A second turning point of this debate occurred during the 1980s and 1990s, when other researchers considered informality an expression of "another" globalization, since it linked grassroots economy-related activities to the markets constituted by large corporations operating worldwide. This is often referred to as the so-called "globalization from below" (Portes 1997; Tarrius 2002). These authors call attention to the fact that informality is not a transitory and fleeting phenomenon but rather an element consisting of the transnationalism of labor and corporate markets.

Coterminous to the second moment, another group of authors questioned the horizon of the modernization theories, thinking differently about how to include informality through business, entrepreneurialism and credit means. The end target is also the labor norm of European countries but with business concerns taking a leading role in consideration. One of the main players was the Peruvian economist Hernando de Soto and his Institute of Liberty and Democracy (ILD) (De Soto 1987, 2001). Institutional outputs began in the 1980s–1990s. The author's own production is opposed to modernization theories and proposes to analyze the economies of the "South" as specific. The appeal and huge success of his proactive analyses come, however, from a theoretical construction sui generis on considering the informal economy as more dynamic and efficient than the formal, despite the oppressive, excessive regulation and state intervention (De Soto 1987). The proposed solution to lingering inequalities was to act on legalization and ownership rights, to release the assets and convert "dead capital" into "living capital" by financialization of such assets (De Soto 2001).

The success of De Soto's proposals was based on the initial support of the Atlas Foundation for Economic Research, help from economists such as Friedrich Hayek and Milton Friedman, numerous awards received, dissemination and implementation of his model by such agencies as the World Bank and the International Monetary Fund (IMF), in addition to a series of contracts in different countries around the world (Mitchell 2005). In slightly more than two decades, the ILD and its team had become a decisive think tank for the "anti-poverty" and "development" policies on a global scale.

This is well-known history, but the Brazilian experience helps provide a fundamental element related to this shift or change in reference due to the role of force in the case of Brazil. The relationship between formalization through entrepreneurship and the use of force is the contribution of this article to the set of studies on grassroots entrepreneurship (Elyachar 2012; Gago 2018). Thus, the question guiding the following exposition is: What does it mean to consider formalization based on the reference of labor and business? How are the grassroots markets produced and regulated by force? In the case of Brazil, it seems to me that the overlapping change between formalization based on the reference of labor and enterprise can only be understood concretely if we consider the use of force.

The period 1980–1990: regulation of activity and formation of the right to work on the street

In the early 1990s, street vendors figured in both cities as a problem (in terms of a lack or disorganization) of the relationship between urban and labor. Street vendors were regarded as belonging to a fraction of the population in between unemployment, vagrancy and survival activities, rather than workers. This is why the main form of interface between these vendors and the State was founded on policies and instruments to produce public law and order. The control of street vending was established as a role of city hall inspectors, and curtailed by the nascent municipal officers,[2] mobilized on occasion during the frequent clashes between inspectors and street vendors. The clashes are not incidental, because the laws regulating street vending as a professional activity are implemented later than those regulating control and inspection.[3] Yet even when the laws did begin to regulate activities, they focused on the use of public spaces rather than the labor standards. This means that, under strong sanction for people who are now situated outside the law, the governmental goal and heart of the dispute became the use of urban space. This established legal-political territory where disputes would occur and the control of the street vendors' points of sale was up for grabs.[4]

In another study, I discussed the heuristic importance of points as a descriptive-analytical category of the various modalities of the so-called informal and illegal markets (Hirata 2018). The specificity of the notion of the points in relation to street vending is that it is a market submitted to specific forms of legal and extra-legal authorization of buying and selling. The municipal authorizations in São Paulo are referred to as *TPU* (permission to use), and in Rio de Janeiro as *TUAP* (permission granted by the municipality for use of public spaces for sale of goods). Unlike other city trade permits, the registration and granting permission for use of public spaces do not attend the street vendors due to three main factors: the non-inclusive nature of the laws, the contradictory guidelines for decisions regarding concessions and the relatively high number of vendors compared to the quantity of permits provided by city hall. Despite a series of favorable legal decisions, most street vendors have failed to obtain or simply do not have the permits for selling goods in the streets.

Given such restrictions, most street vending points remain outside such regulations. "Outside" does not mean exteriority, since these points do not exist "parallel to" or in "empty spaces of" public institutions; rather, the spaces are deemed illegal by state agents. This leads to cases of bribery to inspectors when arrested (Das and Poole 2004); therefore, I stress the importance of *decisive interaction* between the direct agents of state control and the actors who participate in such markets. In the native or emic term, this decisive interaction between police and street vendors is called "a deal," "the truncheon" or "bootlicking." These interactions that constitute everyday practical agency services form a concept of political merchandise (Misse 2006).[5] The abuse suffered by the street vendors preceded the landmark law, but the street vendor regulations expanded the market of political goods, because it attracted them to extra-legal regulatory forms where the use of force was the explicit rule of creating such markets.

Despite these problems, this is still a legal application of the thresholds between the legal and illegal and sets a parameter for the dispute for the street vendor points. Before the existence of legal inscription, the interactions between agents immediately in charge of inspection and the street vendors possessed no legal parameter, and helps explain why street vendors were completely at the mercy of the inspectors' case-by-case decisions, including: who could or who could not sell goods and which vendors would suffer or not the effects of a sanction. This is the reason why, despite being restrictive, illegible, limited and approved by the mayors without community consultation in both cities, street vendors refer to those laws as the "street vendor act," since they established some kind of regulation and protection, albeit precarious, for people engaged in this activity. The key issue is that the legal framework of the forms of the activity's inspection coincides with a practical-discursive matrix of the "right to work in the street." A political dispute is established regarding the use of public space, considered a right by those workers. The way in which the activity has been regulated, therefore, sets the urban space at the center of the dispute, and the *polarization* between street vendors and the municipality as the main protagonists. This legal-political territory came under the fire of street vendor associations and syndicates, and the entire claims agenda was scrutinized during a series of demonstrations, protests, public complaints, court cases, riots, direct attacks on inspection agents and occupation of commerce spaces. In essence, this became the street vendors' operating repertoire (Tilly 2008).[6]

In the case of São Paulo, it is worth emphasizing that these clashes were directed at the typical extortion schemes of the political markets, in a series of events between 1995 and 2002 known as "the inspectors' mafia."[7] These events radically changed the São Paulo partisan political power game, investigating an entire group of city counselors that culminated in the impeachment process of the mayor Celso Pitta (Cardozo 2000). In Rio de Janeiro, the disputes did not create such a widespread vertical impact, evinced by the higher number of occurrences between street vendors and municipal guards in the Rio de Janeiro City Urban Disputes Chart (Nacif 2011).[8]

What seems to me most important so far in the characterization of the government of street vending is: *first*, coercion as a central state instrument; *second*, municipal regularization of the use of public spaces highlighting the restriction on registration and licenses; *third*, and as a consequence of the first two characteristics, the creation of a conflicting field (which I have called legal-political territory) that crosses through the markets of political goods and the claims to extend municipal licenses.

The period 2000–2010: militarization and entrepreneurialism

The decades 2000 and 2010 are very important in both cities because a series of displacements occurred. The building of the legal-political territory is not demolished but is superposed by a change in the reference that organizes street vendor government. This is because the street vendors are either criminalized or transformed into enterprises. This happened not only by intensifying the grassroots policies through *militarization* of urban space, but also by focusing urban planning and economic integration through the *entrepreneurship* form. The latter are the main shifts of a similar *governmental style* in São Paulo and Rio de Janeiro.

Partnerships, self-government and opportunities

A first fundamental displacement of the *reference* involves the rules establishing parameters, the definition of inside/outside of state norms. Contrary to the relationship built through legal-political territory, which separated the formal and informal by licenses to use urban space, the attempts to regulate the street vendors were now organized differently based on the supplementary law no. 128/80, which amended the General Act of Small and Very Small Businesses (supplementary law no. 123/06), implemented in 2009. This law provides a series of benefits for the so-called "individual micro entrepreneurship" (*MEI*), offering an alternative to street vendors who wish to formalize their status through this new business legal entity. The law is accompanied by a series of "benefits" that are much more "inclusive" and clear, compared to the registration difficulties via concessions for use of urban space: with no restriction of profile, anyone can register via the Internet, with a single annual statement on billing (also by Internet) and exemption of the company's registration fees; therefore, when comparing the difficult and illegible concession forms of the TPUs and TUAPs, registration became much easier and at practically the same cost. With regard to the core of the law, there was a reduction in tax rates compared with larger companies and a promise of widespread social security coverage, promoting a new hybrid form, where social rights are accessed when an individual becomes an enterprise.

This new way of thinking about formality and social rights also included the support of institutions promoting the entrepreneurs' "self-achievement", such as the Brazilian Service for support of micro enterprises and small businesses (Sebrae) and public banks: the former occured through guidance in the formalization process via the aforementioned MEI, in addition to technical support for capacity building of the micro entrepreneurs through courses, business planning, advice and guidelines in order to develop "entrepreneurial capacities and skills." Public banks, such as the Bank of Brazil [*Banco do Brasil*], Northeast Bank [*Banco do Nordeste*] and the Federal Savings Banks [*Caixa Econômica Federal*], offer good credit conditions through special funding lines with reduced tariffs and lower interest rates. Lastly, an "opportunity" emerged through the permission of the joint procurement through consortia, since the law provided for this alliance of micro entrepreneurs for procurement with more favorable terms of payment price for goods procured in larger quantities.

This new formalization diagram displaces the reference that adjusted the way in which the street vendors' regulations had been made up until then. However, it is worth mentioning that this new diagram of formalization does not *substitute* but *superposes* the earlier one, to the extent that work in public places also needs municipal permits. For this reason, there was very little adoption of the business format among the formalized street vendors already installed in the streets. The major impact of the enterprise form as a new way of formalizing the street vendors, however, happened in closed environments, the so-called grassroots shopping malls or street markets, in both cities as a result of the contentious interface between State and street vendors in the matrix of the "right to work in the streets."[9]

It is curious that it was exactly in those spaces where the new entrepreneurial diagram had its strongest effects and the enterprise form was more widespread, either due to the quantity of people who became MEIs, the proliferation of training courses in "entrepreneurial capacities and skills," or to the buying and selling consortia and access to credit. The associations and later the management committees of these closed environments, with a number of members and degree of organization very different to those operating in the streets, very quickly organized themselves within this new entrepreneurial diagram and started up the programs much more intensely than the latter.

The key to the entrepreneurialism diagram is a displacement of the formal/informal reference of the street vendors from a statute of "quasi-workers" to that of "quasi-enterprises." The legal-political territory established, under local permits to sell in public places, a *polarization* between State and street vendor, which provoked major demonstrations and disputes wherever this diagram operated. What the entrepreneurialism diagram produces as an interface of contact between street vendors and State are *partnerships* formed through a convergence of interests to promote the commercial sector.

The street vendors when "quasi-workers" had a "quasi-enterprise," which was the municipality, from where a "quasi-labor relationship" in the measure of the hierarchy was established between them. Even if in the letter of the law the street vendors were considered self-employed, the relations built with the municipality in a specific sense that I attempted to emphasize above, were much closer than employment relations. The dispute for the use of public places demonstrated the asymmetry of the relationship, configuring polarization, and in São Paulo it is no coincidence that street vendors were referred to as "street workers," saying that the "State was the street vendors' boss," and street vendor organizations were called predominantly trade unions, also with union cards linked to the Central Union of Workers (CUT) and the Union Force depending on the political connections.[10]

Inasmuch as government intervention transformed street vendors into "quasi-enterprises," the polarization created by a markedly asymmetrical and hierarchical relationship became a contract between partners. As enterprises that wish to compete in the grassroots market, the associations that manage the internal environments seek to match the parameters set by the municipality, first through training courses that pedagogically instruct how to organize themselves within this new form of state incidence, then as players in programs designed for them as procurement consortia and access to credit.

In both cities, this activity previously regarded as urban disorganization and belonging to the labor world gradually moves to being considered a front of economic development faced with competition from other cities. Thus, an important turning point of the urban renovation projects occurs, incorporating popular markets as part of their strategic objectives. The current projects of São Paulo's "main shopping street" to renew the downtown region, vying with the mega-events in Rio de Janeiro (Olympics and World Cup), are examples of how this shift in interpreting the State changes in the entrepreneurialism diagram. Competition between large cities for economic resources accommodates and places on the horizon the impact of such markets as a relevant item of the urban economy and, consequently, popular commerce now becomes a question of sharing of wealth and no longer a question of poverty and social problems.

Militarization of the urban space

If the incentive for the enterprise form was limited to closed environments, state intervention in the streets proceeded in a very different way. Criminalization of street vendors intensified by further militarization of the forms of control and urban spaces. The territorialized occupation of certain areas by the forces of order and the use of a blatant coercive deterrent power accentuates militarization as a preferential form of controlling the street vendors.

In relation to this militarized state action in public places, three points must be emphasized: first, a new "institutional design" of municipal administration; second, established programs that reorganize their roles and modify their powers to exercise them. Lastly, as a consequence of these first two points, political markets change in function of the *decisive interaction* between the agents immediately responsible for controlling itinerant trade and street vendors.

In Rio de Janeiro, The Special Secretariat of Public Order (SEOP) was created on the first day of Eduardo Paes' term of office by decree 30,339 dated 1 January 2009. This regulatory act revised the entire organizational structure of the municipal administrative power relating to the construction of public order with no Legislative consultation or public participation thanks to its "special" character as allegedly provisional (Nacif 2011).[11] In São Paulo, The Municipal Department for Urban Security (SMSU) had been created earlier in 2002, when Marta Suplicy was the mayor. Both have as one of their main objectives the "upsurge of street vending control." What seems to be clear in the origin of the new institutional design is the concept of coordinated administration of public order, justified by the appeals for improved efficacy of the public order administration (Hirata and Cardoso 2016). This is a new form of urban planning, whose main concern is public security (Oblet 2008), anchored in the "new military urbanism" (Graham 2011), which sets trends and equivalences between military strategies and urban planning.

It is essential to firmly understand how the programs of those secretariats operated. In São Paulo the Delegated Operation program (law no. 14,977/09 and decree no. 50,994/09) allowed the military police on their days off to work up to 96 hours a month for the city government, earning an extra bonus paid by the municipality. However, more decisive was the delegation of tasks that designates the operation, and establishes a transfer of the attributes to control informal commerce from sub-prefecture inspectors and police officers of the metropolitan civil guard to the powerful military police. On the one hand, the agreement harms the constitutional division of each control agency's roles, diluting the specificities of inspection roles in favor of extending the scope of action to the Military Police (*PM*). By centralizing in the action of the Military Police the roles previously shared among the different agents for street vendor control, the delegation facilitates faster and more efficient control in the day-by-day life of the neighborhood. Major Wagner Rodrigues, head of the Center's Administration and Operation Division, said that this way of conceiving inspection was based on the experience of other earlier operations that he himself had commanded, where it was noticeable that role sharing "hindered efficient control." He demonstrated that the so-called "parachutes" – street vendors who extend their merchandise on cloth on the ground in order to escape inspection by wrapping them up – were seldom caught because when the cloth was opened out the role of inspection of street points was the responsibility of the municipal civil guards (*GCM*), and when closed in to kind of "bag" only the Military Police could search personal belongings. It was due to this increase in the military police powers that the structure of the police force was mobilized to operate in the Brás neighborhood, one of the main traditional street markets in the city. Riot police, cavalry, many mobile bases and special units were sent to occupy the neighborhood. Days later the head of the PM announced a decline in petty crime, such as theft and robbery, publicized as undeniable proof of the action's success, which was then extended to other parts of the city. Street vending was also cited as a drop in crime, even though the activity itself is not a crime, but at that time it was no coincidence that the war against piracy was also municipalized under a global anti-piracy program organized by the UN and World Bank recently installed in the Ministry of Justice.

In Rio de Janeiro, the group of operations known as "*Choque de Ordem*" (literally "shock of order") was the main SEOP program. In its first year, the shock referred to a perceptive impact, according to which the city hall attempted to "convey a message" that "everything had changed" (Velloso 2012). In that same first year, the street vendors figured in these operations by way of the major re-registration of street vendors centralized in the Single Register for Street Commerce (*CUCA*). In the second year of the new secretariat, the SEOP operating methods were rearranged in the constitution of the "*choque de ordem II*," where the Public Order Units (*UOP*) were now the most important operating instrument. The *UOP* land use model replaces the itinerant practice that had previously characterized the implementation of the *Choque de Ordem*. In this new model, the permanent occupation of the law enforcement is assumed as a more effective form of operating the secretary's programs and projects.

At first, the Municipal Guard (*GM*) changed the strategy during the early morning hours before the stalls. Tents and tables were set up as a point of sale for the street vendors. The current *GM* commander said that the "territorial domain" prior to opening the market facilitates its role since right from the start it warns everyone who "is boss" there, with far lower "costs" of a later action. After implementing the Unidade de Polícia Pacificadora/Pacifying Police Unit (*UPPS*), the assessment of the efficacy of the territorial dimension confirmed the embryonic experience of the GM. The issue change and thus required a new way of interpretation and instrumentation, since the GM was not designed to act in this territorialized format. The most important item is that as the territorialized format is crystallizing, the GM centrality in the SEOP is even greater, becoming stronger on completion as the main instrument of social-spatial order.

The occupation of the downtown neighborhoods in both cities changes the dynamics of the *decisive interaction* between street vendors and the agents responsible for controlling the activity. Territorialization as a form of control, in both cities, demonstrates that the market of political goods is concentrated as long as the control is now taken in this manner; in other words, extortion is now "wholesale," in negotiations between the military command of operations and the associations controlling the closed environments and concentrating the market flows. The street vendors' associations, less organized and unable to pay the increase in price of political goods, stay outside these negotiations or, in specific cases, also occur in "retail" episodically and uncertainly, with no assurance that it is a reliable exchange and the sale guaranteed.

This means that disputes for points of sale change completely when selecting incitement policies in business format and militarize public order. The trend occurs to the extent that a *certain* steering to the formalization and incentive process for closed environments is coupled with military-security control. It would be exaggerated and wrong to say that such a transformation occurs *to enable* the markets to operate in this way, but there are affinities and convergences that create a specific form of government that *produces effects* in that direction.

Conclusion

This brief overview of the street vendors government in the cities of São Paulo and Rio de Janeiro provides general outlines to the changes in its forms of problematization. This was done by demarcating the boundaries and the reference that separate and compare the practices in and outside the state legal order, and create and regulate the appropriation of wealth circulating in the regions of both cities. On the one hand, this study is based on an important discussion about the production of the neoliberal forms of subjectivity, associated with enterprises form and entrepreneurialism (Dardot and Laval 2010), but it also calls attention to the importance of use of force, decisive for producing and regulating popular markets in Brazil. The shift of the government of street vending between 2000 and 2010 indicates a change in the differentiated management of illegalisms (Foucault 1976); that is, of the balance of tolerance and repression that selectively concerns those markets, marked by the thresholds between legality and illegality, formality and informality (Hirata 2018; Telles and Hirata 2010). This does not mean that dispute is not present in the streets, but rather that the terms in which it is undertaken have changed considerably.

Notes

1 Seeing street vending as a problem or "problematization" relates to a form of constructing objects of research that closely follows a logic described by Michel Foucault. To analyze the conditions of a possibility of multiple solutions for one problem (facts, practices and thoughts) accepts problematization. The Foucauldian question would always be "How was it possible?" See Foucault 2001 as well as "*Polémique, politique et problématisations*" (text 342 of book IV).

2 If at first the role of inspection was a prerogative of the municipal inspectors, the use of force was operationalized jointly with the municipal guards right from the start. In São Paulo, the metropolitan civil guard, an institution dating back to the beginning of the century, is recreated in a democratic context in 1986 as one of the first in Brazil (Law 10.115/86). In the case of Rio de Janeiro, it was created in 1992 (Law 1.887/92), implemented with the first public examination held only the following year.

3 In Rio de Janeiro's case, Law no. 1.876/92, in São Paulo Law no. 11.039/91.

4 The term *camelô* (in Portuguese) is a synonym for street vendor and both imply the same ambiguity, when simultaneously referring to fixed or mobile commerce in the city streets. For the purpose of this text, such differences will be minimized considering that, even those vendors operating on a mobile basis, also generally undertake their work within a defined perimeter, being influenced by the dynamics of the disputes for points of sale. See Mafra (2005) regarding this difference between mobile and fixed street vendors.

5 Political merchandise and the marketing of political goods are concepts discussed by Michel Misse. It is an analytical construction that criticizes the discourse of the "economics of corruption," which generally centers on moral and institutional dysfunctions. Moreover, to consider how this market of specific goods operates, political merchandise are understood not only to be the relations between supply and demand but also "strategic assessments of power, the potential resource to violence and balance of forces; that is, strictly political assessments." See Misse 2006 and Pires 2010.

6 This argument meets what Fernando Rabossi (2011) identified in Ciudad del Leste, where the legal-political territory boosted the formation of associations.

7 The scheme known as "the bribery mafia" coordinated "from below" the payment by street vendors to inspectors of the regional agencies by depositing merchandise, setting up stalls and warning of police checkpoints, while "above," regional administrators who would collect money from the inspectors and pass it on to counselors linked to the government in force. The scheme's purpose was to pay for the election campaigns and personal enrichment of this group, but was, first and foremost, a form of local structuring of the traditional crony capitalist power in São Paulo. See Cardozo 2000.

8 The Urban Dispute Chart in the City of Rio de Janeiro [*O Mapa de Conflitos Urbanos da Cidade do Rio de Janeiro*] is a project of the Permanent Observatory of Urban Disputes (Ettern-Ippur-UFRJ) involving a survey of the demonstrations in the "city as an arena and object," by means of collecting data from the press and Ombudsman's Office, and annals of the relevant public authorities. See www.ettern.ippur.ufrj.br/projetos-em-andamento/38/observatorio-de-conflitos-urbanos-no-rio-de-janeiro. Accessed on November 5, 2019.

9 The Uruguaiana Popular Market, first in the city of Rio de Janeiro, inaugurated in 1994 after a failed attempt in 1984 in Plaza XI, was the result of a liaison of street vendor leaderships with the then governor Nilo Batista. This represented a continuity with state guidance under Leonel Brizola, who regarded these spaces as a form of state action closer to the interests of the street vendors. In São Paulo the *Madrugada* market began operating in 2004, also as a liaison between mayor Marta Suplicy with street vendor leaders, in a recovery process of policies begun in the Luiza Erundina administration.

10 CUT is currently the largest trade union in Brazil, created in 1983 amidst major strikes and the so-called "new trade unionism." The *Força Sindical* (Union Force), the second central union in the country, was founded in 1991 as a reaction and lies more to the center of the political-ideological spectrum in relation to CUT.

11 The secretariat consists of pre-existing agencies in the municipal structure, but which traditionally operated autonomously and separately, namely: the Under-Secretary of Inspection (merger of the licensing and inspection company-CLF, and the parking and trailer inspection company-CFER), urban control (merger of the Urban Control Company agency-CCU); and operations (Municipal Guard).

References

Braudel, Fernand. *Civilização material, economia e capitalism: O jogo das trocas*. Translated by Maria Antonieta Magalhães Godinho. São Paulo: Martins Fontes, 1989 [1979].

Cardozo, José Eduardo. *A Máfia das Propinas*. São Paulo: Fundação Perseu Abramo, 2000.

Dardot, Pierre and Laval, Christian. *La nouvelle raison du monde*. Paris: La Découvert, 2010.

Das, Veena, and Deborah Poole. *Anthropology in the Margins of the State*. Oxford and Santa Fe: James Currey/School of American Research Press, 2004.

De Soto, Hernando. *Economia subterrânea: Uma analise da realidade peruana*. Translated by Gilson Schwartz. Rio de Janeiro: Globo, 1987.

De Soto, Hernando. *O Mistério do capital*. Translated by Zaida Maldonado. Rio de Janeiro: Editora Record, 2001.

Donzelot, Jacques. *La invention du social*. Paris: Seuil, 1984.

Desrosières, Alain. *La politique des grands nombres*. Paris: La Découvert, 1993.

Ewald, François. *L'etat providence*. Paris: Grasset, 1986.

Elyachar, Julia. "Next Practices: Knowledge, Infrastructure, and Public Goods at the Bottom of the Pyramid." *Public Culture* 24, no. 1 (January 2012): 109–129.

Foucault, Michel. *Surveiller et Punir*. Paris: Galimard, 1976.

Foucault, Michel. *Dits et Écrits*. Paris: Gallimard, 2001.

Foucault, Michel. *Segurança, Território, População*. Translated by Eduardo Brandão. São Paulo, Martins Fontes, 2008.

Gago, Veronica. *A razão neoliberal: Economias barrocas e pragmática popular*. São Paulo: Elefante, 2018.

Graham, Stephan. *Cities under Siege: The New Military Urbanism*. London: Verso, 2011.

Guyer, Jane. *Marginal Gains: Monetary Transactions in Atlantic Africa*. London: University of Chicago Press, 2004.

Hirata, Daniel Veloso. *Sobreviver na Adversidade: Mercados e formas de vida.* São Carlos: Edufscar, 2018.

Hirata, Daniel, and Bruno Cardoso. "Coordenação como tecnologia de governo." *Horizontes antropológicos* 22, no. 46 (2016): 97–130.

Hart, Keith. "Informal Income Opportunities and Urban Employment in Ghana." *Journal of Modern African Studies* 3, no. 11 (1973): 61–89.

Hull, Mathew. *Government of Paper: The Materiality of Bureaucracy in Urban Pakistan.* Berkeley: University of California Press, 2012.

Kowarick, Lucio. *Capitalismo e marginalidade na América Latina.* São Paulo: Paz e Terra, 1975.

Latour, Bruno. Science en action. Cambridge: Harvard University Press, 1988.

Machado da Silva, Luis Antonio. "Da Informalidade a Empregabilidade (reorganizando a dominação no mundo do trabalho)." *Cadernos CRH* 15, no. 37 (2002): 81–109.

Mafra, Patricia. "A 'pista' e o 'camelódromo': Camelôs no centro do Rio de Janeiro", Master's thesis, National Museum/Federal University of Rio de Janeiro, 2005.

Misse, Michel. *Crime e Violência no Brasil Contemporâneo.* Rio de Janeiro, Editora Lumen Júris, 2006.

Mitchell, Timothy. "The Work of Economics: How a Discipline Makes Its World." *European Journal of Sociology* 46, no. 2 (2005): 297–320.

Mitchell, Timothy. "The Properties of Markets." In *Do Economists Make Markets? On the Performativity of Economics*, edited by Donald MacKenzie, Fabian Muniesa, and Lucia Siu, 244–275. Princeton: Princeton University Press, 2007.

Nacif, Cristina Lontra, Diego da Costa Cardoso, and Maria Baldo Ribeiro. "Estado de Choque: Legislação e conflito no espaço público da cidade do Rio de Janeiro-Brasil (1993–2010)." *Anais do XIV Encontro Nacional da Anpur*, Rio de Janeiro: ENANPUR, 2011. http://anais.anpur.org.br/index.php/anaisenanpur/article/view/ 696/681. Accessed on November 5, 2019.

Nun, Jose. "Superpoblacíon relativa, ejército industrial de reserva y massa marginal." *Revista Latinoamericana de Sociologia* 5, no. 2 (1969): 174–236.

Oblet, Thierry. *Défendre la ville: La police, l'urbanisme et les habitants.* Paris: PUF, 2008.

Oliveira, Francisco de. "A Economia Brasileira: Crítica a razão dualista." *Novos estudos CEBRAP* 2 (1972): 4–82.

Pires, Lenin. "Arreglar não é pedir arrego", PhD diss., Federal University Fluminense, 2010.

Portes, Alejandre. "Globalization from Below." In *Latin America in the World Economy*, edited by W. P. Smith and R. P. Korczenwicz, 151–168. Westport, CT: Greenwood Press, 1997.

Quijano, Anibal. *Polo Marginal de la economia y mano de obra marginada.* Lima, Universidad Católica, 1971.

Rabossi, Fernando. *Os caminhos da informalidade.* Mimeo, 2006.

Rabossi, Fernando. "Negociações, associações e monopólio: A política de rua em Ciudad del Este (Paraguay)." *Etnográfica* 15, no. 1 (2011): 83–107

Tarrius, Alain. *La mondialisation par le bas: Les nouveaux nomades de l'économie souterraine.* Paris: Balland, 2002.

Telles, Vera, and Daniel Hirata. "Ilegalismos e jogos de poder em São Paulo." *Tempo Social* 22, no. 2 (2010): 39–59.

Thèvenot, Laurent. "Les investisement de forme." In *Conventions économiques*, edited by Laurent Thévenot, 21–71. Paris: PUF, 1986.

Tilly, Charles. *Politique(s) du conflit: De la grève à la revolution*. Paris: Presses de Sciences Po, 2008.

Vatin, François. *Évaluer et valoriser: Une sociologie économique de la mesure*. Toulouse: PUM, 2013.

Velloso, Natalia. "Políticas da ordem: poder e imaginação na criação da cidade olímpica", Master's thesis, Federal University of Rio de Janeiro, 2012.

3 Migrant refugee spatialities lived and legislated in São Paulo

Igor Machado and Derek Pardue

A central element of the human condition is mobility. As a species, we have realized that knowledge, power, resources and networks emerge from strategic movement and meaningful encounters. Such a discourse includes histories and legacies of conquest, colonialism, slavery, capitalism and the so-called modern nation-state. It is also a discourse of inalienable human rights in the face of a "globalized indifference," in the recent words of Pope Francis, who has used his position as an international spokesperson of morality on several occasions to speak out on the issue of immigration and social justice. He and scores of other community leaders and activists have observed that what was once justifiable in the name of "civilization" is now under sharp scrutiny as a threat to humanity and an illegal transgression.

Migration and its politically charged specification of *im*migration represent the glaring contradictions of il/legality as they relate to the spatiality of everyday existence. As scholars such as Shahram Khosravi, Nicholas de Genova and others have argued, immigration has become a politically profitable and publically prevalent manner to "produce criminality and illegality" involving a set of "technologies of anti-citizenship" (Khosravi 2010, 115ff). Ascribed qualities of "primitive masculinity" to Muslims in Sweden or "dangerous" or "worthless Africans" in Brazil help reconfirm an imagined Swedish masculinity and Brazilian whiteness, respectively. We are faced with questions that are both existentially philosophical and pragmatically political. Should the very presence of someone be grounds of legality? Can one just *be* here and try, like everyone else, to live and work? Moreover, for the purposes of this edited volume, what might Brazil contribute to this set of universal questions?

Despite the recent rise in xenophobia among a number of national leaders, including those in Brazil, few, if any, would issue a blanket statement against immigration. That is to say, immigration itself is not an illegal act. "We want to attract the right kind of immigrants," so the political talking point goes, the "legitimate" or useful ones, as Zygmunt Bauman (2004) once described. In the transformation of moral discourse into law and policy, the social or identity categories of race and ethnicity play a definitive role in who constitutes the "right kind of immigrant" (Fernandes 2019).

In Brazil, arguably the "blackest" country in the world outside of Nigeria, the role that racism plays in the delineation of accepted immigrants and refugees is markedly significant. From 2011 to 2017, Brazil experienced a dramatic increase in arrivals of "new" foreigners, those from Haiti, Senegal, Congo (DRC), Mali, Angola, Nigeria as well as thousands of Syrians. In the following, we will demonstrate the multiple dimensions that racism and, more generally, racialization play in the interpretation of the new Migration Law (*Lei de Migração 13.445/17*), as it relates to categorization (refugee versus humanitarian visa) and social service infrastructure (health, residential and Portuguese language services). We attempt to balance policy analysis with prosaic narrative in order to approximate political policy with lived experience, as we see these perspectives as complementary and not separate. This chapter is based on ethnographic fieldwork in the city and state of São Paulo since 2016.[1] Ultimately, we suggest that practices of racialization work to produce both a hypervisibility and an erasure of blackness, which, in concert, twist and contort legalities with real effects on how newly arrived black migrants navigate urban public spaces. In this respect, our chapter enters in dialogue with Hirata from this volume; socio-economic and political marginalities produce certain spatialities. Both texts exemplify current contestations over "legal-political territories."

Legal context

Similar to most countries in the world and all nations on the American continent, Brazil was forged through migration. Coercion, opportunity, escape and religious conversion are only some of the many qualifiers one might use to describe the range of migration constitutive of Brazil. Both creative and violent, migration is undeniably foundational to understanding Brazil. Yet, for many, such movement and encounter belong to the past, a formative period of colonial and post-colonial moments. Until 2017, the last systematic policy on immigration occurred during the military dictatorship under a Cold War episteme highlighting concerns over "subversives" and "Communism." The 1980 Law, referred to as the *Estatuto do Estrangeiro* (Foreigner Statute, Law 6.815/80) frames immigration in terms of a national security threat. In subsequent years, a wide range of communities have argued and succeeded in effecting policy to represent migration as an inalienable "human right." This shift is at the heart of the new Immigration Law in Brazil of 2017. Despite the 20 last-minute executive alterations made by interim president Michel Temer, which have been detrimental to hundreds of indigenous and indo-African (*quilombolas)* communities, already established but undocumented immigrants as well as immigrants seeking health care,[2] many activists maintain that the new law is a step forward (Soares 2017). While a detailed analysis of the particularities of the law itself and their significance is outside the purview of this text,[3] we underscore the relationship between social demographics of migration and legal formation (Zapat and Fazito 2018, 230).

There is an order of different categories in the experience of black immigrants/refugees in São Paulo. When we speak of black immigrants and refugees, we refer to Haitians and Africans of various origins (Senegalese, Congolese, Angolans, Guineans, etc.). Legally, they experience different forms of insertion in the Brazilian visa granting system. Haitians have been formally denied the possibility of requesting refugee status under CONARE (National Committee for Refugees) Regulation 18, unlike the others, and can only apply for refuge in very specific cases. That a mere two Haitian refugees were approved by CONARE until 2018 underscores this difficulty. The other foreigners can apply for refugee status, which does not mean they obtain it. However, with the request for refuge, the foreigner can legally enter the country and work while the case is under review, which lasts on average approximately three years. Thus, there is a time window in which these Africans can legally stay in the country, at the end of which they may or may not have the refugee status approved. If not, they will have to leave the country, or remain without documentation, or try other forms of legalization, such as a work visa, which allows residence for two years (renewable). It is important to add that after four years of residency in Brazil, it is possible to apply for permanent residence.

For Haitians, the Brazilian state created a special category, called a "humanitarian visa" (later extended to Syrians) that allows legal residence in the country. This visa was an alternative to produce documentation for a relatively high number of Haitian migrants in Brazil, while at the same time aiming to contain the influx of more Haitians, since it imposed limitations on the granting of a humanitarian visa.[4]

It is important to highlight here the implications of legal differences in the experience of these foreigners in Brazil. In bureaucratic terms, immigrants and refugees (or refugee seekers) deal with different entities at first. When an African applies for refugee status, the federal police, responsible for controlling the entry and exit of people from the country, refers the case to CONARE, linked to the Ministry of Justice. Meanwhile, the applicant receives a provisional document, which allows for work and residence in the country. Haitian immigrants apply for a humanitarian visa before arriving in the country, or along the travel route (in Ecuador or Peru, for example). The granting of these visas was linked to the CNIg (National Immigration Council), linked to the Ministry of Labor – until it was finally extinguished and incorporated into the Ministry of Finances by the new government inaugurated in January of 2019. However, in both cases the first contact bureaucracy is the federal police, since there is no specific bureaucratic structure of management for immigration in the country. The volume of Haitians was larger than anticipated by the quotas of Brazilian policy, leading the Brazilian State to work in collaboration with Peru and Ecuador to limit the entry of Haitians before reaching the Brazilian Amazonian frontiers (see Fernandes and Faria 2017).

The multiple effects of outsourcing

Having refugee status can be more advantageous than possessing a humanitarian visa status in some situations. The State of São Paulo, where about half the refugee population is concentrated in Brazil (Cavalcanti et al., 2015), has produced laws that allow, for example, a process of recognition of diplomas without the usual high cost in Brazil. In the Brazilian case, assistance to refugees (and in some cases for immigrants) is a policy outsourced by the State, which transfers resources to various NGOs to produce social actions. Often the source of resources comes directly from international bodies such as UNHCR (United Nations High Commission for Refugees), for example. In general, these policies cover receiving refugees and occasionally immigrants, in shelters where they can stay for six months to a year; assistance in accessing Brazilian public services; job search assistance; Portuguese classes; psychological assistance among other services. Some of these policies are offered exclusively to refugees, in which case the legal status would supposedly make a difference. Putting policies into practice have multiple and sometimes contradictory outcomes.

The case of migrant and refugee mental health services is an example of how the agents who produce "reception" articulate other ideas of difference. From the point of view of the attendants, Haitians and Africans in São Paulo belong to the same category of difference, which we could term foreign *negritude*. They are all black and do not speak Portuguese or speak it with an accent. The example discussed by Branco (2019) is instructive. With resources, received from UNHCR, an NGO sets out to offer and manage a refugee mental health policy. This action would happen together with other promoted by the NGO, related to classes of Portuguese and formal assistance in obtaining employment.

Accompanying the day-to-day provision of the mental health service, Branco made two discoveries: first, there was little demand for the collective sessions offered by the NGO, and, second, this small demand was composed mainly of Haitians and other foreigners, but very few "real refugees." The sessions were scheduled and, most of the time, did not happen. On one occasion, a single foreigner attended and offered a lesson in his native language to psychologists, since it was not possible to hold a session with only one person.

On another occasion, there was a UNHCR inspection visit to the NGO to verify the effectiveness of the services provided. For this visit, it was necessary to organize a "real" session with "real" refugees, that is, there should be no Haitians or foreigners who were not refugees present. More Haitians attended the session than refugees; they were essentially "smuggled in" as refugees. This particular example shows that for the NGO workers, Africans and Haitians were within the same semantic field, unconsciously articulated by the issue of blackness. Importantly, there was a sociological reason to group them together: they lived in the same outlying neighborhoods of São Paulo or in the same urban occupations. Consequently, they experienced similar difficulties in the labor market and challenges in adapting to the hostile geography of the city.

We can conclude that the agents of the NGO inserted black foreigners into the Brazilian systems of racial classification,[5] which tend to produce high inequality for the black population. The fact that the urban geography in which these black foreigners circulate is the same geography of exclusion of the black populations in the city of São Paulo facilitates this association between skin color and exclusion, between discrimination directed to Afro-Brazilians and that addressed to black foreigners. Branco calls this process "exclusionary inclusion." In effect, the legal distinction between refuge and immigration when applied to black foreigners disappears. The funds destined exclusively for refugees are often used to serve black African immigrants as well as Haitians, since for the workers of these organizations, there is no real difference between them. They are all black and foreign.

Different nationalities, different languages, different legal statutes are not relevant to blackness, which operates as a first classifier and thus"overrides" all others, organizing another way of classifying and managing the difference represented by these refugees and black immigrants. This other form presupposes more or less as natural the exclusion to which Afro-Brazilians are subjected, naturalizing the difficulties and extreme conditions of vulnerability. According to Almeida (2019), the phrase "is also so for Brazilians," heard constantly by black foreigners, signals this process of naturalization of exclusion, because it means, in effect, "this precarious situation is the same as that of Afro-Brazilians in the favelas."

In the end, legal status, nationality or language spoken by black foreigners are secondary to the primacy of skin color, which places them in the same position of exclusion of Afro-Brazilians. Thus, it is only natural, in the uncritical eyes of NGO workers, that these foreigners suffer as black Brazilians suffer. The transposition of this internalization of racial orders equates the different migration experiences as a single set, marked by the negritude of the foreigners. Thus, to black foreigners, exclusion is seen as natural, as the precarious conditions of insertion into Brazilian society rival what Afro-Brazilians have come to expect.

It is not the case that NGO workers, who provide care and "hospitality," make no distinctions between refugees and immigrants. Local ethnographic research highlights the perception of vulnerability. In practice, such recognition is directed at refugees seen as white in the local conceptions of race and color. Syrian refugees provide perhaps the best example. It is important to emphasize that conceptions of race and color are imminently cultural, as classifications are structured by rules constituted in a local historical scenario and it is only possible to understand it effectively in temporal perspectives.

While there is not enough space to discuss the historicity of color categories in Brazil and specifically in São Paulo, we can direct the reader to the extensive literature on the subject. In the main, this literature spans the

Brazilian slave system and its social consequences (Azevedo 1987) to migration policies of the nineteenth and twentieth century, marked by the concern of the Brazilian elite with "ethnic" composition of the national population (Seyferth 1998; Lesser 2013). With regard to Syrian refugees (and also Palestinians), it is noteworthy that they are part of a relatively established trajectory of Syrian-Lebanese migration in the early twentieth century, which was of great importance both numerically and culturally. That is, the fact that thousands of Brazilians are descended from Syrians and Lebanese and are seen as "white" plays a role in the racialization of the new Syrian refugees.[6]

Seen, therefore, as whites, an imagery of refuge is specially created for them, effectively distinguishing the Syrians from black African refugees. The primacy of race remains significant. This helps explain why black refugees themselves use the categories of "white refugee" and "black refugee" as anemic categories (Branco 2019 and Almeida 2019). Moreover, black refugees/immigrants clearly perceive that there is a preference for the "white refugee" among the workers of the NGOs and even in the Brazilian State.

Almeida (2019) argues this based on quotidian examples. After becoming close to a number of African women while volunteering at a local NGO, she decided to accompany them as they left the shelter due to time limits (as is per normal, see earlier). The challenges of social integration were immense and soon the situation became desperate for some of the women. Almeida then requested that the same NGO help by raising various supplies; however, her efforts fell flat, since the NGO refused to provide "assistentialist" actions. A month later the same NGO organized a collection of groceries for a family of Syrian refugees facing hardship. It all happened as if it were unthinkable to leave a Syrian family in that situation, whereas for African refugee women that was a tolerable situation.

These are not isolated cases and yet they are generally explained away as anecdotal and thus not systematic. In our view, it is probable and certainly plausible that the racialization of the refugee in Brazil, creating distinctions based on Brazilian racial and color classifications, is a structuring force. There is a visible preference for the Syrian "white" refugee, given the historical resonance that this displacement produces in Brazil and there is also a non-acceptance of the black refugee, to the point that, in practice, this is confused with Haitian immigration in the institutions. The practice of living life produces a very marked exclusion of black foreigners, an experience that transgresses law as it simultaneously dispenses with national and religious differences that these migrants express.

In short, Brazil presents a scenario in which the legal reality of Haitian immigrants and African refugee seekers (or refugees) is categorically different. However, ethnographical research reveals that life experiences of Africans and Haitians on Brazilian soil present many similarities, especially in the forms of exclusion to which they are subject. In the case of the city of São Paulo, this means exclusion of a system of popular housing and life in very precarious conditions on the outskirts of one of the largest cities in the world.

The rest of this chapter focuses on the experience of il/legality as it relates to the basic conditions of residence. The key relationship involved are occupation or squatter movements and basic health care. The in/visibility of race is evidently spatial in addition to being entangled in class formations among black foreigners.

(Hi)Stories of residential occupation

Scholars, such as Lúcio Kowarick, Raquel Rolnik, Nabil Bonduki and Luiz Kohara, have written copiously about the impact of immigration historically on the city of São Paulo. The massive growth of the small citadel town to a modernist economic juggernaut from 1870–1920 depended on wild speculation from coffee barons, which caused intense housing crises exacerbated by mismanagement of labor and a lack of urban planning for rental housing. This has been well documented (e.g., Bonduki and Rolnik 1978; Kohara 2010; Kowarick 1979; Rolnik 2008).

Moreover, political scientists and social geographers have analyzed the mobility of financial capital and power away from the downtown areas of Sé, República to Paulista Avenue and then farther to the southwest in the late 1990s and early 2000s to Berrini and Faria Lima avenues. We underscore the relationship between capital mobility and political policies of urbanization represented in municipal Master Plans. The tension between investment capitalism and periodic campaigns of social responsibility from the state has unsurprisingly produced an uneven urbanization. Improvised housing demonstrates what architect Jeroen Stevens has called the "interstitial spaces or pivotal nodes that link formality with informality" (2017, 49). Historically, migrants have adapted to and remade these spaces into vibrant, if precarious, urban spaces. The neighborhood of Bixiga is perhaps the most obvious example of this in São Paulo.

More recently, a new wave of West Africans, Syrians, Colombians and Haitians have found their way to the center of São Paulo and confronted the realities of a major housing crisis. These diverse migrant groups add to a larger presence of itinerant or precarious dwellers, who have, once again, brought improvised housing to public awareness.

The following narrative fragment is an example of ethnographic fiction. The intention is to capture, in this case, the experience of precarity among different immigrant populations within the basic right of housing. Made manifest in many forms, precarity breeds racist stigma, exploitation and violence. Beyond an exercise in thick description of space, the story suggests that sometimes the il/legality of the situation amplifies race and on other occasions it seems to silence race as a determining factor of fate.

The action takes place in an "occupation," a term used by activists and residents to point toward the fact that there are hundreds of abandoned buildings in the downtown area of São Paulo and thousands of people who are homeless or reside in absolute precarity. These spaces have become one nodal point of convergence among immigrants from different countries and the Brazilian urban poor, working classes.

The story focuses on an encounter between Letrice, a Congolese immigrant and concerned mother of three, and Maurice Malabranche, a Haitian immigrant, who is formally educated as a healthcare provider and has recently gained employment through an initiative in the São Paulo city public sector. They met in the corridor depicted below (Figure 3.1). Their conversation and the setting of the occupation provokes certain reflections on the part of Maurice. One of the authors had extensive conversations with a young Haitian health care provider in São Paulo and visited the occupation featured in the story on two occasions in 2017 and 2018.

The sunlight is soft in São Paulo during early June (Figure 3.1). The warmth is welcome in the sub-tropical winter; it helps dry the clothes and brings a

Figure 3.1 Corridor in residential occupation. Photo by Derek Pardue, 2017.

serenity to what is often a place of stress and suspicion. Letrice tended her three small children, each of whom had carved out a small nook for drawing, doll play and cell phone entertainment. Dr. Maurice Malabranche turned his back for a moment, went out into the hall and looked at the assorted hanging clothes. His professional title had yet to be recognized officially and he felt like a wrinkled shirt hung out to dry. The slight breeze emanating from a broken window ruffled the clothes from the nearby lines. The adult wear did not budge, steadfast in its weight and obdurate in its position to outside suggestions. Dr. Malabanche contemplated his own family in all its fragmentation. "The term is diaspora," his history professor had explained in the Port-au-Prince boarding school. He was American, had come from New York City, liked to wear his *Akademi Ayisyen* ("The Haitian Academy") uniform and knew absolutely nothing about Haitian families. Dr. Malabranche strained to recall the last time he had seen his own clothes hanging next to those of sweet Michèle and sons Sylvestre and Emmanuel. São Paulo could have been the final destination.

"*Viens ici*!" Letrice commanded. Dr. Malabranche had abandoned her, lost in his own nostalgia. The light was too subtle to divert his attention, as he drifted from subject to subject. Realizing a loss of determination, he reentered the squatter apartment and sat down in a corner chair. He promised himself that he would just listen.

Letrice adeptly code-switched between French and Lingala as she balanced the formal meeting with child rearing. Her husband Paul held sporadic short-term contracts as a maintenance worker, often scheduled in excess of 60 hours a week for a month or so and then dire unemployment and indolence. Dr. Malabranche had been hired also on a temporary basis.

During a moment, albeit brief, in São Paulo's city government history, mayorFernando Haddad raised the visibility of immigration within public policy initiatives. Of course, we should say that it was a multi-faceted, multi-interest conversation involving agents of the State, NGOs, the private sectors and other civil society groups, including immigrants themselves, who created the kinds of initiatives of inclusion leading to Dr. Malabranche's employment contract. However, internal departmental records showed that clerks had registered the building where Letrice resided on Redentoura Street as the home of Bolivians, Paraguayans, Syrians and a few veteran Portuguese families.

"I told you, Letrice, that you probably will get better service if you go with me to the clinic than me coming here." The doctor had cut Letrice short, again.

Letrice nevertheless continued.

> I want you to see where I live, where a couple hundred of us Congolese live. We have been here for three months. We pay four hundred *reais* a month for rent. It's fine, it's a space but sometimes we all pass around a strange kind of cold or flu. I don't know what it is.

Letrice proceeded to escort the doctor around the building. They stopped and chatted with a few housewives along the corridor, with whom Letrice was friendly. "Who's this fine man? Hmmm, Letrice. What does Paul have to say about all of this? You coming up in the world. Hmmm." Everyone laughed at the jibe that was at once a joke about Paul's diminutive height, a somewhat puny 1.60 meters, conflated with the perception of a formality and class of the markedly taller Haitian man. The women looked the doctor up and down, assessing his peculiar spectacles, freshly ironed shirt with a left breast pocket and clean, formal shoes. His blackness was an afterthought.

The women quickly turned their backs and engaged in small talk about recipes. Supposedly, someone on the fifth floor makes a delicious *ngombe*. As they wondered about what magic ingredient or the mode of preparation involved, the doctor stopped paying attention at that point, (and they had already switched into Lingala), and noticed that few, if any, of these apartments had windows that could be opened. "Hmm, this explains why people leave their front doors open and why, on a few floors, the hallway windows were missing selected panes," the doctor thought to himself as he found himself lightly hypnotized by the rhythmic rattle of the window underpinning the melodic Lingala language.

Circulation. Lack of. Hanging clothes. Too much shared air. Stagnant space residents tried to animate. Young men sat at the end of the fourth floor hall in lawn chairs sipping tea. One fiddled with a cellphone battery. Cobalt and ion batteries, "the trauma that courses through facts, is the image of subterranean riverbeds of gold and fossil objects" (Taussig 2004, 250).

Letrice and the doctor stepped quickly but carefully up and down the winding, angular staircase. Almost pitch black even at midday. The damp conditions accumulated in these close quarters and the experiences of residents moving were captured in the smudges on the wall and streaks on the floor. Dirt, light debris and water mixed into little piles pushed to the corners of the stairwell. The building collected these residues of human movement and everyday life. With few cleaning brigades organized by the residents (or by the mysterious, most probably nefarious rent collection agencies, in this case), the concrete surfaces of the building, originally intended to be a hotel, animated to tell a different story. That which might be called "the setting," a conjuncture of hard, unforgiving surfaces, became a protagonist.

After the tour the pair returned to Letrice's apartment. The oldest daughter and her teenage friends from down the hall slipped away signaling that their babysitting duties had ended. Hernan, one of the few Bolivians in the building, had a very cool cell phone app that just had to be seen.

And, there they were. An unexpected calmness descended. The infant had dozed off and the toddler was intently focused on drawing a circle with the crayons Maurice had brought in his pressed shirt breast pocket. The apartment furniture, which had previously appeared thrashed, permanently in use by the children and deployed for multiple purposes by Letrice and Paul, seemed somehow to be at peace. A lull in the corridor chatter. All was still.

> You see, Mr. Malabranche, I need a different address. I live here but I cannot say that I live here. This place does not exist for many employers and hospitals. Surely, you can understand that. Tell me, where do you live?

The doctor disregarded the question and made an exaggerated production to retrieve his notebook and hospital forms. By creating a bit of noise, he hoped to divert Letrice's attention to stuff that mattered, something he could check off and mark as accomplished. "Right, so it looks like you along with the mothers in the building need packages of diapers. The families also urgently need basic cough and flu medicine. This, we can do right away," the doctor said without looking at Letrice. He scanned his papers again and read aloud, "Madam, I am sure you know the benefits of *cesta básica*.[7] It's a simple matter of registering your address. You and your friends here can do that, can't you?"

Letrice was silent. Blank. Unyielding like the hanging clothes.

> I promise I will also ask an electrician friend of mine to come by later that week to see if it were possible to provide electricity to all floors and tidy up the webs of loose wires dangling from the ceiling in various corridors.

Maurice continued elaborating on his claims as an agent of power. He could get things done.

Letrice interrupted,

> Dr. Malabranche, thank you for coming. I am not special. I simply am bolder than most of the others. I know you are an immigrant, a refugee perhaps? You are educated and have found a place here in São Paulo. I see that. Everyone here sees that. Do you see me? You don't know me but do you see me? Do you see us?

Silence returned. A breeze kicked up. There was nothing left to say. On his way out, the doctor passed by the lobby and noticed flyers advertising an upcoming religious service. Taped to the walls were pictures of a reverend, a rotund man with a broad smile that belies his stern, horn-rimmed glasses. An overweight, bawdy evangelical leader. A storyteller.

As Maurice approached the partially unhinged gate to the street, a little girl sprinted across his path. Her beautiful braids swung back and forth as a cohesive unit offering a compelling rhythm in sync with her gait. She briefly looked up at the doctor and Maurice heard the repeated sounds of "Michèle". Sustain. "My daughter's name. This girl's name. A simple coincidence," he pondered. Turning quickly, the doctor saw no one but the elderly man, who had been collecting wire and cardboard since the doctor arrived. Folding and unfolding.

Dr. Malabranche delivered his report to the public health post. The electrician never made a visit to the building and, now as I write to you, it is unclear if he ever truthfully asked him …

Reworking stories into theory and analysis

The above elaboration from field notes attempts to perform textually the contingencies of migrancy and the dynamics of spatial production that is the city. The encounter of Dr. Malabranche and Letrice reveals partially a spatial expression of a heterogeneous Congolese presence in São Paulo, a particular rearticulation of an abandoned area. This constitutes one more example of transforming a "non-space" or a space of abjection into a meaningful, albeit marginalized, basis of residence, a home.

Through the conversations between Dr. Malabranche and Letrice one can feel certain struggles on both sides to just live and get through the day. For example, rights to basic food stuff, that is, *cesta básica*, are made more complicated by Letrice's liminal residential status. She is unsure and asks for a favor. The (il)legality of healthcare, the reason for Dr. Malabranche's visit in the first place, is featured throughout. The two protagonists are sympathetic to each other but also hold a mistrust or, at least, a skepticism of the other's intentions.

While blackness does not appear as an explicit topic of conversation or interaction, racialization acts as a background of social positioning both in terms of implicit approximation and differentiation. The doctor is afforded greater mobility in Brazilian society, albeit seemingly ephemeral due to the short-term contracts from the new, innovative city initiatives related to immigration and healthcare. It is implicit that Dr. Malabranche indeed relies on these contracts and despite his formal education is not so far removed from Letrice and her husband Paul. Racial stigma can be negotiated through class, education and other forms of social capital, but it is a continual process, one that weighs on each character in different ways. The reader has more access to Malabranche's experience through reflection, as he tends to wander off in memory triggered by occasional empirical observations of Letrice and the scenes within the residential occupation.

The case of Dr. Malabranche and Letrice, as well as thousands of other West African and Haitian migrants, constitute moments of mobility ideology in what geographer Tim Cresswell has called a "critical geosophy" (2006, 21).[8] There is a dynamic "geography of knowledge" and each episteme defines mobility as a personality type in certain ways. Mobility marks people in terms of class and morality and we can quickly discern the potential intersectionalities.

Scholars from various disciplines have been increasingly sensitive to the spatial agency of migrants. As a theoretical counterpoint to categorization, migrant's spatial navigation of the city connects the everyday empirical evidence of labor and apprenticeship (e.g., Buhr 2017) to the politics of integration. Such analyses dialogue with a cadre of Brazilian and Brazilianist scholarship, which has discussed local mapping strategies of various social classes. From discourses of *pontos* (Hecht 1998) to *pedaços* (Magnani 1992) to *trajetórias* (Frúgoli 2006), it is clear that urban inhabitants work with and sometimes against institutional categorization in order to capitalize on the socio-spatial resources the city has to offer. While relatively small (but meaningful) victories occurred in São Paulo, especially, during the Haddad administration, the current regime both at the municipal and federal level has become extremely antagonistic to any projects in the name of "popular housing." Urbanist and public scholar Raquel Rolnik published on her blog and broadcasted on her radio show about the PL ("law project" or better translated as bill) that proposes absolutely no federal money for public housing in 2018.[9] Such economic and infrastructural constraints result in greater pressure for precarious occupations to take place. Migrant agency is thus reduced to a limited number of channels of expression.

Conclusion

In simple terms, commercial interests located in the national borderlands and racism against new *africanos* shapes legality as it pertains to immigration. The maintenance of the status quo, despite the redressing of the law in humanitarian terms, is consecrated in the fact that the federal police continues to be the managing agency, a situation that represents a lack of institutional understanding that the rights and realities of migrants are outside the purview of the federal police. It is simply not within their expertise. These matters require a specialized, qualified set of agents who are in dialogue with the global dimensions of human mobility. With that said, we can begin to imagine the complexities of what constitutes "legality" as an already uneven playing field for immigrants and refugees. Access to basic rights such as healthcare and decent housing, in many instances, can only be gained through "illegality," since what is recognized as legal excludes many migrants, often based on race. Our discussion of local NGO operations and daily experiences in squatter apartment buildings demonstrate that this lack of recognition easily becomes a daily violence and a source of desperation.

This il/legality is made manifest primarily in the confusion around migratory status related to Haitians and Africans in São Paulo. In everyday life, they tend to be placed in the same box, as it were, a situation of social exclusion, despite the relative advance in public policies. Ethnography demonstrates that the real progress has occurred with "white refugees" (e.g., Syrians). The experience of racialization among black foreigners is spatialized in the city, whether one considers squatter occupations and the accompanying precarious conditions in the city center or life in the extreme periphery neighborhoods where police violence is common and access to basic, public services continues to be a challenge. While such difficulties are certainly present for native Brazilians, they have the advantage of kinship and friendship networks, which for the most part is out of reach for immigrants thereby making the situation even more hostile and ultimately, in many cases, creating a force of expulsion. It is thus not surprising that in recent months, many Haitians have left Brazil in search of better conditions in countries such as Chile and the United

States, and many African refugees have turned their attention to Europe as a potential haven.

Notes

1 Igor Machado has been conducting individual research on Brazilian immigration law since 2005, and also coordinates a project on refuge in São Paulo with funding from FAPESP (São Paulo Research Support Foundation), of which Almeida and Branco's researches cited here are part. Derek Pardue has conducted several different research projects in the city of São Paulo since 1995. Beginning in 2016, he used a research sabbatical from Aarhus University (Denmark) and funding from FAPESP and Eurias (European Institute for Advanced Studies) to turn his focus to issues of visibility and presence among recent African and Haitian migrants in the city.

2 See, for example, Erika Yamada's "Veto na Lei de Imigração aumenta a criminalização de indígenas," published online: www.unicamp.br/unicamp/ju/noticias/2017/10/03/vetos-podem-desfigurar-lei-de-migracao-alertam-especialistas (accessed October 5, 2017). As explained by Yamada, one of the provision of the original law was to allow "free circulation" of indigenous groups, many of whom live and manage lands (estimated at 180 different plots) on the border with other South American countries. See the comments by Jobana Moya, member of the Warmis Colective and Deisy Ventura, professor of International Law at the University of São Paulo (USP) in Soares 2017 related to undocumented residents and health care, respectively.

3 On July 26, 2019, the Minister of Justice, Sérgio Moro, published a legal order, an addendum (*Portaria 666/2019*) to the current 2017 Migration Law, which states that immigrants considered "dangerous" can be summarily deported. Several legal experts (www.bbc.com/portuguese/brasil-49134995?ocid=socialflow_facebook&fbclid=IwAR12SUgU15vs8JmQ8RQUTt4HLjxz9a0KPMgXjduxKY3AMym_-M_Xxrz5fdU), the Committee on Migration and Displacement within the Brazilian Association of Anthropology (www.portal.abant.org.br/2019/07/27/nota-do-comite-de-migracoes-e-deslocamentos-da-associacao-brasileira-de-antropologia-sobre-a-portaria-no-666-2019-do-ministro-de-estado-da-justica-e-seguranca-publica-sergio-moro/) and many others have issued statements condemning this act precisely because it contradicts fundamentally the current law in that it presumes a possible illegality or suspicion from immigrants. This is, in effect, a return to the Cold War tone of Brazil's military dictatorship. As Marina Faraco, professor of Constitutional Law at the Pontificate Catholic University in São Paulo (PUC-SP), explains such addenda (*portarias*) "cannot create new hypotheses for punishment." Moreover, many activists and NGO leaders warn that upon consideration that the new proposed time for defense is 48 hours rather than 60 days, any sort of infraction could effectively lead to deportation.

4 For a discussion of migration policies for Haitians in Brazil, see Fernandes and Faria (2017) and Trabalon (2018).

5 For a discussion of Brazilian racial systems, see, among others Hasenbalg (1996), Sansone (1996), Nogueira (2007) and Guimarães (1999).

6 On Syrian-Lebanese immigration in Brazil, see Truzzi (1997).

7 A standardized supply of foodstuffs for low-income families provided by the State.

8

> It is this status of a necessary social production, I argue, that makes knowledge surrounding mobility (like that surrounding other fundamental geographical concepts such as space and place) so important and so deeply implicated in the politics of the modern world. Stasis and mobility, fixity and flow, are the subjects of deep knowledges that inform any number of ways of seeing the world. For this reason, an understanding of the ways in which ideas about fixity and flow provide a profound undercurrent to thinking (which is closer to the surface of cultural life – law, medicine, activism, film, photography, planning, architecture, philosophy, and even geography itself) enacts a critical geosophy.
>
> (Cresswell 2006, 22)

9 https://raquelrolnik.wordpress.com/2017/09/18/governo-propoe-zero-reais-para-moradia-popular-em-2018. Accessed on February 6, 2018.

References

Almeida, Alexandra C. G. "'É uma longa história, quem sabe um dia te conto' – Mulheres estrangeiras e suas vivências na cidade de São Paulo." PhD diss., Federal University of São Carlos, 2019.

Bauman, Zygmunt. *Wasted Lives: Modernity and Its Outcasts.* Cambridge, UK: Polity Press, 2004.

Bonduki, Nabil and Raquel Rolnik. *Periferias* [Cadernos de Estudo e Pesquisa 2]. São Paulo: FUPAM/FAU-USP, 1978.

Branco Pereira, Alexandre. "A antropologia em um serviço de saúde mental para refugiados: a invenção de um não lugar". Master's thesis, Federal University of São Carlos, 2019.

Buhr, Franz. "Using the City: Migrant Spatial Integration as Urban Practice." *Journal of Ethnic and Migration Studies* 43, no. 14 (2017): 307–320. http://dx.doi.org/10.1080/ 1369183X.2017.1341715.

Cavalcanti, Leonardo, Antônio Tadeu de Oliveira, Tânia Tonhati, Delia Dutra (eds.). *Relatório Anual 2015 – A inserção dos imigrantes no Mercado de Trabalho brasileiro.* Brasília: Observatório das Migrações Internacionais (OBMigra), 2015. https://portaldeimigracao. mj.gov.br/images/dados_anuais/relatorio_OBMIGRA_2015_final.pdf. Accessed on October 23, 2019.

Cresswell, Tim. *On the Move: Mobility in the Modern Western World,* New York: Routledge, 2006.

De Azevedo, Celia Maria Marinho. *Onda negra, medo branco: O negro no imaginário das elites, século XIX.* São Paulo: Annablume, 1987.

Fernandes, Duval, and Andressa Virgínia de Faria. "O visto humanitário como resposta ao pedido de refúgio dos haitianos." *Revista Brasileira de Estudos de População* 34, no. 1 (2017): 145–161.

Fernandes, Sujatha. "The Right Kind of Immigrant: The Narrative of Deserving and Undeserving Immigrants," BESE, June 14, 2019. www.bese.com/the-right-kind-of-immigrant-the-narrative-of-deserving-and-undeserving-immigrants. Accessed on October 23, 2019.

Frúgoli, Heitor Jr. Centralidade em São Paulo: trajetórias, conflitos e negociações na metrópole. 2nd ed. São Paulo: Edusp, 2006.

Guimarães, Antônio Sergio Alfredo. "Raça e os estudos de relações raciais no Brasil." *Novos Estudos CEBRAP* 54 (1999): 147–156.

Hasenbalg, Carlos "Entre o mito e os fatos: Racismo e relações raciais no Brasil." In *Raça, ciência e sociedade*, edited by M. C. Maio and R. V. Santos, 235–249. Rio de Janeiro: FIOCRUZ/Banco do Brasil, 1996.

Hecht, Tobias. *At Home in the Street*. Cambridge: Cambridge University Press, 1998.

Khosravi, Shahram. *Illegal Traveller: An Auto-Ethnography of Borders*. New York: Palgrave, 2010.

Kohara, Luis. "Relação entre as condições da moradia e o desempenho escolar: estudo com crianças residents em cortiços." PhD diss., University of São Paulo, 2010.

Kowarick, Lúcio. *Espoliação Urbana*. Rio de Janeiro: Paz e Terra, 1979.

Lesser, Jeffrey. *Immigration, ethnicity, and national identity in Brazil, 1808 to the present*. Cambridge: Cambridge University Press, 2013.

Magnani, José Guilherme Cantor. "Da periferia ao centro: Pedaços & Trajetos." *Revista de Antropologia* 35, no.1 (1992): 191–204.

Nogueira, Oracy. "Preconceito racial de marca e preconceito racial de origem: Sugestão de um quadro de referência para a interpretação do material sobre relações raciais no Brasil." *Tempo Social* 19, no. 1 (2007): 287–308.

Rolnik, Raquel. "O Direito à Moradia no Brasil e no Mundo." *Oculum Ensaios* (2008): 147–163.

Sansone, Livio. "Nem somente preto ou negro: O sistema de classificação racial no Brasil que muda." *Afro-Ásia* 18 (1996): 165–187.

Seyferth, Giralda. "German Immigration and the Formation of German-Brazilian Ethnicity." *Anthropological Journal on European Cultures* 7, no. 2 (1998): 131–154.

Soares, Nana. "Apesar de vetos, nova Lei da Migração é um avanço para migrantes no Brasil." Portal Aprendiz, June 2, 2017. https://portal.aprendiz.uol.com.br/2017/06/02/apesar-de-vetos-nova-lei-da-migracao-e-um-avanco-para-migrantes-brasil. Accessed on October 23, 2019.

Stevens, Jeroen. "Cortiços: Interstitial Urbanization in Central São Paulo." In *The Political Meaning of Informal Urbanization*, edited by R. Rocco and J. V. Ballegooien, 45–58. New York: Routledge, 2017.

Taussig, Michael. *My Cocaine Museum*. Chicago: Universtyof Chicago Press, 2004.

Trabalón, Carina. "Política de visado y regulación de las fronteras: Un análisis desde la movilidad de haitianos en Sudamérica." *Polis – Revista Latinoamericana* 51 (2018): 163–186.

Truzzi, Oswaldo M. S. "The Right Place at the Right Time: Syrians and Lebanese in Brazil and the United States, a Comparative Approach." *Journal of American Ethnic History* 16, 2 (1997): 3–34.

Zapat, Gisela P. and Dimitri Fazito. "Comentário: O significado da Nova Lei de Migração 13.445/17 no context histórico da mobilidade humana no Brasil." *Revista UFMG* 25, no. 1 and 2 (2018): 224–237.

4 *Jeitinho* revisited

Georg Wink

> *There is no possibility of social domination without explicit and implicit ideas that legitimize and justify domination, and which therefore allow its timely reproduction. Thus, to criticize the dominating ideas must be the first step to change unjust socio-economic domination.*
>
> *(Souza 2018, 151)*[1]

The *jeitinho* is the most famous umbrella term for social practices in the gray zone between legality and illegality in Brazil. The term has been translated into English as "little way out," "clever dodge," "knack," "adroitness," "dexterity," or similar. In common understanding it means an especially Brazilian, creative problem-solving strategy to circumvent norms and rules with the purpose of attaining personal objectives. The practice is understood as persuading others on personal and egalitarian basis without threatening interpersonal harmony (Amado and Brasil 1991). Even though the *jeitinho* is said to be applied in challenges of everyday life, it usually responds to handling difficulties with representatives of the state in situations of "bureaucratic overreaches" (Smith et al. 2012) and "excessive legalism" (Duarte 2006, 512). These involve two parties: the citizen who needs a problem solved and the representative of the state who is expected to solve it (Torres and Dessen 2006). Consequently, the inadequacy of the normative system generates the need for the adoption of creative tactics (Ferreira et al. 2012). Another common assumption is that the *jeitinho* does not imply corruption, as no payment should occur between the involved parties and as it does not intend to harm others (Motta and Alcadipani 1999). Rather the person who gets convinced to solve the problem is imagined to act based on an evaluation of the personal needs and the (in)adequacy of the official rule to attend them. Therefore, the core mechanism of *jeitinho* is explained as the transformation of individuals in a purely rational relationship into persons in an emotional relationship (Pedroso et al. 2009).

The *jeitinho* is believed to be widely present in all kind of social interaction in the Brazilian society. It is not only celebrated but also seen as an atavistic lack of the exercise of citizenship or, in short, a development problem, which can only be overcome by cultural change toward the full materialization of citizenship and good governance (Alcântara et al. 2015; Azevedo et al. 2018). Notwithstanding this ambivalence, the *jeitinho* has been build up as an icon of Brazilian identity through a long tradition of Brazilian social and cultural thinking. The original inspiration stems from the literary character of the *malandro*, the Brazilian trickster, with a strong presence in Brazilian literature at least since the mid-19th century.

Today, the *jeitinho* has become somehow démodé in scientific writing, mainly because any attempt to define all-encompassing Brazilian identity features has become somehow obsolete in the more differentiated, process-oriented, constructivist and less essentialist perspectives (such as, e.g., the special issue on "Cordiality and Intimacy in Contemporary Brazilian Culture," edited by Dennison 2018). Thus, skepticism prevails toward inferring socio-cultural phenomena just from supposed "national traits":

> In this sense, the use of epistemological shortcuts like the "Brazilian jeitinho" or the "cordiality," commonly accepted to give final explanations for all of our problems, sounds less and less plausible. This type of argument has been used without rigour and with the aim to explain the most varied phenomena.
>
> (Rodriguez 2016, 61)[2]

However, within academia the *jeitinho* has had a curious revival in Brazilian and international management literature, now promoted as "Brazilian management practice" and a magic formula for succeeding in business (see, among many others, Glenn 2009, 9; Mansur and Sobral 2011; Balbinot et al. 2012). Not by coincidence, this happened in the wake of the BRICS-Hype in the early 2000s and came along with the promise to enable businesses to access these "difficult" markets. This banal use of the concept compares *jeitinho* to other "indigenous management practices" such as Chinese *guanxi*, Arabian *wasta* and Russian *svyazi* (Araujo et al. 2014). To illustrate this, these authors realized – almost for the first time – a large number of empirical surveys, however with limited methods and ambivalent results, as will be shown later. Given the nature of management literature, few texts take a critical position.

The *jeitinho* is frequently presented as hermeneutic key of the Brazilian culture. Any understanding would require a deep familiarity with Brazil, usually not available for outsiders. This might of course be true, but also signal a possible lack of conceptual coherence and evidence for its concrete practice. Therefore, the *jeitinho* could also be a deep-rooted cultural cliché. In this regard, when revisiting the phenomenon, allow me the defeatism to occupy the epistemological standpoint of doubting its existence in the ways usually taken for granted. Having said that, I understand my contribution as an exploratory study with the objective to raise through a critical literature review some questions that might shed further light on this cultural phenomenon and turn it more objectively intelligible, though subjectively less familiar.

First, I will explore the *jeitinho*'s construction as idiosyncratic characteristic of Brazilian culture and central component of national identity, as convincingly argued by Barbosa (2005), so far the most complete work on this aspect, first published in 1992. By doing so I will go beyond the commonplace reference Roberto DaMatta (1980, 1984, 1987, 2004), who not only coined the concept, but also played a decisive role in romanticizing it (Godois 2015, 3). Second, I will examine the evidence given for the *jeitinho*'s alleged endemic perception and use as a social practice (Ferreira et al. 2012, 332), which is usually taken for granted. Finally, I will scrutinize its uniqueness as a Brazilian phenomenon. My hypothesis is hereby that the *jeitinho* constitutes, primarily, a specific cultural topos, which in the fourth concluding part needs to be analyzed with regard to its function for veiling and preserving asymmetric power relations and the status quo of social inequality.

Cultural roots of the *jeitinho*

Guerreiro Ramos (1966) appears to have been the first scholar to attempt a "sociology of the *jeito*." His argument is that under the social conditions of Brazil and Latin America the validity of norms is formally proclaimed and practically denied (Ramos 1966, 373). This formalism, the discrepancy between social, political, juridical institutions and social practices, and consequently the *jeito* as solution strategy, is presented as a result of Portuguese colonization and the implementation of the patrimonial state, as explained in detail by Faoro (1979 [1958]).[3] Therefore, the problem would disappear as soon as these societies (as elsewhere before) were compelled to adopt realistic legal structures through a socioeconomic development process (Ramos 1966, 381). Differently from his predecessor, João Camilo de Oliveira Torres in his *Interpretação da realidade brasileira* (1973), though still based on the causality of the rigid bureaucracy that leaves no other choice, glorifies the *jeitinho* as proof of Brazilian ingeniousness in adapting to situations and even more as a philosophy of life. As Roberto DaMatta a few years later, Torres associates this philosophy to carnival, as a temporary flexibilization and even inversion, supplementary (but not contrary) to the rigid social hierarchy. Furthermore, he contributed the anecdote that later became the *jeitinho*'s foundational myth:

> During the war, in the campaign of the Apennines and with the winter coming, many soldiers had to be released because of frozen feet. The healthcare services took action and in a very American way started by collecting data. The result was a surprise: higher incidence among American soldiers, familiar with snow, than among Brazilians, who saw it for the first time. Analyzing the fact, they got to the astonishing information: the Brazilian soldiers wrapped their feet in newspapers as soon as the cold started, while the Americans waited for instructions from the medical services ...
>
> (Torres 1973, 213)[4]

As I will show later, this famous anecdote does not describe properly what is commonly understood as *jeitinho* – and this quite meaningful. Francisco José Lustosa da Costa in his *Ideologia do favor, curral e cabresto* (1977) continues Ramos' argument and applies it to the political realm, with the difference that he does not see the solution in the improvement of legality without taking into account how the formalism (as *jurisdicismo*) serves the interests of the economic elite (Costa 1977, 75).

Roberto DaMatta (1980), first published 1978 and translated into English in 1991, then gained laurels for his synthesis of the debate (however none of the previously mentioned authors is cited by him), echoing Ramos' problematization of the historical roots and carrying forward both Torres' ambivalent interpretation of *jeitinho* as solution and Costa's concerns that the ritual is not likely to disappear through any modernization process. DaMatta elevated the *jeitinho* to the core element of what he calls the "Brazilian dilemma." One side of this dilemma is the existence of drastic laws, impossible to be rigorously abided, so that "the Brazilian" ends up always negotiating exception to the law. He does so by using or the authoritarian *Você sabe com quem está falando* (known in English speaking contexts as "Do you know who you are talking to"), taking advantage of higher social status to pressure the lower status representative of the law.[5] Or he uses its "cordial variant," the *jeitinho* (DaMatta 1991, 188). The other side of the dilemma is that this generalized behavior provokes distrust of universal rules, even though hope remained that at some point in the future these laws will be implemented (DaMatta 1991, 188). How does the *jeitinho* work? Here DaMatta brings in the literary character of the Brazilian *malandro*, more precisely the folktales about the mythical figure of Pedro Malasartes. His function is to personalize "the general, universal law in cases where it *should* be personalized, because the affected person is not just any individual but the child of some family or, in this case, a 'Malasartes'" (DaMatta 1991, 235, original emphasis). To explain this personalization, he draws on Sérgio Buarque de Holanda's concept of Brazilian "cordiality," in the etymological sense of linked to the heart, proceeding from the sphere of intimacy, familiarity and privacy, which governed relations in Brazil's society through networking (Holanda 1976 [1936] 106–107, footnote 157).

Thus, between the law (which has to be preserved) and the personal situation (which needs to be resolved) mediates the *jeitinho* by just demoralizing the law a tiny little bit (DaMatta 1984, 80; DaMatta 2004, 45–46). This dichotomy is the basis of his argument. One could even say that it is the basis of his entire opus, just as in the distinction between the spaces of private "casa" (home) and public "rua" (street) (DaMatta 1987). In his later work DaMatta turns the tragic dilemma into an equilibrium:

> The result is a socially divided and even *equilibrated* system between two basic social units: the individual (the subject of universal laws which

> modernize society) and the person (the subject of social relations, which conducts to the traditional pole of the system).[6]
>
> (DaMatta 1984, 64, my emphasis)

By doing so, the *jeitinho* formerly known as "something embarrassing, close to favor and corruption" is finally transformed into a cachet of "*malandra* [female adjective of malandro] social and political ingenuity, something as positive for the constitution of our identity as Carnival and Football"[7] (DaMatta 2005 [1992], xxiv).

It is important to notice that none of these mentioned authors ever worried about collecting any representative data to give evidence to his thoughts. All these are exclusively based on anecdotes or constructed typical scenarios (sometimes the distinction is unclear), as the ones mentioned above. Vieira et al. (1982) were the first ever to provide at least some empirical basis for the phenomenon (instead of just assuming it), which they obtained by doing 20 semi-structured interviews with public servants. This allowed them to revise to a certain degree the common understanding of the *jeitinho* by including information on how these informants actually evaluate the mechanism and how they – at least say to – apply it in their daily routine. With regard to four aspects the data did not corroborate the earlier assumptions: first, the *jeitinho* does not exclude monetary payments, which relativizes the carefully avoided distinction with corruption; second, the *jeitinho* is perceived as "Latino" if not universal practice and manifest wherever hierarchical systems and personal networks encounter; third, the *jeitinho* is considered mainly a negative social practice, though the informants argue that they are "constrained" to use it, because bureaucracy is not able to attend all requests; and fourth, the *jeitinho* is a power instrument, used against the hypothetically neutral and egalitarian state to get privileged access to the redistribution of public goods and services and as such provokes negative results for society (Vieira et al. 1982, 21–22). At this point, it becomes clear that a social science perspective is deeply needed to supplement the culturalist interpretation. As Souza (2001, 56) provokes:

> Let us assume, as hypothesis, that unfortunately the degree of corruption in Brazil is higher than in other countries. Should the cause not be more the lack of efficient control mechanisms than a mysterious atavistic efficiency of traditional personalist cultural patterns inherited from Brazil's colonial times?[8]

Social perception and practices of the *jeitinho*

The *jeitinho* is necessarily defined within a trifold model, spreading between legality and illegality. For example, Barbosa (2005) distinguishes the *jeitinho* on one side from *favor* (arguing that the favor implies in reciprocity, is only requested from known and trusted person and does not involve a transgression of norms) and "corruption" (implying material or pecuniary gain and infraction) on the other. Flach (2012) separates between the use of the *jeitinho* on the levels of emergency (no harm), *malandragem* (minor infraction, possible harm, tolerated by common sense) and corruption (major infraction, harms others, against consensus of society). What limits these definitions is that all indicators can only be measured gradually and depend on subjective evaluation. What determines if a personal relationship is trustful and if an infraction is "minor" or "major"? What is the limit of a "small amount" and how to quantify the damage caused to society? In fact, it is most difficult to define the difference between *jeitinho* and corruption, if we apply a more comprehensive definition of the latter. Silva (1994) in his functional definition as *conluio* (collusion) goes farthest beyond what he calls the "moralist, legalist and revisionist paradigms" on corruption, all somehow vague when it comes to defining what moral, law or benefit is actually the reference.[9] Functionally, corruption is "deviation from an institutionalized pattern of conduct, mainly characterized by the utilization of the public sphere in benefit of the private, and with the clear goal of achieving personal or group advantages"[10] (Silva 1994, 21).

The only reliable parameter seems to be the (assumed) common sense perception. Heidenheimer (2001 [1970]), in his introduction to the seminal volume *Political Corruption*, makes this the decisive criterion for his definition of three forms of corruption. They all are considered corruption by law, but not necessarily by social norms: On the first level ("white") the perception is non-corrupt; on the second ("gray") no consensus has been reached so far; on the third ("black") consensually corruption is detected (Heidenheimer 2001 [1970], 27). Therefore, we can conclude almost tautologically that a *jeitinho* exists when the respective practice is not perceived unanimously as legal, neither as illegal.[11] This does not only mean that illegal practices are perceived by some as legal, but also the other way round.

As mentioned, most of the above-mentioned pioneer texts refer to invented scenarios to give evidence to their definition and explanation of the *jeitinho*. Later works include at least to some degree empirical surveys, usually confronting interviewees with *jeitinho* samples.[12] Significantly, most of them are *de jure* not situated in the intermediate space of the legality-illegality spectrum – and also known by other, less stigmatized names. One of them is the *gambiarra*, a "make do," usually a temporary technical solution to solve a problem with precarious but own means, under absence of formal control and in many cases implying elevated risk for the user (Boufleur 2013). The ur-*jeitinho* of the newspaper-lined boots fits this category, just like many other harmless cases presented as *jeitinho* in the specialized literature. Another is the *permuta*, a barter to substitute monetary payments by the exchange of goods or services, which is a legal institution.[13] The hard sales strategies Souza et al. (2014, 64) analyze in the informal marketing among micro-entrepreneurs apply *cum grano salis* to the formal sector too. A payment deferral or credit purchase are not *jeitinhos*, as Duarte (2006, 523) makes us believe, but century old commercial institutions. Just like the consecutive interpretation of a customer requests of expatriated monolingual US managers, afflicted with Brazilian rental and internet provider contracts, until a helpful native colleague helps out and does the magical *jeitinho* call – obviously in Portuguese (Araujo et al. 2014). Nor is it the workaround to avoid major harm in a situation of emergency, as in the case of a father who urgently needs a birth certificate to bury his deceased child (Lima et al. 2016, 906), but just bureaucratic proportionality in the sense of Max Weber (as I will show in the next section). The same goes for signing a purchase order on behalf of a traveling colleague (Duarte 2006, 510). There seems to be a confusion between *jeitinho* and simple lobbying, as in the case of an NGO inviting a senator for dinner and convincing him to endorse politically their work (Duarte 2006, 523). Finally, one should not just subsume all political wheeling and dealing as *jeitinho*, just because they happen to occur in Brazil (in Fauré 2012), as not to overgeneralize it. All these pseudo-*jeitinho*-types have in common that they are universally present legal human practices.[14] Why are they then perceived as *jeitinho*?

With regard to those samples that exceed formal legality, the majority of interviewees is quite hesitant to legitimize them, when asked to evaluate. Rather they are seen as "linked to deceitful actions carried out with the objective of gaining personal benefits while harming the counterparty involved" (Park et al. 2018, 413). In a study carried out among Brazilian university students, Freire et al. (2018, 234) come to the conclusion that actually very few scenarios are perceived as legitimate by their informants: only downloading media from pirate sites and unwrapping consumer goods purchased abroad in order to cheat the customs control were classified as such by a relative majority, but not jumping a queue, parking in a lot reserved for elderly, cheating in an exam, short-changing, plagiarizing online material for a student presentation and falsifying a medical pardon to skip work. Borrowing a student ID, bribing a police officer and buying a driver's license were clearly recognized as corrupt practices. If asked for their own practices, one could expect that Brazilians say to use the *jeitinho* more strategically or often than a comparable group. However, this is not corroborated by studies such as Nishioka and Akol (2019) who found no significant use of *jeitinho* to cope with acculturative stress among Brazilian students in the United States. Lourenço (2014), one of the very few studies including participatory observation of real practices, detects in the interaction between retailers and patronized (never unknown) customers the existence of *jeitinho* practices (such as to jump the queue, buy medicine without prescription, ask for adding a little something), but they are perceived as embarrassing by the staff and other clients. The second study I was able to find which also observes real behavior instead of taking statements as reality, deals with *jeitinhos* in conciliation hearings in Consumer Defense Disputes (Abritta and Oliveira 2012). However, the strategies used by the mediators do not point to any semi-illegality. Surprisingly, even the queue – here in the context of public health services – is defended as icon of social equality, only to be jumped in serious cases of life or death (Pinto and Najar 2011, 4379). The same authors stress the perception of the *jeitinho* as "justification for the non-compliance of laws"[15] (Pinto and Najar 2011, 4381) which evidences a condemnatory evaluation.

In sum, there seems to be no evidence for the *jeitinho* being seen in the Brazilian context as in between legality and illegality. The available data suggests that the tendency is to distinguish clearly between both sides. If people are confrontated with scenarios or real situations, legal *jeitinhos* are consensually celebrated as ingeniousness, illegal *jeitinhos* condemned as corruption. It is the cultural topos alone to blur the limits to such a degree that both legal practices and corruption are transformed into *jeitinho*. Should this confusion be no coincidence? My hypothesis, which I will test in the concluding section, is that the main function of the topos is to relativize and distract from corrupt practices which otherwise would be perceived only as such (and not associated to the *jeitinho*). Moreover, this function explains why the topos has been included prominently into the construction of collective identity. As Barbosa claims convincingly (2005, 32), the *jeitinho* is perceived as "defining us as country and people."[16] The interesting question is by whom and what for.

Supposed uniqueness of the Brazilian *jeitinho*

Roberto DaMatta concludes his famous chapter on the *jeitinho* with a famous historical source, the letter written by commander-in-chief Pedro Álvares Cabral's secretary, Pero Vaz de Caminha, to King Manuel, informing about the so-called discovery of Brazil. In this letter, Caminha ends up asking the King to pardon his son-in-law Jorge de Osório and to allow him to return from the island of São Tomé where he had been banished due to an unknown crime or misdemeanor. "Do we need to say anything more?"[17] asks DaMatta (1984, 89) rhetorically in his last sentence. With all due respect, I would answer that there are still many things to say about this episode. For example, to question whether this plea, rather than a typically Brazilian proto-*jeitinho*, might not have been just a common convention in the communication with monarchic rulers in the beginning 16th century. At least this is what the specialized literature suggests as reciprocal principle of "Do ut Des" for France and Germany even until the late eighteenth century (Davis 2000, 136; Büschel 2007). The fact that DaMatta does not even consider this possibility (even though he refers to an earlier book written by Natalia Z. Davis when he discusses the function of carnival) is paradigmatic. Without comparing to the world outside Brazil, every phenomenon must appear to be exclusively Brazilian.

Yet the problem might even be deeper, because most apologists of the *jeitinho* do include a comparison, just in a quite abstract way. They use to refer to the United States, sometimes also to Britain, France and Germany, as places where the *jeitinho* (among other cultural phenomena) is non-existent or even unthinkable.[18] Already a common place is the affirmation that in Brazil some laws apply, some not, despite existing: "In the United States, France and England, just to give three good examples, rules are either followed or they do not exist"[19] (DaMatta 1984, 81). This construction of the "other" is never supported by any evidence, apart from anecdotes that evoke popular fantasies about the "First World." The proof is given, by most authors, through a theoretical treaty, Max Weber's chapter IX about the "Sociology of Government" in his main opus *Wirtschaft und Gesellschaft: Grundriß der verstehenden Soziologie*. This text, written at the end of World War I and the very beginning of the first formally democratic government ever in Germany, analyzes the international process of modern bureaucratization and based on this elaborates an ideal type of "good bureaucracy" under the conditions of rational and legal government, including both the administration in the public and private sector (!). Max Weber's treaty is not an ethnography of bureaucratic realities in the German Empire and the Weimar Republic (not exactly a consolidated democracy at that time), and at no point he affirms that the German bureaucracy is immune against favoritism, personalism or corruption. Taking him at his word, even in the twenty-first century his vision of a rational administration of the state (and private companies) is only partly realized, of course in different degrees depending on each country (and company). What also deserves attention in his work is that even though he defines functional rationality, hierarchy, impersonality and distinction between public and private spheres as main pillars of bureaucracy, he also includes – less prominently – several dimensions that the above-mentioned contemporary authors believed to be in opposition to rational bureaucracy: the flexible application of the rules by the bureaucrats to the best of their knowledge (Weber 1972 [1921–22], 552) and, if not possible, by the careful evaluation of objective and means (Weber 1972 [1921–22], 565). This shows that Max Weber was aware that even as ideal type the bureaucracy means more than just applying rules to individuals. Bureaucracy is, in his words, the "rational administration of interests" (Weber 1972 [1921–22], 125).[20]

With this relativization of the imaginary "other" in mind, the Brazilian peculiarities of leading with a necessarily always deficient bureaucracy might still be on a higher level of intensity and frequency, but not different in their nature. Actually, most of the so far discussed samples appear to be fairly common practices, even from a German or Danish perspective.[21] Even attempts to prove that Brazilians identify to a higher degree with the *jeitinho* than elsewhere have so far not delivered convincing results. Smith et al. (2012, 195) had to admit at the end of their comparative study that *jeitinho* was considered more typical in Lebanon than in Brazil itself. Even more surprising, Chen et al. (2017, 75) found support for the – in their eyes – counter-intuitive hypotheses that relative to their counterparts in the United States, employees from Brazil perceive less positive consequences and less justice in *jeitinho* samples. Even Barbosa (2005, 19) admits the possible existence of "functionally identical and morphological situations"[22] outside Brazil, but then argues that the difference lies in the awareness of the practice as culturally significant or not.[23] However, is the denomination of a social practice and its incorporation in the construction of national identity really decisive?

I sincerely doubt this. One of my ex-supervisors at a German university did not need to know the terms "jeitinho" (and "Caixa 2") when he asked me to find a strawman to receive a honorarium for a fictive service and to return the amount (save for 10% commission) in order to have funds for spontaneous expenses (like inviting guest lecturers for dinner) without passing through the regular bureaucratic process. He just presented it as the way things are done at the department. The *jeitinhos* Pereira (2018) detected in the indirect land acquisitions by foreign agribusinesses in Brazil did not need to be framed as such. "These legal strategies facing the Brazilian legislation demonstrate that the fame is Brazilian, *but the jeitinho comes from abroad*"[24] (Pereira 2018, 173, original emphasis). If a society is not aware of corruption (showing a low perception index), this does not mean that corruption does not exist. It could also show the lack of realistic self-perception or even more the strong existence of an alienating self-image, both blatantly present in any selective construction of national identity. It is not the significance attributed to a phenomenon that creates a cultural practice. The signification just allows for giving a *certain* meaning to the practice.

The main question is therefore not why some societies mediate between formalities and dysfunctional realities (they all can be expected to do, as I hope to have shown *ex negativo*) but, rather, why the Brazilian society turned this mechanism of bending legal norms to expediency not only into a "highly prized paralegal institution" (Tobolowksy 2016, 413), but into an institution with the aura of a national identity feature, and others not. In addition, as Barbosa (2005, 35) remarks, it should be asked why despite the undeniable progress of good governance "the *jeitinho* shows to be far from extinction and more present in the media and the everyday discourse than ever?"[25]

Conclusion: the social function of the *jeitinho*

The most fascinating aspect of the *jeitinho* is probably its assumed egalitarian character. Every Brazilian is expected to be able to make good use of it, independent of his or her social status which makes it more likable than showing off authority by claiming the *Você sabe com quem está falando* (Barbosa 2005, 99–100).[26] It suggests that even the powerless are in a position to subvert the discriminatory hierarchy (Torres et al. 2015, 80–81). As such, the *jeitinho* promotes a myth of equal opportunities, a comforting and maybe even empowering promise.

> We believe that the "jeito" can be considered the showpiece of a society marked by juridical inequality among citizen. It is not only a tool to bypass the law or inverted ethics, but many times the only means to achieve basic rights and the only access to a juridical system in which every legal person acts as "every man for himself", whenever and however possible.
>
> (Alvim and Nunes 2017, 21)[27]

This assumption depends however on the premise that the position of individuals in society is a negligible variable. Logically, all arguments that sustain the idea of *jeitinho*, as part of the Brazilian national character, must avoid making any distinctions within this notoriously heterogeneous group. Nevertheless, behind the "generic Brazilian" exists a complex system of class, race, gender, *habitus* and other differences, which establish a spectrum with the extreme poles of fully integrated supra-citizen and excluded sub-citizen.[28] In reality, not all Brazilians have the chance to apply the *jeitinho* when interacting with the police, to give just one example – for some of vital importance. The famous *despachantes* (professional bureaucracy facilitators) offer a fast track only for those who can pay them. The majority of Brazilians whose taxes and contributions are automatically deducted from the salary payment (or who do not earn a salary and only contribute through exorbitant consumption taxes) do not have the opportunity to reduce their burden with a little help from consulting firms specialized in *jeitinhos* of tax avoidance or even fiscal evasion (Braga and Bezerra 2017, 29). As Vieira et al. (1982, 28) observe, "In this sense, the 'jeitinho' is clearly discriminatory for the majority of the population which almost never has available these resources."[29] Against the myth, those who primarily benefit from the *jeitinho*, belong to a wealthy minority of Brazilians. Maybe this is the reason why the *jeitinho* is always praised as sign of peaceful avoidance of conflicts (Amado and Brasil 1991, 56) – reminding the "reconciliação," the traditional Brazilian political strategy to maintain the social status quo. Sometimes, the justification of the *jeitinho* reminds worryingly the so-called neoliberal discourse, for example when

> a labor inspector overlooks the failure of a marginal firm in an area of high unemployment to pay the official minimum wage on the theory that strict enforcement would be likely to throw many employees out of work and perhaps shut down the plant altogether.
>
> (as cited in Rosenn 1984, 386)

Here appears explicit what usually remains in between the lines: the *jeitinho* as a solution to an imaginary conflict between patrimonial-corrupt state and a virtuous "market."

The folkloric popularization of an instrument of power, which lies mainly in the hands of the elite, has far-reaching effects: First, it legitimizes social inequality by accepting the scarcity of public services and transferring the responsibility to overcome the bottleneck to the citizen (Vieira et al. 1982, 28). This is especially intriguing, because as such it also stimulates a passive and resigned attitude, "reproducing and fueling the ideological belief transmitted by the dominant bureaucracy: that the common people will not complain, because they are creative enough to give in and find a little way out when dealing with problems of life"[30] (Vieira et al. 1982, 28). A second effect is the naturalization of corruption by ascribing it to the "formation of the Brazilian character and its natural dishonesty"[31] (Filgueiras 2009, 390). These effects gain in importance when seen in a context of democratization, which reduces means of formal discrimination: strengthened civil rights and good governance demands imply in the relative loss of extraordinary rights for a formerly privileged minority which only can be compensated through informal ways of limiting access to power and resources. Paradoxically, these can only be justified if promoted as open to everybody (after all, arguing that everybody is somehow corrupt, suggests that nobody is really corrupt), which could explain the parallelism of modernization and the rise of *jeitinho*, addressed earlier in this chapter by Barbosa (2005, 35).

This last effect is even to some degree quantifiable. Filgueiras (2009, 413) analyzes data about the perception of corruption in different social groups and institutions. While predictably the economic and political elite (or institutions linked to them) score highest, it is remarkable that "o povo brasileiro" occupies a position in the upper third, even above the federal police, the middle class and the media. Asked about practices, "bribing a police officer," one of the most typical promoted *jeitinho* samples, scores highest in the corruption perception, while a significantly lower score is given to "evade taxes," not part of the traditional *jeitinho*-repertoire (Filgueiras 2009, 415).

What we can conclude based on these reflections is that the *jeitinho* fulfills the aim opposite to that promised, corroborating Vieira et al. (1982, 28) who warned:

> [T]he "jeitinho" is a power tool, an intimate ritual of power, which on one side equalizes in discourse and discriminates in practice and on the other side liberates creativity in the discourse and neutralizes the reaction, harmonizing conflicts and consolidating dominion.[32]

In this perspective, the legitimizing topos of the *jeitinho* is admittedly a Brazilian peculiarity, as claimed by several authors above, just not with a subversive, but a reactionary purpose, because it contributes to hide "the domination of a few over the rest" and "the root of all inequalities which in fact stem from the unequal access to economic and cultural capital, a premise turned invisible in this theory"[33] (Souza 2017, 56). Given these characteristics, the *jeitinho* should be better addressed in a skeptical way, similar to recent approaches on the functionally similar topos of "racial democracy," a formerly progressive social utopia which today is reframed to disable affirmative action policies (Wink 2018). Anani Dzidzienyo (1971, 14) prophesized early:

> [t]he Black Brazilians' position in white-dominated Brazil differs from that of Blacks in similar societies elsewhere only to the extent that the official Brazilian ideology of non-discrimination, by not reflecting the reality and, indeed, by camouflaging it, achieves without tension the same results.

This is a topical advice, as it applies *grosso modo* to the ideology of the *jeitinho*. The comparison is not as farfetched as it appears: the *jeitinho* also belongs to a self-exoticization and only apparently emancipating-recognizing process, which at the beginning drew heavily on Afro-Brazilian cultural roots like the *ginga* (Laplantine 2015). Indeed, tracing the first mentions of *jeitinho* in Brazilian newspapers,[34] they refer overwhelmingly to Samba-musicians and black female dancers, until generalizing the gift as national character feature, surprisingly in the aftermath of the screening of Walt Disney's animation movie *Saludos Amigos* (1942) which favored Brazilian culture with its most popular *malandro*, the humanoid parrot Zé Carioca.

The cultural narrative of a peculiarly Brazilian and somehow winsome folkloric space between legality and illegality is a seductive object of study. However, as antidote we might need to apprehend the manipulative social function of this rhetoric. This goes for not only the celebration, but also the condemnation of the *jeitinho*. In times when we don't yet know the extent to which state power is being appropriated for the benefit of a marginal elite (see Jean Wyllys' contribution to this volume), we should suspect when those social actors, who are executing a selective lawfare in order to "clean up" Brazil, justifying the means by the end, call for a fight against the *jeitinho* as "small corruption." As discussed above, the topos can have not only an absolving, but also a distracting function. Contrary to what is believed, the blurred distinction of which practices can be framed as *jeitinho* and redeemed as culturally legitimate or not, seems to depend not on the crafty man on the street, but on the authority of "who is talking."

Notes

1

> Não existe dominação social possível sem ideias – explícitas e implícitas – que a legitimem e justifiquem, e que permitam, por conta disso, sua reprodução no tempo. Assim, fazer a crítica das ideias dominantes é o primeiro passo para mudar uma dominação socioeconômica injusta.

All translations are by the author, unless otherwise stated.

2

> Nesse sentido, a utilização de atalhos epistemológicos como o "jeitinho brasileiro" ou a "cordialidade", que costumam ser tomados como explicações definitivas para todos os nossos problemas, soa cada vez menos plausível. A utilização desse tipo de argumento tem sido feita sem grande rigor com a finalidade de explicar os mais variados fenômenos.

3 Souza (2000) reconstructs how the notions of Iberian inheritance, personalism and patrimonialism conquered a dominant position in the academic Brazilian self-interpretation (especially – in my eyes perhaps involuntarily – through Sérgio Buarque de Holanda, Raymundo Faoro and Roberto DaMatta) and turned into unquestioned common sense.

4

> Durante a guerra, na campanha dos Apeninos, entrado o inverno, ocorreram sucessivas baixas de soldados com os pés gelados. O serviço de saúde começa a trabalhar e, muito americanamente, principia levantando estatísticas. O resultado inicial foi surpreendente: a maior incidência entre os americanos, que conheciam a neve, do que entre brasileiros, que a estavam vendo pela primeira vez. Analisando o fato, veio a informação espantosa: os pracinhas, ao avanço do frio, cuidaram logo de enrolar os pés em jornais, enquanto seus camaradas americanos esperavam orientação do serviço da saúde…

5 The typical scenario, which illustrates the "Você sabe com quem está falando," is the following:

> Several people are in the waiting room of a bank diretor. Another man comes in, waits impatiently for a few minutes, and then says in a loud voice: "Do you know who you're talking to?! I'm So-and-So." The nervous secretary hurries to the director immediately and the man is soon ushered in.
>
> (DaMatta 1991, 161)

6

> O resultado é um sistema social dividido e até mesmo *equilibrado* entre duas unidades sociais básicas: o indivíduo (o sujeito das leis universais que modernizam a sociedade) e a pessoa (o sujeito das relações sociais, que conduz ao pólo tradicional do Sistema).

7 "[A]lgo vergonhoso, próximo do favor e da corrupção"; "malandra engenhosidade social e política, como um dado tão positivo quanto o carnaval e o futebol como elemento constitutivo de nossa identidade."

8

> Admitamos, por hipótese, que, desgraçadamente, o grau de corrupção no Brasil seja maior do que em outros países. Não seria a causa desse fato uma ausência de mecanismos mais eficazes de controle, antes que uma misteriosa eficácia atávica de padrões culturais personalistas tradicionais da vida colonial brasileira?

9 For example, managers working in countries with high levels of regulation may consider arguably unethical mechanisms to reduce transaction costs as a source of competitive advantage and thus not consider them as corruption (Cuervo-Cazura 2016).

10 "[O] desvio de um padrão de conduta institucionalizado que se caracteriza principalmente pela utilização do público pelo privado com um manifesto propósito de favorecimento pessoal ou grupal."

11 For this reason, it is irrelevant that Keith Rosenn (1971), author of the most comprehensive study of the *jeitinho* from a law perspective, evaluates all cases he examines as one or another form of corruption, because he operates in a binary system of juridically legal vs. illegal.

12 Due to methodological flaws (e.g., not distinguishing between what people say about their action and what they actually do), these results can't be submitted to scientific scrutiny, but still can shed a light on common perceptions and expected practices.

13 If that were a *jeitinho*, most academic peer-reviewers in the Anglo-Saxon World who are so fortunate to be compensated by the editor with free book copies would enter this category.

14 Miura 2012 as well as Maciel and Picelli 2014 get to similar results.
15 "[J]ustificativa para o descumprimento de leis."
16 "[N]os definindo como país e como povo."
17 "Será que é preciso dizer mais alguma coisa?"
18 If not corruption, at least the *jeitinho* is unthinkable outside Brazil, as Barbosa (2005, 32) affirms in her revealing syllogism: "To say that the *jeitinho* corresponds to or facilitates corruption is the same as to say that societies and people who do not have and practice the *jeitinho* are honest ipso facto."
19 "Nos Estados Unidos, na França e na Inglaterra, somente para citar três bons exemplos, as regras ou são obedecidas ou não existem."
20 Until today, any public servant in Germany is officially empowered to use the so called "Ermessensspielraum" (meaning a margin of autonomous discretion) to fully apply (or not) the rules, depending on each case. In my own lifelong interaction with the German bureaucracy, I experienced that this flexibility is widely deployed. It would be interesting to collect reliable data about how exactly this "Ermessensspielraum" is stimulated by the citizen and when it is granted by the representative of the State. My hypothesis is that this depends on the effectiveness of personalizing the relationship, which would match the definition of *jeitinho*.
21 The German newspaper *Süddeutsche Zeitung* launched in 2012 an interactive anonymous forum to collect personal corruption experiences in business. Soon it accumulated 884 statements, which represent the whole spectrum known from Brazil (SZ 2012). Obviously, these experiences are not quantifiable, but it is impossible to deny that they exist in both countries. They are just deemed to be more or less typical, based on our preconceived idea of each culture. Even when numbers are available, being fully accurate or not, they are largely ignored from a Brazilian perspective, such as the cost of corruption in Germany equal to 104 billion Euros or 4% of the GDP (The Greens 2018, 26), an amount close or even above the numbers usually reported for Brazil. The main problem seems to be to assume *a priori* differences, instead of searching for comparable data.
22 "[S]ituações morfológicas e funcionalmente idênticas."
23 She however relativizes this in an endnote, informing that apparently *jeitinho* is known in Algeria as "chtara" (Barbosa 2005, 37, endnote 1).
24 "Estas estratégias legais perante a legislação brasileira, evidenciam que a fama é brasileira, *mas o jeitinho é estrangeiro.*"
25 "[O] jeitinho, longe de se mostrar em extinção, está mais presente nos meios de comunicação e no discurso do cotidiano do que em qualquer período anterior."
26 Souza (2001, 50) analyzes in detail the DaMatta's dichotomy and its several appearances (like in this example) and problematizes that implicitly the personal/hierarchical element is presented as dominant over the individual/equalitarian, but without discussing at any moment how these two sides are articulated and how they concretely relate to each other.
27

> Acreditamos que o "jeito" pode ser considerado o cartão postal de uma sociedade marcada pela desigualdade jurídica entre os cidadãos. Não é somente instrumento de burlar a lei, ou uma ética às avessas, mas muitas vezes, veículo único de alcance à direitos fundamentais; única via de acesso a um sistema jurídico no qual cada sujeito de direito "salva-se quando e como puder."

28 Of course, the criticized authors do not pretend this dimension. However, we have to keep in mind that such interpretation must always remain incomplete:

> The idea of a deep social grammar only makes sense if it was possible to determine the evaluative hierarchy which governs the instituionalization of selective stimuli for the conduct of the individuals in society. This selectiveness requires to consider the variable of relative power of the social groups and classes that are involved in the social struggle for ideological and material hegemony. [...] After all, the task is to clarify the interconnection between ideological dominion and differential access to scarce ideological or material goods.
>
> (Souza 2001, 51)

29 "Neste sentido, o 'jeitinho' é uma prática nitidamente discriminatória para a maioria da população que quase sempre não pode dispor desses recursos."

30

> [R]eproduz-se e alimenta-se da crença ideológica transmitida pela burocracia dominante segundo a qual o povo não irá se queixar, pois é criativo o suficiente para resignar-se e dar um "jeitinho" nas dificuldades "produzidas pela vida."

31 "[F]ormação do caráter do brasileiro e sua natural desonestidade."

32

> [O] 'jeitinho' é um instrumento de poder, um rito íntimo do poder que, por um lado, igualiza no discurso e discrimina na prática e, por outro, liberta a criatividade no discurso e neutraliza a reação, harmonizando os conflitos e consolidando a dominação.

33 "[A] dominação de alguns sobre outros"; "a raiz de todas as desigualdades advindas, na verdade, do acesso desigual aos capitais econômico e cultural que se tornam um pressuposto invisível nessa teoria."

34 Using the digitalized material available in the archive of the *Fundação Biblioteca Nacional*, I verified the occurrence of the words "jeito" and "jeitinho" until the publication year of the first academic treatise on this subject (Ramos 1966). Even though methodologically not exaustive and any possible discussion going beyond the scope of this chapter, the preliminary result might indicate a tendency.

References

Abritta, Carolina Scali, and Maria Do Carmo Leite de Oliveira. "Reaching an Agreement through the Brazilian Way of Dealing with Problems," *Calidoscópio* 10, no. 2 (2012): 186–193.

Alcântara, Valderi de Castro, José Roberto Pereira, and Érica Alline Ferreira. "Gestão Social e Governança Pública: Aproximações e (de)limitações teórico-conceituais," *Revista de Ciências da Administração* 17 (2015): 11–29.

Alvim, Joaquim Leonel de Rezende, and Tiago de García Nunes. "O jeitinho brasileiro, o homem cordial e a impessoalidade administrative: encontros e desencontros na navegação da máquina pública brasileira," *Revista de Direito Público Contemporâneo* 1, no. 2 (2017): 120–140.

Amado, Gelles, and Haroldo Vinagre Brasil. "Organizational Behaviors and Cultural Context: The Brazilian 'Jeitinho'," *International Studies of Management & Organization* 21, no. 3 (1991): 38–61.

Araujo, Bruno Felix von Borell de, Maria Luisa Mendes Teixeira, Poliano Bastos da Cruz, and Elise Malini. "Understanding the Adaptation of Organisational and Self-Initiated Expatriates in the Context of Brazilian Culture," *International Journal of Human Resource Management* 25, no. 18 (2014): 2489–2509.

Azevedo, Elis Bianca, Antonio Gonçalves Oliveira, Camila Lima Buch, Thiago Cavalcante Nascimento, and Christian Luiz da Silva. "Corrupção, governança e desenvolvimento: Uma análise seccional de dados para o Brasil," *Journal Globalization, Competitiveness & Governability* 12, no. 1 (2018): 48–62.

Balbinot, Zandra, Luciano Minghini, Rafael Borim-de-Souza. "Indigenous Brazilian Management Practices," *Journal of Technology Management & Innovation* 7, no. 4 (2012): 132–147.

Barbosa, Lívia. *O jeitinho brasileiro: A arte de ser mais igual que os outros.* Rio de Janeiro: Elsevier, 2005 [1992].

Boufleur, Rodrigo Naumann. "Fundamentos da gambiarra: A improvisação utilitária contemporânea e seu contexto socioeconômico", Master's thesis, University of São Paulo, 2013.

Braga, Sergio Pereira, and Eudes Vitor Bezerra. "O jeitinho brasileiro: As pequenas corrupções diárias e seus reflexos na morosidade da justiça," *Revista de Política Judiciária, Gestão e Administração da Justiça* 3, no. 1 (2017): 17–33.

Büschel, Hubertus. "Die sanfte Macht der Machtlosen: Rituale, Glückwünsche und Geschenke. Preussens Untertanen und ihre Könige um 1800," *Historische Anthropologie: Kultur, Gesellschaft, Alltag* 15, no. 1 (2007): 82–102.

Chen, Chao C., Joseph P. Gaspar, Ray Friedman, William Newburry, Michael C. Nippa, Katherine Xin, and Ronaldo Parente. "Paradoxical Relationships Between Cultural Norms of Particularism and Attitudes Toward Relational Favoritism: A Cultural Reflectivity Perspective," *Journal of Business Ethics* 145, no. 1 (2017): 63–79.

Costa, Francisco Lustosa da. *Ideologia do favor, curral e cabresto.* Fortaleza: Stylus, 1977.

Cuervo-Cazurra, Alvaro. "Corruption in International Business," *Journal of World Business* 51, no. 1 (2016): 35–49.

DaMatta, Roberto. *Carnavais, malandros e heróis: Para uma sociologia do dilemma brasileiro*. Rio de Janeiro: Zahar, 1980 [1978].

DaMatta, Roberto. *O que faz o brasil, Brasil?* Rio de Janeiro: Rocco, 1984.

DaMatta, Roberto. *A Casa e a Rua: Espaço, cidadania, mulher e a morte no Brasil*. Rio de Janeiro: Guanabara, 1987.

DaMatta, Roberto. *Carnivals, Rogues, and Heroes, an Interpretation of the Brazilian Dilemma*. Translated by John Drury. Notre Dame: University of Notre Dame Press, 1991.

DaMatta, Roberto. *O que é o Brasil?* Rio de Janeiro: Rocco, 2004.

DaMatta, Roberto. "Prefácio" In *O jeitinho brasileiro: A arte de ser mais igual que os outros*, Lívia Barbosa, xviii–xxv. Rio de Janeiro: Elsevier, 2005 [1992].

Davis, Natalie Zemon. *The Gift in Sixteenth-Century France*. Madison: University of Wisconsin Press, 2000.

Dennison, Stephanie (ed.). "Cordiality and Intimacy in Contemporary Brazilian Culture" [special issue], *Journal of Iberian and Latin American Studies* 24, no. 3 (2018).

Duarte, Fernanda. “Exploring the Interpersonal Transaction of the Brazilian Jeitinho in Bureaucratic Contexts,” *Organization* 13, no. 4 (2006): 509–527.

Dzidzienyo, Anani. *The Position of Blacks in Brazilian Society*. London: Minority Rights Group, 1971.

Faoro, Raymundo. *Os donos do poder: Formação do patronato político brasileiro*. Porto Alegre: Globo, 1979 [1958].

Fauré, Yves-André. “Jeitinho and Other Related Phenomena in Contemporary Brazil” In *Neopatrimonialism in Africa and Beyond*, edited by Daniel C. Bach and Mamoudou Gazibo, 169–185. New York: Routledge, 2012.

Ferreira, Maria Cristina, Ronald Fischer, Juliana Barreiros Porto, Ronaldo Pilati, and Taciano Lemos Milfont. “Unraveling the Mystery of Brazilian Jeitinho: A Cultural Exploration of Social Norms,” *Personality and Social Psychology Bulletin* 38, no. 3 (2012): 331–344.

Filgueiras, Fernando. “A tolerância à corrupção no Brasil: Uma antinomia entre normas morais e prática social,” *Opinião Pública* 15, no. 2 (2009): 386–421.

Flach, Leonardo. “O jeitinho brasileiro: Analisando suas características e influências nas práticas organizacionais,” *Revista Gestão e Planejamento* 12, no. 3 (2012): 499–514.

Freire, Denilson Aparecida, Renata Monteiro Martins, and Vitória Rezende Lopes. “A percepção dos atuais e futuros gestores da região do Triângulo Mineiro sobre as práticas de corrupção no cotidiano e no ambiente organizacional,” *Revista de Carreiras e Pessoas* 8, no. 2 (2018): 227–238.

Glenn, Doug. “Jeitinho: Succeeding in Brazil.” *Industrial Heating* 76, no. 1 (2009), 118.

Godois, Leandro. “Corrupção no Brasil: Uma abordagem culturalista a partir da sociologia de Roberto DaMatta,” Presentation at III Colóquio de Ética, Filosofia Política e Direito, University of Santa Cruz do Sul (25–26 Aug 2015). https://online.unisc.br/acadnet/ anais/index.php/efpd/article/view/15027/3648. Accessed on August 6, 2019.

Heidenheimer, Arnold J. “Perspectives in the Perception of Corruption.” In *Political Corruption*, edited by Arnold J. Heidenheimer, 3–28. New York: Holt, Rinehart and Winston, 1970.

Holanda, Sérgio Buarque de. *Raízes do Brasil*. Rio de Janeiro: José Olympio, 1976 [1936].

Laplantine, François. *Life of the Senses: Introduction to a Modal Anthropology*. Translated by Jamie Furniss. London: Bloomsbury Publishing, 2015 [2005].

Lima, Daniella Munhoz da Costa, Valderez Ferreira Fraga, and Fátima Bayma de Oliveira. “O paradoxo da reforma do Judiciário: Embates entre a nova gestão pública e a cultura organizacional do jeitinho,” *Revista de Administração Pública* 50, no. 6 (2016): 893–912.

Lourenço, Cléria Donizete Da Silva. “Cultura Brasileira e Marketing de Relacionamento: Um Estudo Etnográfico no Varejo,” *Revista Brasileira de Marketing* 13, no. 5 (2014): 47–64.

Maciel, Wellington Caixeta, and Isabelle Alline Lopes Picelli. “Representações sociais do ‘jeitinho brasileiro’ por trabalhadores de repartições públicas de Brasília,” *Arquivos do Centro de Memória Digital* 2, no. 2 (2014): 146–161.

Mansur, Juliana Arcoverde, and Filipe João Bera de Azevedo Sobral. “Política na terra do ‘jeitinho’: Consequências dos comportamentos políticos em organizações no Brasil,” *Revista de Administração Mackenzie* 12, no. 6 (2011): 165–191.

Miura, Marco Akira. “Entre a Simpatia e a Corrupção: Análise das dimensões constituintes do Jeitinho Brasileiro”, Master’s thesis, University of Brasília, 2012.

Miura, Marco Akira, Ronaldo Pilati, Taciano Lemos Milfont, Maria Cristina Ferreira, and Ronald Fischer. “Between simpatia and malandragem: Brazilian jeitinho as an individual difference variable,” *PLoS One* 14, no. 4 (2019), 1–16. https://doi.org/10.1371/journal.pone.0214929.

Motta, Fernando C. Prestes, and Rafael Alcadipani. “Jeitinho brasileiro, controle social e competição,” *Revista de Administração de Empresas* 39, no. 1 (1999): 6–12.

Nishioka, Silvia Alves, and Defne Akol. “Jeitinho as a Coping Strategy Used by Brazilian International Students for Dealing with Acculturative Stress,” *Journal of International Students* 9, no. 3 (2019), 1–19. https://doi.org/10.32674/jis.v0i0.675.

Park, Camila Lee, Mauro Fracarolli Nunes, Maral Muratbekova-Touron, and Valérie Moatti. “The Duality of the Brazilian *jeitinho*: An Empirical Investigation and Conceptual Framework,” *Critical Perspectives on International Business* 14, no. 4 (2018), 404–425.

Pedroso, José Pedro Penteado, Márcia Shizue Massukado-Nakatani, and Fabrício Baron Mussi. “A relação entre o jeitinho brasileiro e o perfil empreendedor: Possíveis interfaces no contexto da atividade empreendedora no Brasil,” *Revista de Administração Mackenzie* 10, no. 4 (2009), 100–130.

Pereira, Lorena Iza. “O jeitinho estrangeiro: As estratégias do controle do território por estrangeiros no Brasil,” *Pegada – A Revista da Geografia do Trabalho* 19, no. 1 (2018): 162–181.

Pinto, Allesandra Maria Silva, and Alberto Lopes Najar. “Cultura e instituições de saúde: Estudando a participação de traços culturais da sociedade brasileira no processo de trabalho de serviços de atenção básica,” *Ciência & Saúde Coletiva* 16, no. 11 (2011): 4375–4384.

Ramos, Alberto Guerreiro. *Administração e estratégia do desenvolvimento.* Rio de Janeiro, FGV, 1966.

Rodriguez, José Rodrigo. “Contra o fanatismo textualista: Corrupção, jeitinho brasileiro e estado de direito,” *Novos Estudos* 104 (2016), 61–76.

Rosenn, Keith S. “The jeito: Brazil’s Institutional Bypass of the Formal Legal System and Its Development Implications”, *American Journal of Comparative Law* 19 (1971): 514–549.

Rosenn, Keith S. “Brazil’s Legal Culture: The Jeito Revisited,” *Florida International Law Journal* 1, no. 1 (1984): 2–43.

Silva, Maurício. “Corruption: Attempting a Functional Definition,” *Revista de Administração Pública* 28, no. 1 (1994): 18–23.

Smith, Peter B., Hai Juan Huang, Charles Harb, and Claudio Torres. “How Distinctive Are Indigenous Ways of Achieving Influence? A Comparative Study of Guanxi, Wasta, Jeitinho, and ‘Pulling Strings’,” *Journal of Cross-Cultural Psychology* 43, no. 1 (2012): 135–150.

Souza, Jessé. *A modernização seletiva: Uma reinterpretação do dilema brasileiro.* Brasília: Ed. da UnB, 2000.

Souza, Jessé. “A sociologia dual de Roberto DaMatta: Descobrindo nossos mistérios ou sistematizando nossos auto-enganos?” *Revista Brasileira de Ciências Sociais* 16, no. 45 (2001): 47–67.

Souza, Jessé. *A elite do atraso: Da escravidão à lava-jato*. São Paulo: LeYa, 2017.

Souza, Jessé. *Subcidadania brasileira: Para entender o país além do jeitinho brasileiro.* São Paulo: LeYa, 2018.

Souza, Gustavo Henrique Silva de, Jorge Artur Peçanha de Miranda Coelho, Nilton Cesar Lima, and Jamerson Viegas Queiroz. "Informal Marketing: A Commercialization Model Guided by Brazilian Jeitinho, Informality and Entrepreneurship," *Revista Brasileira De Marketing* 13, no. 3 (2014): 63–77.

SZ – Süddeutsche Zeitung. "Schmutzige Geschäfte: Ohne Korruption geht es nicht?" March 2012. www.sueddeutsche.de/wirtschaft/korruption-1.986060. Accessed on August 6, 2019.

The Greens/EFA. "The Costs of Corruption Across the EU". Dec 7, 2018. www.greens-efa.eu/files/doc/docs/e46449daadbfebc325a0b408bbf5ab1d.pdf. Accessed on August 6, 2019.

Tobolowsky, Zachary B. "Brazil Finally Cleans up Its Act with the Clean Company Act: The Story of a Nation's Long-Overdue Fight Against Corruption," *Law and Business Review of the Americas* 22, no. 4 (2016): 383–413.

Torres, João Camilo de Oliveira 1973. *Interpretação da realidade brasileira.* Rio de Janeiro, José Olympio, 1973.

Torres, Claudia V., Solange Alfinito, Galvão, César Augusto de Souza Pinto Galvão, and Bruna Chie Yin Tse. "Brazilian jeitinho versus Chinese Guanxi: Investigating their Informal Influence on International Business," *Revista de Administração Mackenzie* 16, no. 4 (2015): 77–99.

Torres, Claudia V., and Maria Auxiliadora Dessen. "The Brazilian jeitinho: Brazil's Sub-Cultures, Its Diversity of Social Contexts, and Its Family Structures" In *Families Across Cultures: A 30-Nation Psychological Study*, edited by James Georgas, John W. Berry, Fons J. R. van de Vijver, Çigdem Kagitçibasi, and Ype H. Poortinga, 259–266. New York: Cambridge University Press, 2006.

Vieira, Clóvis Abreu. "The Brazilian "Knack" as a Power Resource," *Revista de Administração Pública* 16, no. 2 (1982): 5–31.

Weber, Max. *Wirtschaft und Gesellschaft: Grundriß der verstehenden Soziologie.* Tübingen: Mohr, 1972 [1921–22].

Wink, Georg. "Looking for More Brazilian Solutions: Rhetorical Strategies against Racial Quotas in Brazilian Higher Education," *Brasiliana – Journal for Brazilian Studies* 6, no. 2 (2018): 3–41.

5 Political sexology

Márcia Tiburi

Introduction

The objective of this text is to introduce the concept of "political sexology" that would allow us to understand in what ways sex becomes the goal of political power play in the current period. I will show how sex plays a part in the scene of "illicitudes" that have taken Brazil over during the present moral and ethical crisis, which is intimately linked to the political crisis. What place does sex occupy and how has it been used as a weapon in games of power that have disturbed Brazil in recent years, which led to a judicial coup d'état in 2016 and allowed for the fascist rise to power headed by Bolsonaro? I use "games of power" to refer to discursive and media games, in which sex is the main action piece.

The analysis of such aspects of a symbolic war in which sex is embedded demands an urgent attention to the "illicitudes" that dominate the battleground within the neoliberal laboratory that Brazil has become. In this manner, I hope to shed light on the tension between democracy and authoritarianism by showing that sex is a weapon against the category of "gender," which, indeed, is a dangerous analytical category for the patriarchy, a class that uses all of its might to try to annihilate this category, including the very notion of sex.

It is in this context that the concept of "political sexology" assumes an urgency that starts from an interdisciplinary approach that includes psychoanalysis, aesthetics, philosophy, anthropology, semiotics, ethics and politics. As a science, sexology is committed to producing knowledge, having an ethical impulse at its base, namely, confronting the use of sex and gender as distorted categories used in mystification processes.

Political sexology treats sex as a category of political analysis, just as it does with gender. The hypothesis of this text is that these categories are today part of the discursive and practical production of democratic or authoritarian regimes. Sex has also become a kind of communicative category, a discursive, repetitive and performatizing "tropo." In this sense, it comes to be a transmission device, a kind of code that can be used to trigger mental disorders in populations with a precarious educational and cognitive level. I am referring to the masses that allow themselves to be passively taken to television and computer screens in the current times and cancel urgent processes of reflexive thinking.

In the following, I outline a constellation, a topical cartography from which we can understand this field of analysis in epistemological and semiotic terms.

Mutation

Sex occupies a new political place in our society. It is new in contextual relation to the old conflict associated with sex. In the past people engaged in "the war of the sexes" and discovered later that the war against sex was a war against pleasure and the body. For centuries, sex was the evil against which certain worldviews position themselves. This is to say that that power was oppositional to sex. Afterwards, political actors learned to fight with sex and make it a mechanism for struggle.

Michel Foucault (1994) demonstrated that sex was a manipulated object that degraded and offered excess value based on the necessities of power. Many people fell into the trap to condemn sex by discussing it as impure, dirty and abject. Power tried to negate, hide and withdraw sex from the scene. However, it appears that sex has made a comeback. It has had a facelift. Since the 1960s, sex has been indomitable and it seems that power has tried to reappropriate sex as pleasure and make it a weapon of seduction. Power and pleasure are "plastic" forces that then stiffen, when threatened by knowledge, democracy or, if we were to use political-economic terms, the redistribution of wealth. Given that sex is an object easily exploited – be it for purposes to dominate bodies, be it to profit in industry or in the marketplace – power must take it up again from time to time. And, this recuperation has everything to do with what we might consider the "game of power" involving sex. A dirty game of power. Herein one finds the essential link to the theme of the present volume: illicitudes.

My hypothesis is that a change has occurred with regard to the positioning of sex, even as it remains a mechanism. Despite the "sexual revolution," a return to the perspective of "sex for procreation" has occurred, but now in terms of purification. Ranging from the religious defense, above all the neopentecostal position concerning the reproductive family, the hatred toward women who choose abortion, to the defense claiming "natural" sexes, what we see is a rehabilitated discursive field of sex. This rehabilitation is certainly a tactic to reinforce the ideology of heteronormativity and heterosexuality underscored by the Law, to which everyone feels an obligation after having passed through inevitable processes of *genderification* (Butler 2003). What is curious is that for heterosexuality to be guaranteed as Law, illicit mechanisms are always directed toward unruly *bodies or bodies disciplined by Law*. From a moral and ethical standpoint, violence is always on display in the processes to sustain heteronormativity.

In today's world, sex is not demonized as it once was. How did such a mutation take place? Sex was divided and classified; therein, the process of purification occurred. Sex was treated by science, by philosophy and even the church, which always dedicated a discourse of hate. Over time, sex was accepted. However, such acceptance did not include an opening up toward the body or toward pleasure, but rather solely, because these institutions are institutions of power, they could not waste the opportunity to exploit sex. As motivations continue to be excuses, we should be skeptical that the power games have come to an end.

On the one hand, we see that sex has returned as "naturalized," as "clean sex," in opposition to un-, anti-natural or dirty sex, in other words, all types of non-standard sexuality that lies outside of the sexual pyramid about which Gayle Rubin (2011) discusses in her scholarship concerning the political economy of sex. Beyond this, one finds a more profound mutation. Even dirty sex holds some exceptions that were previously inadmissible. In prior periods, deviant sex, when practiced, occurred in hidden places. The nature of taboo. Nowadays, "abnormal" sex is still considered abject and is attacked in many societies, but if the actor is in a position of power, it need not be hidden.

In this sense, there is both a purification of sex for procreation and another purification, one even more curious. *The power that dirties sex is also the same power that purifies it.* It is the image of sex that ends up being manipulated to serve power: what was illicit becomes licit.

But what does this really mean? Due to varying political conditions, the image of sex changes as its function changes. What we need to ask is: if the psychosocial and concrete conditions that lead to fascism return in a particular historical moment in Brazil, what happens to sex, what function will sex play in authoritarian power? In my view, it is necessary to think about sex as a mechanism in the authoritarian context. Above all, we must keep in sight that cynicism plays a role in sex's performativity and that this is typical of the growing fascism in Brazil.

Power games

Patriarchy and family both depend on and give support to the idea and practice of heteronormative sex. Patriarchy, family and sex are images that require repetition. As a political weapon manipulated and denigrated by the church, sex has changed roles to adapt to this new political scene.

The old mechanism has returned as protected and without the negative stigma of the past. This mechanism must be saved as it could serve a useful function in its renewed condition. The generation that is accustomed to the idea of sexual freedom, who naturalized sexual acts, is not necessarily aware of the fact that during the twentieth century sex was liberated from moral and religious bonds that had controlled it for a long period of time.

My intention is to offer a brief analysis of the use of sex as a weapon in the psychic and cultural war, which is also an epistemological battle within the overall war, a "hybrid war" (Korybko 2018) against "gender" and bordering on a war against democracy as a whole. In this case, it is not just a war against sex as seen in the past involving Christian history and sexuality (Ranke-Heinemann 1996, 368), but also a war using sex to attack gender and twist epistemologically "gender" to dismantle democracy. In the following, I will discuss briefly the important aspects within the context of a political sexology.

Illicitude

The new wrinkle in the story of political sexology is that "gender" has become a dangerous category for the status quo and heteronormativity. While sexism has found an acceptable and even useful place – sex morphed into "natural" or "normal" within fundamental perspectives – gender is now "anti-natural," "abnormal" and even "ideological" in a truly theoretical anamorphosis designed by religious leaders with the objective to combat gender, the new evil and the main danger to the power project of their churches.

One must note: perhaps sexual liberation resulted in a situation in which sexism, as the operator of patriarchy, transferred an inherent hate to gender. In truth, sex as a category weakened after sexual liberation. Just as anguish is a fluctuating factor in neurosis, hate is a dynamic factor in patriarchy and it is for some time that gender has been the repository of hate, which had been directed at sex. This is a hate also directed toward women as the special carriers during certain historical periods such as the Middle Ages, when it was necessary to control working women. In essence, hatred toward sex has been redesigned and repositioned.

Now gender as a category that must be destroyed and those who want to carry this out have discovered that the quickest and most effective way toward this end is to wage an epistemological war utilizing the closest element to gender. Sex. The goal of this war is to destroy the mentality and capacity to discern and to think analytically, which differentiates the bodies and lives of those they wish to dominate.

Moreover, the war on gender departs from the "epistemological cheat" – an illicitude at its core – that directly relates to the symbolic violence and patriarchal logic, whose form is a cunning of reason bordering on cynicism.

The attacks on gender studies in our times are part of the maintenance strategies of the hegemony of patriarchal reason. We must strive to understand this.

Cunning

The war against gender goes further. By dismantling gender studies, the objective is to destroy democracy itself, that which was always sustained by reflections against mystification, that which depends on shared knowledge and critical depth. We could say that gender studies represents today what philosophy represented during the dictatorship in the 1960s and 1970s. What is in common is critical thinking.

We are thus discussing a kind of cunning. The war against gender is like the Trojan horse placed in the city in order to win the war by ruse. Hate discourse and fake news about gender contribute to the current context in which cunning is more important than reason. It is an attempt to remove gender from the scientific field and rearticulate it as mere ideology. The sciences, in fact, are at risk in such circumstances, faced with the destruction of reflection by mystification, which itself stems from the impoverishment of language thereby serving the interests of authoritarianism and, by association, patriarchy.

Gender is one of the essential terms in the history of knowledge production that acts as the base of a democratic society. There is no democracy without critical thinking, analysis, without science and art, without the fostering of debate of a high theoretical level that is then circulated by an equally responsible press. Unfortunately, all of this has been lost in Brazil and lies in the hands of the linguistic/discursive owners of production, such as the church, mass media, the juridical sector. In a phrase: the economic elite and their system of oppression.

Political technology

The case of Brazil deserves special attention because sex has emerged as a weapon in the current return to authoritarianism. What kind of authoritarianism has no moral commitment with sex but knows how to use it as a weapon? Or, by contrast, how could such a form of politics liberate sex from destruction and the status of evil? The dictatorial State returns but sex is not its target; rather sex is a medium by which the State seeks to destroy that which is more dangerous: gender and democracy.

The toppling of democracy in Brazil and in other countries with similar situations of a resurging authoritarianism has occurred in a comparatively more sordid fashion with the inappropriate use of democratic tools. In this instance, I employ "inappropriate use" in reference to the authoritarian deployment of concepts, such as "freedom of expression" as well as the production and dissemination of "fake news" in social media with the intention of manipulating opinion and influencing political acts like voting. This specific issue is outside of the purview of the particular essay. What I will discuss is the significance of sex in media operations of fake news. It is true that there are other key phrases such as "corruption" in the manufacturing of fake news, as it, like sex, is also associated with "dirtiness." At the writing of this essay, most people know that Bolsonaro illegally used the media application of Whatsapp to send millions of messages with fake content. But, why did these messages contain "information" about the infamous "Gay Kit" and "Penis Baby Bottle" as well as a charge that Fernando Haddad had raped an 11-year-old girl? Why were all the main pieces of fake news sexual in content?

How did Bolsonaro become important in this manner? How did he rise from a relatively unknown to the "myth," as he known by his followers? Why is it that in the subsequent Bolsonaro regime the number of fake news items related to sex has not diminished? Why, even after the electoral victory, is sex used as a tool during Carnaval 2019, for example, in the twitter episode in which president Bolsonaro exposes a "Golden Shower" episode? What function would the outbursts of minister Damares Alves, a woman, who frequently refers to bizarre sexual acts with children, serve, if it weren't mystification?

Certainly, we are talking about a cunning mystification. For those who are unaware of this issue or the case of Brazil and the coup d'état of 2016 that deposed the innocent president Dilma Rousseff, perhaps this text may seem like a "drawer full of curiosities" surrounding a series of weird sexual stories that are ultimately irrelevant. It may seem like a text in which an author decided to cite a few exotic cases from the "cultural trash" associated with sex as part of a rhetorical "style." *Might this be the case in the conceptualization of sex as a weapon used in the so-called "Political Farce," a trend to capitalize on the ridiculous as part of political technology in contemporary Brazil?* The church – historical experts in aesthetic manipulation – also shape the ridiculous approaching limits that are impossible to predict.

Gender ideology

"Gender ideology" (Tiburi 2018) is a fundamental point in the mapping of political sexology. First, it calls attention to a term, somewhat inhospitable, as both "gender" and "ideology" are traditional terms of critique. Scholars in the field of gender studies have mostly been concerned with applying gender as an analytical category with the intention of understanding patriarchy within ideological structure (Rubin 2017; Scott 1986).

The expression "gender ideology" is not a result of theory nor science. From the point of view of epistemology, one might say that it holds the same structure as fake news but applied in the scientific field. What journalists, public relations staff and media militia produce as Fake News is what religious leaders (padres, pastors, reverends, etc.) create under the rubric of "gender ideology".[1] We can affirm that gender ideology is a form of "Fake Theory." There is no context; rather, it creates value by cheating and reaches its target through discursive publicity and high-impact affect. It doesn't matter if the goal is positive or negative. The form implies a certain truth-value only because it was said in a truth function and framed as truth.

The goal is pragmatic to cause conceptual confusion. There is a pragmatic use of a distorted perspective as if we were facing an anamorphosis. There is a confusion produced in the point of view that hides the true perspective. Those who created the expression "gender ideology" hide that they are the original "gender ideology". The use of this expression by fundamentalist sectors serves to attack gender and hide the very ideology that the category of "gender" analysis deconstructs. Again, the aim is to combat the gender studies that today are devoted to a serious epistemological violence. The objective is also to make feminists once again seen as "witches" as the Church did in the past.

This rhetorical game produces a logical illusion, which I described above as an anamorphosis. It involves an abusive masking of violence without precedence, now emboldened by new weapons of digital technology fueled by the increasing interest of people in social networks. In Brazil, "gender ideology" occupies noble spaces, such as schools and universities. Congress members and militant fundamentalists of neopentecostal churches have succeeded in banning the term from governmental texts and have created a real witch hunt. Witches are thus anyone who still speaks of gender like the author of this text and so many others.

Pedophilia

Another element in the cartography of political sexology is pedophilia. I do not intend to discuss the concept of pedophilia from a psychological or criminological perspective. Moreover, my goal is not to consider the history of pedophilia or how it has become a topic in the society of the spectacle (Verdrager 2013), but rather simply to describe the role pedophilia has played in the ruination of democracy.

The term pedophilia appeared in Brazil as a synonym of monstrosity. Foucault (1999) discussed the social production of the monster that always serves multiple purposes. Fundamental in the manufacturing of common sense by the owners of mainstream media, pedophilia also follows a double logic in Brazil. At times, it is depicted as an illness, other times a crime and thus the agent is deserving of punishment. Still, other times pedophilia, when associated with "monstrosities," such as rape, incest, homosexuality and intersexuality, disappears. It is essentially erased.

For example, Sílvio Santos, a man of nearly 90 years of age who is still the host of a popular television show shown on his network channel, occasionally disrespects children morally. Recently, he asked a seven-year-old girl if she preferred "sex, power or money."[2] While the incident was received with disdain across social media platforms, there was no critique from governmental authorities, who in public discourse regularly invoke pedophilia as a serious disgrace in Brazil.

The horror of pedophilia looms as part of a milieu of partially elaborated fears within a society of manipulated emotions and prohibited reflections. The pastor Damares Alves, the acting Minister of Women, Family and Human Rights, speaks in melodramatic verse that girls should wear pink and boys blue[3] but also declares in the same tone that she watches video of babies being raped like never before in Brazil.[4] I cannot pass judgment on the validity of the cases she has mentioned publicly, but what calls my attention is Alves' underscoring of the "shock value" inherent in these examples.

Through her discourse, Damares Alves promotes a deep mystification of pedophilia and with it a particular politics regarding "women, family and human rights." Another example involves a primer in which the Dutch teach how to masturbate children.[5] Alves goes on to comment that girls on the Island of Marajó (state of Pará, located in the north of Brazil) are abused because they do not have underpants to wear. In fact, there is a well-known system of child abuse on the island,[6] not unlike many other places in Brazil. Be that as it may, my principal concern is to understand why these crimes need to mystified. Indeed, the defense of children is vital to government in the struggle against violence; however, the discursive tone of the minister avoids this sort of questioning. There is a total lack of responsibility for policy development in concert with fundamental human rights and the security of children youth and all groups who constitute the victims of sexual violence.

Pedophilia has a similar function to "gender ideology" within the fundamentalist sector that has risen to power in 2018 in Brazil. In addition to the misleading defense of children, we also see in the anti-abortion propaganda, which is, in fact, not a defense of children, because, of course, such power players do not align themselves with children in scenarios such as school, impoverishment, hunger, favela assassinations, an attack against women and any critics under the banner of "gender ideology." One might say that there is an Order of Fundamentalist Discourse carried out by Brazilian neopentecostalism, which goes well beyond Edir Macedo, the richest and most established of all of such figures.

Our focus must remain on the role of violence in the imaginary of the patriarchal and authoritarian society. What is the place of children in this imaginary? Brazilian society knows violence at various levels of fear facilitated by the needs of the system of power. Simultaneously, the cult of childhood as a time of innocence has always comprised an important of Brazilian culture. We know that today the great majority of rape victims in Brazil are children. The current government has not made any sort of pronouncement supporting schools and children's/youth rights, nor has it provided any statement on the increasing number of black and poor youth murdered in favelas during the years of 2018 and 2019. Such death that has shocked a portion of society has been greeted with mere silence by the State.

Neopentecostal groups promote a discourse of pedophilia – and other criminalized practices – as a weapon against feminists, homosexuals and LGBT people.[7] The impact of mystification among certain socio-cultural classes, above all among the working poor, is immense. Moreover, the impact is functional and programmatic.

One interesting example along these lines involves the pastor/mayor of Rio de Janeiro, a person known for never appearing in his own mayorial office and who actively censured a book because it contained a homosexual kiss.[8] This was all done to call attention to himself and to his constituency, who, despite being forsaken by an administration that has done nothing substantially, absorb the moralism as political fodder. More than 30% of Brazilian claim to be evangelical Christians and the number of pastors who have become politicians has increased dramatically,[9] which goes to prove that the machinations of power urged on by religion are agile.

Artifacts

While people are used to a certain relationship with sex as spectacle through media, such as television *novelas* and social networks, sex has lost its impact in real life. Having turned into something banal and trite, sex has lost its force. All the interest directed toward sex of youth, couples, the bourgeoisie, women, the religious, lovers, artists, kings and queens, it has all become less important in the face of one sole topic, the perversion of pedophilia.

The strategic use of pedophilia emerged in 2017, when members of the extreme right-wing group MBL (Movement of a Free Brazil) entered into the exhibition entitled "Queer Museum, Mappings of Difference" that took place at the Santander Cultural Center.[10] Accused of inciting pedophilia and zoophilia, the exhibition was closed down by the government causing various protests. The curator received death threats and it is this group stalked me throughout the year of 2018. Since January 24, 2018, when they broke into a radio studio where I was giving an interview, they followed and harassed me in all the spaces where I spoke to promote my book, "Feminism in Common." Group members assaulted people in the audience and threatened me with death. This culminated in my current exile outside of Brazil effective in December 2018. Meanwhile, the MBL leader became a federal congressman with a high number of votes. This is not a religious group, but an extreme right-wing group that activated a trigger of hate toward art and gender.

We should not forget the case of Wagner Schwarz, who during the same period was attacked in connection with his performance entitled La Bête, a piece that had already been performed in many places inside and outside of Brazil. In the performance, which was inspired in "Bichos" of Lígia Clark, the body is manipulated by the public. The detail that became the object of mystification was the actor's nudity. *Nudity quickly was transformed into an eroticization of the body, considered unnatural and stigmatized.* Other artists were attacked at the same time in a movement, which implies a kind of orchestration with electoral goals,[11] given the context of the unjust imprisonment of Lula, the odds favorite candidate for president. As one can see, the field and range of illicitudes is immense, involving a judicial order capable of defiling itself and destroying democracy in the name of power and willing to exploit everyday habits. This leads us to the next example.

During the presidential campaign of 2018, something called the "penis baby bottle" became a center of public debate. A video showed a baby bottle in the form of a penis that, according to the narrator, would be distributed by the Workers Party (PT) in daycare centers under the guise to combat homophobia. The narrator affirmed that this was part of the so-called Gay Kit created by Fernando Haddad (the eventual presidential candidate of the PT).

The narrator thus incited people to vote for Bolsonaro to "make our children into real men and women."[12] The baby bottle, which can purchased in sex shops, was supposed to be a central part of the Gay Kit. There are several sources of disinformation circulated via social networks.

Moreover, a video of an interview with Jair Bolsonaro by *Jornal Nacional*, the well-known news program on the Globo network, features Bolsonaro showing the audience a book that is supposedly a centerpiece of the "Gay Kit."[13] Some journalists published corrections[14] exposing the lies of Bolsonaro's claims about the baby bottle, the Gay Kit as well as the book, which never was part of Haddad's project Education without Homophobia (*Escola sem Homofobia*).[15] Bolsonaro employs similar tactics as Damares Alves in the video as he alerts the viewers of the shocking content of the book. He attests that the book incites pedophilia and demonstrates how one should utilize pedophilia in the classroom as part of sexual education. Bolsonaro performs around the object to emphasize its shock value.

These electoral campaign examples demonstrate the lack of ethical limits within current power politics. In addition, it shows the limitless imagination of a perverse obsession against leftist politics. The fabricated nexus in between sexual perversion and political position also appears in the discourse of "gender ideology." Leftist politics is translated for common citizens as an evil image composed of symbolic categories such as pedophilia.

It is not enough just to say slander. It has to be provoke a scandal, a scene that persuades people through objects. Hence, there is a need to perform and create iconography of perversion. The pornographic object (penis baby bottle) became a series of jokes during Carnaval against which Bolsonaro waged a discursive war in 2019. The politician dressed up again and rekindled his performative flame in the famous video called "Golden Shower,"[16] which he later deleted after he realized that the actors would sue him.

Misogyny

With the disposal of president Dilma Rousseff misogyny became a central logic of the State. A wide gamut of misogynist strategies were used during the defamation of Rousseff. The most basic strategy circulated throughout the mainstream press was to associate the president with craziness, a practice with a long historical precedent. But, it did not stop there.

There was one image in particular that focused on sex that was surprising in its creativity and transparent misogyny. As part of the production of hate against Rousseff, who had previously enjoyed markedly high levels of approval, there were scores of cars sporting a sticker with the face of Rousseff and the image of a woman's body with legs spread. In the place where the genitalia would be was the gas tank. In essence, the gas nozzle acted as a penis. To fill up was to penetrate the president.

This occurred during the time of an imagetic construction working toward impeachment. Rousseff necessarily was a target of hate. This image displayed on these cars combined a hatred of Rousseff with the banalization of rape. Violence against democracy moved via sex into a weapon. On April 17, 2016, during the congressional vote regarding the impeachment of Rousseff, Bolsonaro mocked the president by praising the known torturer (during the military dictatorship), Colonel Ustra, as the "terror of Dilma Rousseff."[17] When it was his turn to vote, Bolsonaro also cited that his vote was for the "innocence of Brazilian children" in order to establish the symbolic connection between the defense of children and torture with one phrase. Very few observed this link at the time, but the entire function of Bolsonaro since this incident has been to produce insanity and bewilderment with a public appeal.

By invoking Ustra, Bolsonaro created a climate of panic while simultaneously guaranteeing a place for perverse ridicule. It is as if he were warning everyone that his future sadistic project would ensure a place for perversion and terror.

Bolsonaro had appeared in headlines in 2003 and 2011 when he attacked congress member Maria do Rosário of the Labor Party (PT). He stated that she wasn't even worth raping and punctuated this slander with the epithet of "*vagabunda*" (lazy scoundrel). Bolsonaro regularly uses an aggressive tone to claim a place of virility and supplements his tone with facial expressions of disgust, interruptions during interviews and muttering words and phrases of military command.

The link between the discourses against Dilma Rousseff and Maria do Rosário is clear. It is necessary to accost a woman to guarantee one's place in power, as an aggressive "macho" with the expected result of admiration. In Brazil, the articulation of violence is a value. Bolsonaro deploys in his discourse of rape an imaginary of promise and threat that become political weapons. The deployment of aggression against women as a performance of authoritarianism fits perfectly within patriarchy, a field that ceases to exist without violence against women. In sum, violence against women is both a means and an end in political patriarchy and thus is one theme within the investigation of political sexology.

Homophobia

One can detect the machinations of power games also with homophobia. Again, what should be fought is fostered as if the improper, the absurd, in a word, the illicit becomes the rule. To transform the illicit into legal, in terms of being cool and "ok" represents the political technology in vogue today in Brazil.

It is not homosexuality *per se* that is morally important to those who lambaste it in public. Many detractors are, in fact, homosexual. They simply hide their sexual practices. Homosexuality is the lever, the pivot to broadcast homophobia as hate speech. And, it is hate speech, as discussed earlier, that is essential in the psychic conflicts that define contemporary politics and politicians, following the work of Chantal Mouffe (2013) regarding agnostic pluralism.

Such a theoretical base helps one understand the oppositional positions of ex-congressman Jean Wyllys, defender of LGBT issues currently living in exile after receiving numerous death threats, and current congressman Alexandre Frota, a former porno actor and former member of PSL (Bolsonaro's political party). Frota was elected on a platform of family values while his pornographic photos and videos circulated the internet. Wyllys has always been "out" and his clear and courageous rhetoric was vilified and criminalized while the pornographic and bisexual sexuality of Frota – as an inevitable element of homosexuality, as declared by Frota himself – was never interrogated. The logic of power is obviously contradictory.

For his part, Jair Bolsonaro had been a minor figure in the national congress for decades. No one believed that he could possible win a presidential election. It is clear now that Bolsonaro's rise in terms of media capital began with his confrontation with Wyllys, which featured Bolsonaro's incendiary homophobia. The wildly circulated scenes of this confrontation catalyzed a relatively latent homophobia in the country.

Celebrities need only "appear" to achieve symbolic capital. In this case, Wyllys' fame emerged in part due to his participation in one of the first BBB (Big Brother Brazil) programs, which reached millions of Brazilians. This was all Bolsonaro needed to break out of his insignificance and enter into the national scenario.

Other homophobic members of congress attacked Wyllys repeatedly over the year and this cannot be understood as a simplistic form of prejudicial spontaneity. Homophobia functions as a weapon. It is not unlike the conventional, material weapons that Bolsonaro's sons often wear around the waist for everyone to see. Be it in political rallies or on television programs, homophobia (just as arms) are weapons in plain sight.

In the case of Jean Wyllys, homosexuality was an object of prejudice but not exactly due to homosexuality itself. Among men, there are various homosexual practices that are tolerated as long as they are not publicly embraced or supported. By declaring his sexual orientation in public, Jean Wyllys broke a tacit agreement and thus threatened the power block of "tradition, family, property" that defines Brazilian politics. Wyllys exposed and disrupted the hypocrisy and committed a heresy at levels comparable to the gender politics of Dilma Rousseff, a transparent, center-left politician, who dared to be a leader in an authoritarian and sexist republic led by media corporations and now militias under the command of Bolsonaro.

The election of Alexandre Frota introduced a new element. Occasionally, moralist people not only reject but also desire homosexuality, as long as homosexuality plays a subservient role within authoritarianism and does not become cynical à la Jean Wyllys. The situation can be explained this way. It is as if the "crime" is allowed, that is, the illicitude is the norm as long as the truth is never admitted. The truth is also prohibited in Brazil.

The model of "traditional family of procreation," led by the macho as represented by Bolsonaro, is also a part of political sexology. Masculinity is a value in the political scenario. The example of João Dória, the current governor of the state of São Paulo, helps clarify. During the election period of 2018, a video was leaked featuring Dória nude in bed with four or five women. At the time, his chance of election was fading, but suddenly he won the election. There are rumors that he himself leaked the video to fortify his heterosexual image, as there had been public suspicion as to his possible homosexuality.

Wyllys is hated for politicizing his homosexuality while Frota, who does not politicize his sexuality and continues to let his pornographic videos flourish online, is adored.

Hypocrisy, then, is a necessary veil to maintain the status quo, and this is why Frota has become an essential player at this time. He is proof that homophobia claims no victims if they are on the side of the oppressor. In this manner, is it not homosexuality that will be punished but those who are not afraid to call out sexuality and say its name.

Corruption displays similarities. It is not corruption that is evil but simply the corruption of the "other" when s/he becomes a political enemy.

In sum, sexuality presents us with complex levels of meaning and power due to its ambiguous relationship with desire. Desire, if prohibited to flourish in a healthy manner, tends toward hate. For its part, hate is an affect marked by projections – to hate what one desires and cannot possess due to a lack of external or internal authorization. To destroy what one desires but cannot have is a rule of the unconscious.

Notes

1 This term was first used in the "Episcopal Conference of the Catholic Church" held in Lima, Peru in 1998. The theme of the conference was "La Ideologia de Género. Sus peligros y Alcances" [Gender Ideology. Its danger and range]. www.aciprensa.com/controversias/genero.htm. Accessed on March 28, 2018.
2 www.youtube.com/watch?v=fndRwVM6XmM. Accessed on October 10, 2019.
3 www.youtube.com/watch?v=CUXdwdnogBM. Accessed on October 10, 2019.
4 www.youtube.com/watch?v=il62J_Yr1T0. Accessed on October 10, 2019.
5 www.youtube.com/watch?v=6HsrRwj35fM. Accessed on October 10, 2019.
6 https://www2.mppa.mp.br/noticias/operacao-resgate-marajo-prende-envolvidos-em-abuso-sexual-de-criancas-e-adolescentes.htm. Accessed on October 10, 2019.
7 According to Tatiana Lionço (2016, 150):

> Argentinian writer Scala (2011) as well as the US reverend Sheldon (2012) exemplify this distortion. They allege that feminist and LGBT movements are attempting to destroy morality by the elimination of all limits regarding sexuality, including pedophilia, zoophilia and even necrophilia and aligning this with homosexuality. Such arguments incite violence against these groups that are supposedly involved in a real moral abomination in an affront to the church and family order." ["O livro do argentino Scala (2011) e do reverendo

norte-americano Sheldon (2012) são exemplos dessa deturpação: alegam que movimentos feministas e LGBTs visariam destruir a moralidade por meio da abolição de quaisquer limites sobre a sexualidade, pendendo para a legalização da pedofilia, zoofilia e mesmo a necrofilia, além de associar linearmente homossexuais a pedófilos. Tais argumentos incitam o ódio social contra aqueles grupos, que estariam supostamente empenhamos em uma verdadeira ruína moral por meio da afronta à igreja e à ordem familiar"]. All translations are by the author, unless otherwise stated.

(2016, 150)

8 www.bbc.com/portuguese/brasil-49650286. Accessed on October 10, 2019.
9 Bolsonaro himself was baptized recently with his family in a ceremony located in Israel. The alliance between politicans and evangelical leaders is increasingly common, as the election of neopentecostal leaders who promise to support only their own churches. See www.youtube.com/watch?v=Yl2nBsPvuyg. Accessed on October 10, 2019.
10 https://brasil.elpais.com/brasil/2017/09/11/politica/1505164425_555164.html. Accessed on October 11, 2019.
11 https://oglobo.globo.com/cultura/artistas-atacados-em-2017-criam-peca-em-resposta-agressoes-22394490. Accessed on October 11, 2019.
12 www.youtube.com/watch?v=bhPF4zlrwqE&oref=https%3A%2F%2Fwww.youtube.com%2Fwatch%3Fv%3DbhPF4zlrwqE&has_verified=1. Accessed on October 10, 2019.
13 www.youtube.com/watch?v=kJB53Mw1Clk. Accessed on October 10, 2019.
14 https://aosfatos.org/noticias/e-falso-que-haddad-criou-kit-gay-para-criancas-de-seis-anos. Accessed on October 10, 2019.
15 The book in question is *Sexual Apparatus and Company*, by Swiss author Philippe Chappuis (known as Zep) and the French writer Hélène Bruller, which was never adopted by MEC (Brazilian Ministry of Education) nor included in Haddad's project. https://brasil.elpais.com/brasil/2018/08/29/politica/1535564207_054097.html. Accessed on October 10, 2019.
16 www.bbc.com/portuguese/brasil-47662013. Accessed on October 10, 2019.
17 www.youtube.com/watch?v=54KUDU-u1P0. Accessed on October 10, 2019.

References

Butler, Judith. *Problemas de gênero: Feminismo e subversão da identidade*. Translated by Renato Aguiar. Rio de Janeiro: Civilização Brasileira, 2003.

Federici, Silvia. *Calibã e a Bruxa: Mulheres, Corpo e Acumulação Primitiva*. Translated by Coletivo Sycorax. São Paulo: Editora Elefante, 2019. http://coletivosycorax.org/wp-content/uploads/2019/09/CALIBA_E_A_BRUXA_WEB-1.pdf. Accessed on October 28, 2019.

Foucault, Michel. *Histoire de la Sexualité: La Volonté de Savoir*. Paris: Gallimard, 1994.

Foucault, Michel. *Les Anormaux. Cours au Collège de France, 1974–1975*. Paris: Seuil/Gallimard, 1999.

Korybko, Andrew. *Guerras Híbridas: Das revoluções coloridas aos golpes*. São Paulo: Ed. Expressão Popular, 2018.

Lionço, Tatiana. 2016. "Criminalização do assédio ideológico nas escolas: Ideologia de gênero como argumento central na disputa fundamentalista da política de educação." In *A política no corpo: gêneros e sexualidade em disputa*, edited by Alexsandro Rodrigues, Gustavo Monzeli, and Sérgio Rodrigo da Silva Ferreira, 145–160. Vitória: EDUFES, 2016.

Mouffe, Chantal. *Agnostics: Think the World Politically*. London: Verso, 2013.

Ranke-Heinemann, Uta. *Eunucos pelo reino de Deus. Mulheres, Sexualidade e a Igreja Católica*. Rio de Janeiro: Ed. Rosa dos Tempos, 1996.

Rubin, Gayle. *Deviations: A Gayle Rubin Reader*. London: Duke University Press, 2011.

Rubin, Gayle. *Políticas do Sexo*. Translated by Jamille Pinheiro Dias. São Paulo: Ubu, 2017.

Scala, Jorge. *Ideologia de gênero: o neototalitarismo e a morte da família*. São Paulo: Katechesis, 2011.

Sheldon, Louis P. *A estratégia – o plano dos homossexuais para transformar a sociedade*. Rio de Janeiro: Central Gospel, 2012.

Scott, Joan W. "Gender: A Useful Category of Historical Analysis." *The American Historical Review* 91, no. 5 (1986): 1053–1075.

Tiburi, Márcia. "The Functionality of Gender Ideology in the Brazilian Political and Economics Context." In *In Spite of You: Bolsonaro and the New Brazilian Resistance*, edited by Conor Foley, 134–146. New York/London: Ok Books, 2018.

Verdrager, Pierre. *L'enfant interdit. Comment la pédophilie est devenue scandeleuse* [series Individu et société]. Paris: Armand Colin, 2013.

Part II
Representing (il)legalities

6 Drinking lime juice to throw up, and the right way to beat an old lady

Policing punk in late dictatorial Brazil (1978–1982)[1]

Alexander S. Dent

The line between the "offensive" and the "illegal" can be difficult to draw. Drinking lime juice mixed with milk in order to induce public vomiting is obnoxious, but not illegal. Beating up an old lady is both. This chapter argues that the growth of punk rock in Brazil offers a fertile place to examine how actors negotiate illegality in real time according to diverse orientations toward the state and its laws. Punk rock arose, in Brazil and around the world, right at the moment in which neoliberal theology began its rise as the hegemonic mode of governance – tying economic and personal life more tightly together, privatizing institutions that were once public, shrinking the regulatory functions of government, and promulgating competition as the primary modality through which to govern daily life. These social and political transformations, although portrayed as "natural" outgrowths of human nature, required force. Though punk's politics were often difficult to discern, punks were broadly opposed to authority, and the police were the state's chief instrument for exercising authority. Punk, as a rebellion against this way of thinking and being, therefore, required disciplining.

This Brazilian case helps us understand the dependency of contemporary capitalism on policing, some of which is violent; in Brazil, the policing practices, which were developed as the military dictatorship transitioned into a violent democracy, have proven to be remarkably durable.[2] Furthermore, we will see how the injunction to police punk is linked to its portrayal as something from "outside" Brazil, allowing it to be laminated together with other dangerous external forces such as communism and socialism. In this sense, therefore, this chapter will advance a theory of how policing, and the decision about what is legal and what is illegal, may be linked to what is viewed as local and what is viewed as external.

In terms of this volume's aim to parse illegality in Brazil – a worthy task in a location in which informality accompanies the capricious enforcement of often quite strict laws (Dent 2018, 2012) – we should note that the maintenance of illegality requires clarity; an officer of the law must make a decision to act that will be supported by law and accompanying judicial infrastructures. The decision about what constitutes illegality gets worked out in real time, between police and those they must simultaneously protect and control. This working out is a difficult task. A full critique of neoliberal policing requires understanding it dialogically, and not as monolithic and predetermined. Only sometimes do officers know what they are going to do *before* they start walking their beats or driving their routes.

In this ambit, we begin with a newspaper article and its aftermath: In May of 1982, entertainment columnist and reporter Luiz Fernando Emediato published an article about punks in the broadly circulated *Estado de São Paulo* newspaper of São Paulo. The article was part of a series entitled "The Abandoned Generation," and aimed to describe youth culture in Brazil at the time. Numerous youth groups received unflattering attention, but punks seemed to get special treatment. The portions of the article that concerned punk contained inflammatory statements about their aggression, contrariness, and cruelty. Loathing was apparent in every line. As a way of establishing how mainstream Brazilian society might have perceived punks in the early 1980s as in need of policing, the article is worth quoting at length.

> Disciples of Satan, the idol that they venerate, they don't see much difference between god and the devil, between Marx, Kennedy, or Hitler, between good and evil. They like to fight – little else, and the cruel ones beat up old ladies and think it's funny. Punks [the author calls them *punkers*] hate alcohol and drugs, though they like sex. They prefer drinking milk mixed with lime juice, and often, after drinking this mixture, they vomit on themselves, or they throw up the coagulated milk into the faces of their victims.
>
> (Nascimento and Paiva 2016, 88)[3]

In another portion of the article, Emediato suggested that punks enjoyed destroying buses. To the reporter and his sympathetic readers, this was no doubt an example of what happens when society breaks down, leading to the abandonment of a generation. Kids who are left to their own devices, without strong parenting, get into trouble, and punk was a particularly disturbing form of that trouble.

Interviews with punks from the period, together with photographic evidence, suggest that the article was, at the very least, hyperbolic. In some places it was downright inaccurate. Brazilian punks, and punks around the world, drank (and drink!) plenty of alcohol.[4] They did not worship Satan – that was a propensity of metal music. Though many of them had not necessarily been to college, they had a perfectly clear understanding of the differences between Hitler and Marx, and a highly developed sense of good and evil. And reports of routinized puking appear nowhere in documents or films from the period (though some puking does show up from time to time). So inaccurate was the portrayal that a group of contemporaneous São Paulo punks encouraged Clemente – bass player for the band Inocentes – to write a reply, which he did, and which was subsequently published in the newspaper. In his reply, Clemente argued that the reporter appeared to have little real knowledge of punks, and that punk was more of a social movement opposed to the arbitrary constraints of society than a hateful group of old-lady muggers and recreational vomiteers. Sure – many (though by no means all) of them espoused anarchism as a mode of governance. But that didn't mean that they destroyed the buses they needed to get around. Furthermore, Clemente suggested that reporters should do a better job of getting to know their subjects before representing them on paper. As a remedy for the reporter's ignorance, Clemente invited him and his readers to come and hear a few shows and figure out what punks were actually up to.

In present day histories of punk, the article and its reply stand for the ways in which the mainstream press, and often middle-class readers, entirely misunderstood punks in late dictatorial Brazil (Essinger 1999; Moreira 2016; Nascimento and Paiva 2016). However, at the risk of offending my punk friends, I should say that had the misunderstanding been total, Clemente's letter would never have been published at all. Furthermore, there was a sort of truth to the article. As we shall see in more detail in a moment, punks *did* like to fight; many of them had seen the movie *Warriors* and were attracted to its artful portrayal of gang combat. And punks *did* often flout the mores of society, particularly through music, art, and comportment. They were not particularly neat in their dress – wearing clothing that was deliberately torn, and often performatively patched with safety pins. Brazilian punks, like elsewhere, often sported mohawks, with a prominent stripe of hair down an otherwise bald head: a hairstyle that was meant to be shocking. And in terms of boorish behavior – the vomiting incident is not difficult to imagine as a dramatic one-off.[5] Indeed, one poster advertising a punk show from the period, and included in a "scene report" sent to an international punk magazine in 1983, contains the phrase "I want to vomit in the repression" (the desire was expressed in English; Bivar and Sampaio 1983). Whether the author meant that oppression made him sick, or that he wanted to vomit *on* the oppression as a way of punishing it, is not clear. But the vomiting is. Though they may not have spent time assaulting the elderly with their firsts, they spent plenty of time displaying a calculated lack of respect for authority of any kind – including the authority that might come from old age. Indeed, while punk often sounded politically inscrutable to middle-class listeners – with no clear "politics" to speak of – its platform was clear enough: down with authority! And in the context of an authoritarian regime run by a loose coalition of military groups prone to feeling threatened by social movements of any kind, this rebelliousness was bound to pose problems.

Contemporaneous punks would have been fine with being portrayed as offensive. Indeed, they often embraced it. Where Emediato's punk interlocutors disagreed with him, however, was in his characterization of punks *entirely* according to offensive behaviors while ignoring several traits which are often celebrated in democracies, and even in dictatorships wishing to *appear* democratic: social cohesion, political critique, organizational skills, resistance to authority, and artistic renovation. Indeed, in the present, it is precisely these features of punk which have led to recent non-fiction, documentary film, and blockbusters celebrations of early punk in Brazil.[6] Furthermore, a series of Brazilian bands with deep roots in punk became crucial to the unfolding of Brazil's music in the mid-1980s, and well into the 1990s (among them Titãs, Legião Urbana, and Paralamas do Sucesso).

At the time, then, Emediato's selectivity was a middle-class attempt to circumscribe something that must have looked dangerous – in part because it was offensive *by design*. Although Emediato does not come right out and say it, his article suggests that punks, as one of the most profoundly "lost" groups within a generally "abandoned generation," required authority figures to set clearer boundaries establishing acceptable behaviors. Punks were naughty. But sometimes, they were worse than naughty. Although many of the sins listed by Emediato are not precisely illegal, they could easily *lead* to illegality, so the story went; general boisterousness might become fighting, and perhaps an old lady might find herself in the wrong place at the wrong time. Furthermore, even behaviors which were simply anti-social (public vomiting) or ignorant (failing to understand the difference between Marx and Hitler) could be bad for society, and might require some sort of intervention; surely people of this sort lacked a moral compass. And if parents weren't there to discipline their kids, perhaps the state would have to take over the disciplinary role. It was this mainstream approach to punk that supported stronger policing, and led to a ubiquitous aspect of punk life that Emediato fails to mention. One of the fundamental experiences of Brazilian punks in the late seventies was getting at the very least locked up, and sometimes, *beaten* up, by the police. Indeed, despite the fact that much punk behavior could be classified as obnoxious though not necessarily illegal, getting locked up by the police for the night was so common as to make it fundamental to punk identity at the time. All São Paulo punks from the period talk extensively about their run-ins with the law.

By analyzing the relationship between punk behavior in this period, and police responses *to* that behavior, we can learn more about illegality in late dictatorial Brazil – a formative period for current Brazilian policing (see, e.g., Linger 2003). The remainder of this chapter will focus on four major areas spread across three major cases of policing: the portrayal of punk as a dangerous foreign influence in the context of a political climate in which communism was also an omnipresent and dangerous foreign influence; the understanding of punk as way too loud – against the backdrop of a rapidly expanding city in which sound was increasingly the subject of discussion; disgust about punk's ribald sexuality, even in a nation that ostensibly prided itself on its permissiveness; and upset over punks' dress, which was perceived as sloppy, degraded, and, once again, foreign.

Illegalities

The story Brazilians tell themselves and outsiders about their permissiveness is considerably more complex than "flexibility." The very question of the relationship between legality and illegality in Brazil is more accurately specified as a question of the situational appropriateness of the application of a law, policy, or procedure. Precisely *where* the line gets drawn has political and even material consequences. Another way of saying this is that the Brazilian state and its affiliates have detailed laws on the books. Saying what the law *is* is rarely the problem; enforcing it is another matter. These laws are sometimes culled from European and North American models, and are sometimes the result of creative self-generative projects (along these lines, see the relatively new set of laws governing the Internet; Omari 2018). But in Brazil, the sorts of laws that might divide the legal from the illegal are almost categorically applied unevenly by those called upon to do so. This is enacted at both explicit and implicit levels: the college-educated go to different prisons, and are even entitled to private cells. But the truth is that the importance of the fluidity of the illegal manifests mostly in quotidian circumstances. This is elicited in part by DaMatta's notion of the authoritarian micro-ritual "do you know who you're talking to?" – *sabe com quêm está falando?* (DaMatta 1979, 138). This is a statement that is uttered when an authority figure (a clerk at a bank, a traffic cop, a door-man) has attempted to enforce a rule. When this statement comes into play, the applicability of a particular law is being negotiated in the context of the encounter *according to aspects of the personal relationships of the participants.*[7] Along similar lines, a common expression: "for my friends – anything. For my enemies, the law!" In this context, the very applicability of the law becomes *not* something that applies in all places and all times, but rather, a kind of mobile standard of recruitment *to* broader projects – either the reinforcement of certain kinds of kinship (fictive or otherwise – "I know your aunt!" or "we are from the same town") or the reinforcement of affiliations to institutional or state power ("I had dinner with your boss last night," or "I'm very close with a federal judge").

DaMatta's discussion gets us only part of the way there; it has been problematized by some scholars for its simplistic structuralism (see Wink, this volume). Another problem with the model is that it focuses largely on discursive contexts in which the application of power impacts a parking ticket or a bank clerk's attentiveness; whereas the application of power is often lethal in Brazil. In the context of this important frame, Daniel Linger's exploration of what he calls "wild power" offers further perspective on the question of the importance of the relationship between legality and illegality in Brazil. Linger investigates the decidedly capricious and always potentially murderous application of state power. The combination of unevenness with mortality is crucial. You may, or may *not*, be in violation of the law, and you may, or may *not* die for it. He draws on the Brazilian social science classic *Rebellion in the*

Backlands [*Os Sertões*] by Euclides Da Cunha, wherein a relatively harmless millennial movement in Brazil's abject Northeast is entirely eradicated by the state in the late nineteenth century – its adherents slaughtered and its resources scattered (Cunha 1944 [1902]). Da Cunha argues that the state should have collectively sent the millennials to an asylum, not slaughtered them in cold blood. This, Da Cunha argued, was one of the central problems of the Brazilian state – that it lacked the capacity to determine a true threat, but behaved as though *any* threat required ultimate force. In calling on Da Cunha, Linger's point is that a capriciously murderous state cultivates a perpetual readiness to die on the part of those subject to its power – which is all but the wealthiest. Furthermore, wild power embeds itself in the bodily hexis of its subjects. However, what is crucial for our purposes is the way in which that "wildness," or capriciousness, is frequently the result of a decision made by law enforcement about the distinction between the obnoxious and the illegal. Recall Da Cunha's argument – wherein the state should have known the difference between a real threat and an irritation.

The usefulness of "wild power" to this discussion of legality/illegality can be explained by the fact that violence in some guise is never very far from punk in most of its forms and locations. As has been discussed in detail in the Brazilian scene (as well as many others) fights continually broke out on street corners and at shows – often among punk groups. In the Brazilian case, rival gangs of young punk men ferociously policed neighborhoods, as well as access to women that resided in those neighborhoods. As noted above, many of these punks had watched the movie *Warriors*, and enjoyed its theatrical violence combined with the sartorial differences between the competing gangs (some distinguishing themselves from their peers by wearing matching baseball jerseys, leather vests, or jean jackets). Thus, punks did, indeed, beat people up with some regularity – mostly each other. But, one thing we can notice about punk is that violence often forms part of its expressive practice, too – not in terms of people getting beaten up, but in terms of how punks occupy space. With respect to the musical practice itself, guitars and drums are often played violently, while the singer sounds pissed off: "sonic dominance" of a particular sort (Henriques 2011). This expressive practice is sometimes aimed explicitly at the state, but frequently is more amorphously focused on "the system," or "the people who put us down." This is especially true of early São Paulo punk, which tended toward hardcore in its instrumental practice and lyrics – by which I mean short songs that tend to be faster, louder, and more aggressive in tone than mainstream punk.

It is this amorphousness of punk's violent rebellion that made it inscrutable to the Brazilian authoritarian state. Police just weren't sure what to make of it. Political amorphousness had, to some extent, worried the authorities with tropicália music as well (Dunn 2001; Schwarz 1992b). But whereas, with *tropicália*, the authorities' problems were in decoding lyrics that obliquely referenced politics, the problems with punk were more immediate. In this case, here were a bunch of kids who were angry about being treated badly, and were also angry about the complicity of the culture industry with the state in *facilitating* that bad treatment. And where Veloso and Gil had been flowery and obscure in their language, part of the point of punk was to be *blunt.* Add to this the aforementioned fights, and the fact that affiliations with explicitly political left-wing student movements sometimes took place, and the police really seemed to have a problem of intelligibility. Just what the hell *was* punk? Had it been generated by Brazilian society, or had it come from somewhere else?

Othering Brazilian punk

As punk was getting started in Brazil, local journalists reacted negatively. At an early punk show in Belo Horizonte in 1977, for example, two journalists felt that the Brazilian band playing was being unoriginal, and rather, was borrowing a genre from elsewhere (the United Kingdom), repeating the age-old capitulation to cultural imperialism that had plagued the nation since at least the 1800s (Schwarz 1992a). Their argument was that Brazil had its *own,* home-grown, musical attempts to tackle its marginality; borrowing someone else's marginality was offensive, since it furthered marginalization. Their remarks are worth quoting at length since they reveal the ways in which many Brazilians responded to Brazilian punks:

> If punk is poverty, garbage, and violence, then we can say without fear of error that Brazil is the punk vanguard. (…) Punk in Brazil is a contradiction – totally absurd … We import punk from Europe – while having it as part of our daily affairs. Our life is punk, our music is punk, our roads are punk, our cities, the very system that we live in.
>
> (Essinger 1999, 92)[8]

Reversing the belittling intentions of the authors of this passage, Brazilian punks themselves sometimes embraced such statements, reading them as support for the notion that punk was, indeed, local. Clemente, the bass player for early São Paulo band Os Inocentes (and the author of the reply letter analyzed above) stated that "if they hadn't invented punk in the London and New York, we would have had to do it here" (Moreira 2016).

However, in other moments, Brazilian punks made it easy for critics of cultural imperialism by appropriating punk *precisely because* it came from somewhere else; this was what made it attractive. Brazilian punks *hated* MPB – finding it far too flowery and oblique – and wanted to return to the roots of rock and roll. Punk's otherness, then, was part of the *point.* Here we have a practice, then, which is simultaneously claiming its indigeneity while embracing its otherness, all in the context of Brazil's emergence from a military dictatorship part of the purpose of which had been to protect its citizenry from communism (Fausto 1994, 1999, 2006; Skidmore 1967, 1988), a strategy the dictatorship employed in order to distance itself from and isolate the Brazilian left. In other words, strategic othering was not only a tool that cultural critics used to downplay the importance of what they took to be lower class popular culture. It was a tool for rendering certain practices illegal within the ambit of the increasingly neoliberal authoritarian state. Labeling punks as "other" was a way to circumscribe and control them with a long history, and real consequences.

Policing punks 1 – the green Chevrolet

This otherness was discernible in the ways in which police handled Brazilian punks. At one famous show on October 17, 1982, in the Bom Retiro neighborhood of São Paulo, a green Chevrolet apparently nearly hit a punk at the entrance to the music hall where the bands Ratos de Porão, Ulster, Fogo Cruzado, Lixomania, and Estado de Coma were about to play. After-the-fact reports by punks who were there lack detail, but apparently a conflict between those in the car and the punks turned violent, and the police showed up to shut the whole show down.

Inside the hall, the police first sought to control the sonic space. The volume and force of punk music needed to be neutralized before order could be restored. It is quite impossible to imagine the policing of the space without this first step; the police couldn't have shouted their commands over the noise. Next, the separation between men and women needed to be enforced; the two groups were placed in different parts of the hall. It is unclear whether this was common practice or whether this was carried out because this was a punk show. Nevertheless, what is clear is that the police select a social category which they then impose on the gathering as a pretext for disaggregating it. Next the police had the punks remove their sartorial distinction; clothing set them obviously apart from civilians. The police had the punks remove their combat boots – an important badge of identity that indexed their affiliation with British punk, in particular. The police ordered the punks to place their boots into a giant pile in the middle of the floor. The police then added some panache to their efforts by mixing the boots up, such that later, when punks who had not been arrested were told to get out fast, they grabbed whatever boots they could find. Clemente laughingly remembers that one guy left with two left boots of different sizes. The whole incident was accompanied by the threat of violence. One punk remembers that if you said anything at all to the police, "you got punched in the eye" (Moreira 2016). The strategies in play here were silencing, disaggregating, striking, and undressing.

Policing punks 2 – the beginning of the end of the world

Brazilian punks frustrated with the amount of violent policing they received did not make it easy on themselves. A feud characterized early Brazilian punk, between the more urban punks from the northern portions of São Paulo, such as Vila Carolina and the area around Freguesia do Ó, and the punks from the satellite cities of the ABC; namely, Santo André, São Bernardo do Campo, and São Caetano do Sul. Resembling fights in other Latin American punk scenes (Greene 2016) this fight revolved around the ABC group's feelings that they were more authentic, because they emerged from more obviously working-class roots; indeed, some of their parents were metal workers, and were involved in the union activities that gave rise to Lula. In any case, the feud reached absurd levels, such that, at one show, the lead singer of ABC group Passeatas blew off his arm while attempting to throw a bomb at São Paulo fans.

Eventually, record store owner Fábio Sampaio (also the lead singer of band Olho Seco), together with playwright and punk documentarian Antonio Bivar, organized a show to bring the dueling factions together. "The Beginning of the End of the World" presented ten bands from urban São Paulo and ten bands from the ABC to play a two-day festival that would also include punk art and photography. The duo recorded a live record that would musically embody the mixture of the two scenes. Attendees commented on the shock of seeing so many punks in one place at one time; they had thought their "scene" was smaller, but there were about 3,000 punks there. Overall, the event was a tremendous success – given that all the bands played and fighting was minimal. Residents close to the community center where the event was held were alarmed by the punks, however – plus there may have been some bottles of wine stolen from a nearby bar. Whatever the case, the riot police appeared and began indiscriminately grabbing punks and locking them up. When they tried to escape on the Metro, the police waited in nearby train stations to snatch kids dressed as punks; once again, dress proved an easy way to identify targets. In contemporary interviews, those who were there express confusion about the appearance of the police, and chalk it up to the way in which the police clearly had come to hate punk rock. Here was an event the purpose of which was to install peace in what had been a conflictual social field, and *still* the police decided to get involved. Sampaio and Bivar wrote a report about the festival for American punk zine *Maximum Rock 'n Roll*, and dubbed the event a tremendous success (Bivar and Sampaio 1983).

Policing punks 3 – kicking the commies

In 1982, a punk show at Salão Beta, at PUC-SP (the Pontifical Catholic University of São Paulo, Zona Oeste) was organized by the institution's student government. In this case, the politics were more easily recognizable, since the explicitly socialist student government had a history of clearly demarcated political action. Clemente describes the show as having "a different kind of public," one that seemed more united, as evidenced by the fact that everyone sang the Inocentes song "Panic in São Paulo" together (Nascimento and Paiva 2016). In any case, toward the end of the show, a fire started, and the police used the fire as an excuse to break up the show entirely. Clemente would later speculate that the police had wanted to destroy some archives at the left-leaning PUC-SP university, and that this had provided an option to weaken a confessedly anti-government institution, the students' representation (the DCE, *Diretório Central dos Estudantes*) at PUC-SP, all the while pinning the fault for that destabilization on punks. It seems likely that the police set the fire. This did not emerge until many years later, however, and at the time, the policing itself as well as the media's coverage *of* that policing, made it seem as though dark forces were at work in Brazilian society – dark forces that lacked coherence and organizational capacity, though, as indexed by the fire, were indeed dangerous. The presence of policing was necessary to keep an "order" that was threatened by "enemies of the state." Punk's obnoxiousness could momentarily become intelligible as "illegal."

Conclusion

It is important to understand that, even during the height of the military dictatorship, not all early Brazilian punk interactions with the police seem to have resulted in violence. Some interactions were simply about noise complaints elicited by shows or practices; the police were often called to shut things down. Douglas, from the band Restos de Nada, recalls that routinely, when the band was practicing, a neighbor would come and tell them that he had called the police. They practiced in a different location each time to avoid this, but to little avail. Once they understood that the police had been called, they took advantage of the time to keep on practicing a few songs. This is not the behavior of kids who think they are necessarily going to get beaten up. If they had thought things were going to get violent, they would presumably have fled. Instead they waited around and continued with the offense that had led to the police being called in the first place. All of this reinforces the fact that the line between the obnoxious (practicing loudly) and the illegal (fighting, or acting against the government) required constant enacting. The broad punk platform of continually challenging authority came into direct conflict with police, whose very responsibility was reinforcing the power of the authoritarian state.

By 1982, when police started that fire at PUC-SP, the military regime was in the process of transitioning to civilian rule. The transition was far from complete at this point, however, and punks were easy to identify. During "The Beginning of the End of the World," a female punk is interviewing her friends about the movement, asking them what it means to be punks – what are your politics? Most of her interlocutors are playfully refusing to be pinned down, saying that they dislike those who oppress them, boss them around, and judge them negatively without knowing them. Using fancier language, one might say that they are angry at what they take to be the capricious exercise of authority, and they express this in a ludic mode. At that moment, a police car pulls into the frame and an officer hurriedly gets out of the passenger side. He walks directly up to cluster of kids – apparently blithe about the camera rolling – and without explanation, simply takes a hold of one of the young men being interviewed by the arm, and leads him out of the frame. What happens next, we do not discover, though later in the interview, the woman asking questions derides the police, using a Brazilian sense of the term "race": "I don't like that race [the police]." In any case, the exercise of police authority was a simple as identifying the punks by appearance. For those in the frame – the other young people answering questions, they seem to know they are targets. The simple fact of looking the way they did made the officer's behavior unsurprising, if uninspiring. Placed into the frame of wild power, however, the stakes of the boundary between obnoxious and illegal seem somewhat more dire.

Notes

1 My sincere thanks are due to Derek Pardue for the invitation to contribute to this volume.

2 I would like to note that drawing lines in policing is fraught territory – as has been evidenced of late in informal video recordings of American police officers using lethal force in situations that appear to call for minor, force, or perhaps even simply discussion. For more on policing in Brazil and elsewhere, see Bretas and Rosemberg (2013); Dent (2016); Fassin (2011); Filho and Herschmann (2003); Garriott (2013); Martin (2007); Martin (2018); Quinalha (2016); Schneider and Schneider (2008); Suares (2003).

3

> Discípulos de Satã, o ídolo que veneram, eles não vêem muita diferença entre Deus e o Diabo, entre Marx, Kennedy ou Hitler, entre Bem e Mal. Eles gostam de bater, só isso. Alguns, mais cruéis, roubam e espancam velhinhas – e acham muita graça nisso. … Os punkers odeiam álcool e drogas, embora gostem de sexo. Eles preferem beber leite com limão – e muitas vezes, depois que bebem essa mistura, provocam vômitos em si mesmos e vomitam o leite coagulado na cara de suas vítimas.

(All translations are by the author, unless otherwise stated.)

4 A form of punk called "straight edge" developed in the United States in the early eighties as an outgrowth of a song by Minor Threat of the same name. Straight edge punks chose not to drink, take drugs, or have sex outside the context of a committed relationship. Indeed, the movement – which it has unquestionably become despite the song's author explaining that he had no intention of starting one – has considerable support around the world. The force and durability of straight edge merely prove the rule, however. Lots of punks, today as then, drank like crazy. Indeed, returning to the Brazilian context, Clemente's autobiography is filled with references to alcohol (Nascimento and Paiva 2016).

5 Although the issue does not come up in discussions of early Brazilian punk, spitting was a frequent practice at punk shows in the United States and the United Kingdom, with the fans spitting on the bands, and the bands spitting back. The topic gets discussed at some length in a documentary about early California punk band The Minutemen called "We Jam Econo." One scene discusses a show where singer D. Boone suddenly stops the set because someone has spat into his open (and singing) mouth.

6 See, for instance, the biopic about the lead singer of famous Brazilian bands *Aborto Elétrico*, and *Legião Urbana* – Renato Russo: *How We Were Young* (*Somos tão*

jovens; Fontoura 2013). Other contemporary celebration of early Brazilian punk appears in the fact that early punk singers Clemente and João Gordo both had spots on MTV, and both have recently written memoirs.

7 These aspects are activated either by accident, or through an explicit process of investigation. For example: the speaker might say that she knows the owner of the bank or club, or the chief of police. The point is to temper the application of the law with aspects of the relationship. "I know your boss." Another way around the application of a policy is less authoritarian, and seeks affinities. Instead of asking the (potentially temporary!) authority figure if she knows who she's talking to, the speaker might try to find out where she's from, who her friends are, or even what sort of music she likes. If there is overlap, the application of the policy might get tempered. "Look, we have the same friends/taste in music/place of birth. Could you cut me some slack?"

8

> Se o punk é o pobre, o lixo e a violência, então podemos dizer, sem medo de errar, que o Brasil é a vanguarda do punk ... Punk no Brasil é contradição, nonsense, absurdo total. ... Importamos punk da Europa mêsmo já o tendo em nosso dia-a-dia. Nossa vide é punk, nossa música é punk, são punk nossas ruas, nossas cidades, o próprio sistema em que vivemos.

MPB luminary Chico Buarque is said to have made a similar statement, though despite its frequent appearance on punk websites, I have been unable to trace where he did so. He apparently said the following: "Se o punk é o lixo, a miséria e a violência, então não precisamos importá-lo da Europa, pois já somos vanguarda do punk em todo o mundo" (Buarque n.d.).

References

Bivar, Antonio, and Fábio Sampaio. "Brazil: Punk ao Vivo." *Maximum Rock 'n Roll*, no. 5 (March–April) 1983.

Bretas, Marcos Luiz, and André Rosemberg. "A história da polícia no Brasil: Balanço e perspectivas." *Topoi* 14, no. 26 (2013): 162–173.

Buarque, Chico. "Grito Suburbano." n.d. https://medium.com/come%C3%A7o-do-fim-do-mundo/grito-suburbano-32f0e8893d21. Accessed on December 16, 2019.

Cunha, Euclides da. *Rebellion in the Backlands*. Translated by S. Putnam. Chicago: University of Chicago Press, 1944 [1902].

DaMatta, Roberto. Carnivals, Rogues, and Heroes. South Bend: University of Notre Dame Press, 1979.

Dent, Alexander. "Piracy, Cloning, and Criminal Cats: The Discomforts of Cellularity in Brazil." In *The Linguistic and Material Intimacies of Cellular Phones*, edited by Joshua A. Bell and Joel C. Kuipers, 188–208. London: Routledge, 2018.

Dent, Alexander S. "Piracy, Circulatory Legitimacy, and Neoliberal Subjectivity in Brazil." *Cultural Anthropology* 27, no. 1 (2012): 28–49.

Dent, Alexander S. "Policing the Unstable Materialities of Digital Media in Brazil." *American Ethnologist* [forthcoming], 2016.

Dunn, Christopher. *Brutality Garden: Tropicália and the Emergence of a Brazilian Counterculture*. Chapel Hill: University of North Carolina Press, 2001.

Essinger, Silvio. *Punk – Anarquia Planetária e a cena Brasileira*. São Paulo: Editora 34, 1999.

Fassin, Didier. "Policing Borders, Producing Boundaries: The Governmentality of Immigration in Dark Times." *Annual Review of Anthropology* 40 (2011): 213–26.

Fausto, Boris. *História do Brasil*. São Paulo: Editora da Universidade de São Paulo, 1994.

Fausto, Boris. *A Concise History of Brazil*. Cambridge: Cambridge University Press, 1999.

Fausto, Boris. *Getúlio Vargas*. São Paulo: Companhia das Letras, 2006.

Fontoura, Antonio Carlos da (dir.). Somos tão Jovens. Rio de Janeiro: Imagem Filmes, 2013.

Freire Filho, João, and Micael Herschmann. "Debatable Tastes! Rethinking Hierarchical Distinctions in Brazilian Music." *Journal of Latin American Cultural Studies* 12, no. 3 (2003): 347–358.

Garriott, William (ed.). *Policing and Contemporary Governance: The Anthropology of Police in Practice*. New York: Palgrave Macmillan, 2013.

Greene, Shane. *Punk and Revolution: 7 More Interpretations of Peruvian Reality*. Durham, NC: Duke University Press, 2016.

Henriques, Julian. *Sonic Bodies: Reggae Sound Systems, Performance Techniques, and Ways of Knowing*. New York: Bloomsbury, 2011.

Linger, Daniel. "Wild Power in Post-Military Brazil." In *Crime's Power: Anthropologists and the Ethnography of Crime*, edited by P. Parnell and S. Kane, 99–124. London: Palgrave, 2003.

Martin, Jeff. "A Reasonable Balance of Law and Sentiment: Social Order in Democratic Taiwan from the Policeman's Point of View." *Law and Society Review* 41, no. 3 (2007): 665–698.

Martin, Jeff. "Police and Policing". *Annual Reviews of Anthropology* 47 (2018): 133–148.

Moreira, Gastão Nascimento, Clemente Tadeu, and Marcelo Rubens Paiva. *Meninos em Fúria – e o som que mudo a música para sempre*. São Paulo: Alfaguara, 2016.

Nascimento, Clemente, and Marcelo Paiva. *Meninos em Fúria: E o som que muda a música para sempre*. São Paulo: Alfaguara.

Omari, Jeffrey. "Digital Access Amongst the Marginalized: Democracy and Internet Governance in Rio de Janeiro." *PoLAR* 41, no. 2 (2018): 277–282.

Quinalha, Renan. "Violência policial no Brasil: Herança da ditadura ou escolha da democracia?" *CULT*, November 18, 2016. https://revistacult.uol.com.br/home/violencia-policial-no-brasil-heranca-da-ditadura-ou-escolha-da-democracia. Accessed on November 10, 2019.

Schneider, Jane, and Peter Schneider. "The Anthropology of Crime and Criminalization." *Annual Review of Anthropology* 37 (2008): 351–373.

Schwarz, Roberto. "Brazilian Culture: Nationalism by Elimination." Translated by Edmund Leites and Roberto Schwarz. In *Misplaced Ideas*, edited by John Gledson, 1–19. London: Verso, 1992a.

Schwarz, Roberto. "Culture and Politics in Brazil, 1964–1969." Translated by Edmund Leites and Roberto Schwarz. In *Misplaced Ideas*, edited by John Gledson, 126–159. London: Verso, 1992b.

Skidmore, Thomas. *Politics in Brazil, 1930–1964: An Experiment in Democracy*. New York: Oxford University Press, 1967.

Skidmore, Thomas. *The Politics of Military Rule in Brazil, 1964–1985*. New York: Oxford University Press, 1988.

Soares, Luiz Eduardo. "Novas Políticas da Segurança Pública." *Estudos Avançados* 17, no. 47 (2003): 75–96.

7 Illegal realities in the lyrics by Racionais MC's

Gabriel Feltran

Introduction

The lyrics to the song "I can hear someone calling me" are narrated by a man who is in between life and death. On the one hand, he is reminded of his estranged brother, who studied and started a family; and on the other is the memory of Guina, his partner in the world of crime. On the one side is the worker, and on the other the criminal. If rap is a chronicle of reality in peripheral neighborhoods, as is commonly asserted, after the release of "I can hear someone calling me," toward the end of the 1990s, a true curiosity was incited among Racionais MC's listeners: "After all, was that Guina in the song Mano Brown's real partner?"

Rumors circulated throughout favelas and prisons, but also within sectors of Brazilian middle and upper class that began listening to Racionais precisely at that moment. This was my first year of ethnographic work in São Paulo's peripheral neighborhoods. "Of course he was his partner," some would say. Brown himself had stated that the lyrics concerning Guina were based on real facts. "What nonsense," others declared: Brown himself also maintained that Guina was a fictional character.

Seven years went by until the controversy seemed to have been resolved. In approximately 2005, Guina showed up in flesh, telling his story in evangelical churches in São Paulo. His account relayed the story of an ex-member of Racionais MC's who had recently been converted to Pentecostalism. The supposed character of this mythological song then recorded testimonies of his life, and in 2006 these songs went viral in the religious market. On the street Conde de Sarzedas, where most of evangelical commerce in São Paulo is concentrated:

> amidst self-help books, bibles, "praises and worship" discs in rhythms such as rock, *sertanejo*, *forró*, *axé*, and rap, passersby can, for example, purchase, in CD or DVD format, Guina's story, an "ex-Racionais MC's," in which they will see and/or listen to the "true testimony of a man who lived in the sub-world of crime and drugs, but who learned the truth, with

> the help of the gospel and Christ, and today, committed of his choice, tells his life story."
>
> (Côrtes, 2017 p. 110)[1]

For at least another six years, this Guina drew congregations to churches throughout Brazil. Some were weary of his story. The supposed ex-member of the music group claimed he had spent two days in a refrigerated chamber while dead, and then returned to life; that he had been shot 40 times from the waist down but had no lingering effects from the gunshots. Others knew that God had no limits, that miracles occurred every day. Guina was there, "alive and living." Was it really him? Did Guina really exist? Is rap truly a chronicle of real life? What about sociology and ethnography? What is the relationship of these fields to what is real? These are the questions guiding this essay, which aims to bring attention to the fact that things that seem to be at the margin, such as illegalities, invariably frame an ideal of reality that, supposedly, exists (Pardue, 2013).

"I can hear someone calling me" is the fourth song in the album *Surviving in Hell* (original: Sobrevivendo no Inferno), by the Racionais MC's, released in 1997. Few cultural products mark an epoch and continue to subsist throughout time. This is one of them. At the moment of its release, more than 1.5 million copies of the disc were sold by an independent label, as well as millions of pirated copies. It became the basis for a reading of the world by an entire generation in urban peripheries throughout Brazil and circulated much beyond. Over two decades after its release, it continues to be critically acclaimed by music and literary critiques (Garcia, 2011, 2013), and was recently published in book format (Oliveira, 2018).

The content of the album's lyrics and the rap's format have been discussed in urban studies, in literature, and linguistics, as well as in areas dedicated to racial relations, violence, youth, and religion, within Brazil and aboard (Caldeira, 2006; Feltran, 2013; Gimeno, 2009; Hirata, 2010; Marques, 2013; Takahashi, 2015, 2017). *Surviving in Hell* was recently placed on the list of required readings for the State University of Campinas's entrance exam, one of the most prestigious institutions of higher education in the country.

The title of the album progressively became a meta-title after years of intense transformations in Brazilian cities. More than two decades after its release, the hell the Racionais evoke (the life of black youth in São Paulo's peripheral neighborhoods) changed radically. When it was written, the First Command of the Capital [Primeiro Comando da Capital – PCC] was only hinted at in the hoods. Over the years, it established itself and took over borders, ports, airports, and the world. Global consumption arrived in the favelas; "there you also find whisky, Red Bull, Nike sneakers, and a rifle," as the same group would later sing in the song "Negro Drama"; not to mention that the hoods also have cellphones, and flat screen TVs. Social welfare policies were implemented, and a significant portion of peripheries had access to consumption, and education of a slightly higher quality. There was talk of a "new C-class" in Brazil, a middle class that derived from peripheral neighborhoods.

However, the more profound part of the favela continued – and continues – to be desolating: criminalization, incarceration, conflicts internal to crime, violence, police extortion, premature deaths, and families torn apart. It is from there, in the profound parts of the favela where the poorest groups of the population live, where a hellish cycle of poverty has been reproduced over generations, that Brazilian criminal statistics are compiled. It is from there, consequently, that the most notable reaction to the state of things surfaced in the 1990s: national rap emerged, in parallel to an expansion of the world of crime as an instance that ordinates social life in peripheral neighborhoods, for it ordinates violence in the favelas (Feltran, 2010c). "A voice from the favela, that is a part of it," was the political claim of its representatives. During the 1990s and 2000s, for those from outside the favela, criminal violence was hell while legitimate violence came from the State. For those on the inside, police violence was hell while legitimate violence was conducted by the PCC.

Homicide rates, which for 15 years rose without respite in São Paulo, leaving the bodies of black youth, the precarious workers in illegal markets, lying across alleyways, plummeted over the next decade as of 1997. The "magic formula for peace," recited by the Racionais in the same 1997 album, seems to have been discovered in São Paulo (Feltran, 2010, 2013, 2019b). Many laughed, but it was truly better "not to disbelieve": today there are more people surviving in São Paulo than before. There was a reaction to this expansion in crime, of course. The military police, which was then totally illegitimate in peripheries, began to develop a public counter-narrative targeted at the most well-off sectors of this poor population: precisely that "new C-class," or "new middle class" that began toward the end of the 2000s.

There was a need to separate, in peripheral neighborhoods, those who are "workers" from those who are "criminals." Churches vindicated that there were objective criteria for this distinction. Those who, in the last few years, found themselves back in poverty – from where they had never left? – welcomed the distinction. Police officers, for this exact reason, began to integrate themselves into churches, as well as religious WhatsApp groups, and neighborhoods with predominantly working- and middle-class residents, who had now all become entrepreneurs. There was a need to react toward criminals, as well as toward those that represent them (Feltran, 2007, 2011b). Evangelical police officers won elections for *Conselhos Tutelares*,[2] human rights councils, neighborhood boards, and joined politics in the 2000s. Years later, they won municipal elections in urban peripheries. Finally, in 2018, candidates from the police won elections at the state level, and, against analysts' expectations, at the federal level as well.

On the other hand, the hellish daily experience of peripheries in the more profound parts of the favela, of imminent death in the hands of a thief or the police, ceased to be an issue limited to the state of São Paulo or Rio de Janeiro. Over the last two decades, this reality became ever more present in other states in the country, concomitant to a growth of illegal markets. Homicide rates exploded in the Northeastern and Northern parts of the country during the years 2010s, particularly in regions of interest for the most thriving sectors of this market, of cocaine and arms (Feltran, 2019a). Black meat continues to be the cheapest in Brazil, as another famous song states.

This essay develops a series of theoretical queries regarding reality and fiction, as well as normative ideas about society. More specifically, it is dedicated to exploring the theme of illegalities and marginality, which I have grappled with over the last few years (Feltran, 2010b, 2018; Bertelli e Feltran, 2017). The objective is to consider the reality of that which is illegal, the world of crime, and its functionality for constructing the ideal of an official society. In order to observe these in relation to one another (the real and the ideal, the illegal and the official), I use an empiric object very common to sociology, ethnography, and artistic expressions: the expansion of the world of crime in urban peripheries in São Paulo, amid dynamic social and political transformations over the last few decades.[3]

There is nothing original in taking an aesthetic production from a specific epoch as the point of departure in a sociological essay, as I do here (Arendt, 1958, 2008; Candido, 1976; Fridman, 2014, 2015; Jackson, 2011; Rancière, 2005). What might be unique of this piece is to expect that a significant understanding will result from taking a common object – illegality, defined here as the expansion of the world of crime in São Paulo's peripheral neighborhoods – and submitting it to formally unequal analytic frames: those of sociology, ethnography, and poetry. The effects of this attempt, for the knowledge of those who read it, will demonstrate whether it was worth it. I assume that all three of these formats are equally valid for understanding the "reality" of peripheral neighborhoods.

This equality is not the end point; in other words, it does not imply that sociology, fiction, or ethnography are easily confused or indistinct. This is not an issue of equality reified in format, nor in content. Equality is an issue of epistemological validity; thus, its productive status for knowledge. If clear, sociology, ethnography, and poetry are equally comprehensive forms of "reality"; and equally personal, arbitrary, and subjective. This is due to the fact that, evidently reality exists, though it is very different based on a given perspective, submitted to a given subjectivity, or to judgment, making it so diverse. Distinctively, therefore, reality really exists, in each situation (Drummond de Andrade, 1991; Simmel, 2009[1908]). Formats that are able to translate this reality fulfill their epistemological task.

Fragments of a realistic poem

In the following, I would have liked to depict fragments from the poem "I can hear someone calling me," which could teach us different things about the realities of crime in São Paulo. As we could not obtain formal authorization, instead of quoting the lyrics I have provided the reader the official video link [www.youtube.com/watch?v=txSXj-F7VX8]. This video can function in this article as our guide to follow the poem fragments [only in Portuguese for rights permission reasons].

A. Guina as a frontier

The beats produced by KL Jay, Racionais' DJ, instill an auditory climate of tension, then comes the introductory phrase, stating that Guina sent us something, through someone who is approaching in a threatening manner. The speaker, whom I will name Ice Rock in honor of two other Racionais' members, knows the gun in the hand of the boy who is approaching well. Bleeding and laying on the floor, a "film goes through his mind," as they say in São Paulo's peripheries.

[please watch from the beginning to 1:23]

Guina synthesizes, in the lyrics, many of the fundamental elements of a "renowned thief" in the hood, in other words, of the criminal who is respected in São Paulo's favelas. People I spoke to referenced these elements hundreds of times – disposition, courage, possessions, generosity, humility in character, and ostentation in daily life – during my own ethnographic work. In addition to these characteristics, however, the fundamental aspect of this sociological figure is that he hybridizes poles that are many times understood as opposing one another in dominant social normativity. Guina snorted cocaine nonstop but was reliable. He was crazy, but cold hearted. His desires were hedonistic – motorcycles, women, clothing from famous brands – but he shared what he had with his buddies.

In the dominant frame, a thief is, evidently, not synonymous with respect and good reputation. Nor does craziness rhyme with commitment. Orgies are not associated with Christian values such as generosity, but rather with personal enjoyment for bodily pleasures, the profane. Snorting cocaine like crazy is not synonymous, in the dominant framework, with a reliable and trustworthy person. In order for these characteristics to join together, one needs to denaturalize hegemonic farmworkers for understanding the social world, which commonly separates both things. This is the political aspect of Racionais' rap – to denaturalize not the content, but the established interpretive frameworks. Guina was a teacher, an example of the correct attitudes to be replicated, but according to illegal markers in the world of crime

[please watch from 3:57 to 4:25]

Guina's story goes on, and his training in crime is presented in the format of a curriculum vitae. Once again, he metaphorically breaks with the dominant framework of normative references:

[please watch from 4:26 to 5:24]

Dominant values reproduce themselves in the universe of crime (Sykes e Matza, 2016; Ramalho, 2008; Cozzi, Font e Mistura, 2014). If Guina's existence was the denaturalization of the normative framework officially legitimized, as we see here, it is also, and, *at the same time*, a reproduction of that which structures the framework. Georg Simmel teaches us how this is possible, based on his argument that every action has a series of teleological meanings that are distinct, and oblivious to the intentionality of the original actor in every single association (Simmel, 2009[1908], p. 493). It is as if rappers, like the members of Racionais MCs, are saying, "What a waste for the system not to take advantage of us, what a shame that it reproduces itself without our presence. We could be in the multinationals, growing as professionals within them. Not in jail."

B. Together with Guina, during two robberies

Seeing Guina have all that he wanted and knowing that "in this big world your value is based on what you own," Ice Rock decides to join this universe.

[please watch from 1:23 to 2:25]

The process of initiation into the world of crime, as in most initiating rituals, includes a stage where one is evaluated by peers: "Great performance"; producing new twists in dominant evaluative diagrams. Even if the robbery had not gone as planned, its fatal victim demonstrates that Guina was relentless, as a robber should be. One more burglary is narrated in the lyrics, and, during the third one, problems begin to arise. The criminal trajectories I studied almost always follow this path: many rewards in the beginning with a heavy price to pay at the end.

[please watch from 7:52 to 8:14]

In this case, the victim is not a security guard, considered as "vermin" by those who are involved in crime. Rather, his partner died. He was only sixteen, the same age as Sr. Percival's son, from Jardim Progresso in the city of Ribeirão Preto, who was shot and died during a robbery. The boy's father called me over to the bedroom, opened a drawer, unfolded a newspaper article, and showed me the picture of his son laying face down on the ground in the street, wearing a white and red colored hoodie. The local news article explained that he was robbing a clothing store during the night, and that, when the police arrived, he had tried to escape while shooting. Such accounts are common to any ethnographer of urban peripheries in Brazil. Ice Rock, our narrator, begins to think that life in crime was not as easy as it seems. Therefore, he decides to leave this universe.

C. *'I lived for seven years in vain'*

[please watch from 8:15 to 8:25]

Hundreds of times I heard paranoid accounts by boys who had whimsically joined criminal life, and, after three or four years, found themselves persecuted by their peers and the police, owing time, without money, and with a family torn apart. Any educator or professional that works in juvenile detention centers, prisons, or mental health programs in peripheral neighborhoods knows that these accounts are customary. The lyrics go on, and the agonizing narrator describes other frustrations. His regret is evident, but illegality is his reality.

[please watch from 5:35 to 5:55]

A moment of crisis regarding his choice to enter the universe of crime is also a moment to reframe perspectives of a boundary between normative horizons. On the one hand, a job and education, on the other, the feeling of having to finish what he started, for there is no use in trying to turn back. The narrator oscillates between these two choices, but deep down he knows there is only one option. At the same time, he realizes that the criminal he has become is not, in *reality*, himself:

[please watch from 5:45 to 5:57]

The image of the criminal had become solidified without Ice Rock realizing so. It had taken over his entire identity (Misse, 1999, 2010).[4] The madness, which was previously, with Guina, associated to courage and commitment, to the intensity of the *crazy life* (original expression: *vida loka*), is now madness in the dominant sense, alienation from reality, an attribute of the lost and demented. Things do not end there; the existential question regarding his own identity and his own values in crisis overlap with a religious and moral question: "Does God still look at me?" Literature in the field thoroughly addressed the relationships between crime, morality, and religion, precisely due to the fact that they define this frontier, and, therefore, are active in ethnographic research regarding the universe of crime (Cunha, 2008; Birman e Machado, 2012; Marques, 2015, 2019). A criminal can become a moral preacher in no time, such as Guina seemed to have become, precisely for this reason (Côrtes, 2007; Teixeira, 2014).

[please watch from 5:58 to 6:20]

The development of Ice Rock's journey is also the development of a typical trajectory of low-placed operators from illegal markets in São Paulo's peripheral neighborhoods during the 1990s. Typical of what takes place, still today, in favelas in the states of Brazil where the PCC did not become the hegemonic faction in the criminal world. Two or three years working in these markets, are supervened by conflicts and death threats.

This also takes place in Colombia, Mexico, and other territories marked by incited violence between criminal groups in Central America. This is also the case in disputes surrounding drug trafficking in Peru and Bolivia. The explanation? These low-placed operators and workers are profoundly encouraged to demonstrate courage, bravery, virility, and strength while very young, and can serve as the front line for their employers, who are operators in transnational markets. When these subjects grow older and develop a better understanding of the violent machinery of which they are a part of, they try to claim for themselves positions higher up in the criminal market, placing their own subordinates at the front line. They begin, therefore, to compete with their direct managers and bosses, and commonly face the choice between killing or dying. Ice Rock realizes that he has come to this point:

[please watch from 8:26 to 9:05]

It is at this moment that those who left the criminal universe, particularly those who were able to leave their networks and retrace their life trajectories in the dominant normative world, can claim that "crime is an illusion" (Feltran, 2011b). The verses that follow demonstrate this terribly exposed illusion, that results from the anomie experienced when the values internal to this world, which were so strongly believed to be the "right" ones, are subverted by one's own peers, by one's own existential family:

[please watch from 9:08 to 9:11]

D. The outcome

[please watch from 10:04 to 11:03]

He knows what this is about, for some time now, and this explains why premonitions and nightmares are so common among youth, brothers, partners, women, and family members before these young men die. This is why it is common for *benzedeiras*[5] to have protected their bodies, for the reliance on *Ogum*, on *São Jorge*,[6] "so that the enemy may have hands, but not touch you." The Brazilian popular world seems to create narratives of war structuring even times of peace, and sporadically elect their warriors. Slaves and rebelled leaders, such as *cangaceiros*,[7] popular vigilantes, good thieves, and owners of the land, such as Charles, the 45th Angel,[8] characters narrated in fiction, in documentary, and ethnography (Feltran, 2013), always seem to know that, at some moment in their political paths, the bloody battle would turn against them:[9]

> [please watch from 11:04 to 11:10]

Ice Rock is shot. Countless times did the youth involved in crime I spoke to show me their scars from gunshot wounds. I was never able to forget one of them: Israel showed me the scars from four gunshots to his head, which occurred when a police officer immobilized him and threw him on the ground, after a robbery attempt in Tatuapé. All four of the shots scraped his head, two on each side. The scars were always visible due to his short haircut. I asked him how that happened. He grabbed me by my shirt, near my throat, simulating how the police officer pointed the gun at him point-blank, directly in his face. After the shots, Israel bled and fainted, but he was "delivered," he told me. The term is Pentecostal; it means that God had saved his life. Just as in the song, he also heard someone shouting out his name. But he survived.

The lyrics to the song then speak of what happen to Ice Rock's brother, who opted for legality, a worker's life. Today he is a lawyer, has a son, and a decent life. The contrast is glaring, and Ice Rock agonizes. Morally surrendered, regretful, and existentially dead, he recognizes his error, and repeats the refrain: "If I leave here, I will change," "I can hear someone calling me." It could be a calling from God, deliverance; a brother, a worker; who knows, maybe the person calling is his deceased mother summoning him to join her. It could be a regretful Guina, calling him to an embrace; the voice sounds like him, after all. It could be the devil. In any case, what Ice Rock is seeking is a calling back to life, so that he might have the chance to change, to redeem himself. He seeks redemption of his values, which out of illusion made him flourish in crime, not in the sacred world of a good society.

What every marginal community seeks, though they are undeceived and bleeding between life and death, is the redemption that comes from the recognition of their most profound values. Philippe Bourgois' classic 1995 book on the homeless and crack users in New York not accidentally is called *In Search of Respect*. An aspect that structures repudiated social life is the perverse desire to belong to the world of those who humiliate. Rejected lovers and children rarely forget the love they once had for those who abandoned them, never overcome the loss of this loved face that they projected for themselves as natural (Goffman, 2009 [1952]). Thankfully, some are eventually able to emancipate themselves from this.

Illegality and reality

Many sociological theories have been extracted from fiction (Kirschbaum, 2006), so have ethnographic narratives about concrete subjects such as the ones we meet in the field been fictionalized, in such a way as to protect their identities, allowing, however, for them to be a part of sociological production (Fiore, 2013; Biondi e Marques, 2010, Feltran, 2019, among others). I previously argued for leveling the epistemological validity of fiction and sociological text, for an equality in validity will never be situated in that which differs them: the narrative format of each one, or the content they express through these mediums. Validation of knowledge refers, above all, to one's postulates and one's capacity to translate these to interlocutors. The set of assumptions that frames any narrative format and content, and thus analysis, produces validation, when communicated to one's peers by means of translation, communication, and legibility. The film becomes a good medium, the rap is great, the ethnographic text excellent or problematic.[10] This set of assumptions, evidently, is not merely personal, nor purely social, and presents itself as an interpretive disposition (therefore practical) between these two dimensions. This was the reason why Pierre Bourdieu felt compelled to crystalize, perhaps excessively, the notion of *habitus* in order to develop his theories about *action*. This set of cognitive and sensorial tools for practice elaborate, therefore, each author's own interpretive capacity, each artist's sensitive capacity, forged in lived experience. This is why books and works of art can be considered genius at a given time, and irrelevant at others.

Guina is a character created by the poet Mano Brown, based on empiric situations experienced by his peers during the 1990s. There are many layers to the blurring of fiction and the portrayal of reality, for marginalized artistic expression tends, in many cases, to be read as a literal portrayal of the artist's context, as if there were no personal authorship. As if, at the limit, a plausible author in the peripheral world does not exist, for this world is not made of independent people, but rather of a monolithic mass. Therefore, there was a confusion regarding the author and the narrator of this rap in real life in São Paulo's peripheral neighborhoods during the 1990s and 2000s. People considered that Guina was Brown's peer who then betrayed him, thus an ex-Racionais. As I explained in the introduction, it did not take long for someone to embody the character, "jump out of the book" and, tell his story, claiming to be Guina from the song who had converted to Pentecostalism. This person spent at least six years circulating among evangelical churches in the country giving talks and testimony of his story.

> What can I say about this guy? This guy is a character, he … jumped out of the book. Imagine Pinocchio. Imagine Pinocchio, dude. A wooden toy that begins to talk. That is this Guina. Maybe if I had used the real name of the person involved in song's crime, this guy would not have shown up. But I gave him a fictitious name, and he … really, he … it is sad to know that in Brazil so many people go to church to see this guy, more for this idea [*that he is Guina*] than for the idea itself [*religious*]. Too many lies, this guy does not exist.
>
> (Brown, 10/12/2016)[11]

Mano Brown asserts that the man in real life is a character, and that his Guina is real. It took years to undo the fiction concerning this character, which was created from another fiction that involves a fictional character, though very real, which, in its turn, is based on participant observation. This process took years due to the fact that the fiction in Racionais' rap seemed so real. We know, in a break from positivism, as well as pragmatically, that a situated perspective and authorial desire actively influence the development of what is real. There are ways in which one tries to translate reality, including attempts to fictionalize through numbers, such as in statistical analysis discussed in the anthropology of science. The legendary fictional Guina, not the "real" one who came forward in churches, incarnates the normativity of the real world of crime in São Paulo during the 1990s. There are elements of this normativity that remain in the normative regime utilized in crime still today. There are others, who are no longer valued in the universe of crime under a new PCC hegemony, so prominent over the last two decades. The Guina in the fiction, in addition, is a reference to what many Ice Rocks would like to become, but who, like so many others, will never achieve.

Lyrics in rap are not, as many would say, "portrayals of reality." Neither is sociology, political science, or indigenous ethnology. A community of peers, in all areas of arts and science, evaluate the quality and reality of what is produced based on their own ethical and analytic criteria, representing this as real. Beyond an absolute materiality, a set of assumptions existentially experienced, and politically institutionalized by these communities, constructs what is plausible to see in the world. The vast amount of cultural products related to the theme of illegalities is not a coincidence. There is a need for them to circulate, and with them their statements regarding a fight of good against evil, so that what is legal and what is official might be read as real, or better yet, as ideal.

Notes

1

> ... em meio a livros de autoajuda, Bíblias, discos de "louvor a Deus" com ritmos de rock, sertanejo, forró, axé, rap, transeuntes podem, por exemplo, comprar, vendidos em CDs e DVDs, a história do Guina, "ex-Racionais Mc's," em que poderão ver e/ou ouvir "um testemunho verídico de um homem que viveu no submundo do crime e das drogas, mas através do evangelho de Cristo conheceu a verdade e hoje convicto de sua escolha, conta a sua história de vida.
>
> (Côrtes, 2012, p. 110)

All translations are by the author unless otherwise stated.

2 Literally "Tutelage Councils"; an elected member of civil society that serves on a council responsible for enforcing legislation concerning children and adolescents in Brazil.

3 Hannah Arendt claims that

> though the common world is the common meeting ground of all, those who are present have different locations in it (...) Being seen and being heard by

> others derive their significance from the fact that everybody sees and hears from a different position. This is the meaning of public life (…) Under the conditions of a common world, reality is not guaranteed primarily by the "common nature" of all men who constitute it, but rather by the fact that, differences of position and the resulting variety of perspectives notwithstanding, everybody is always concerned with the same object. If the sameness of the object can no longer be discerned, no common nature of men, least of all the unnatural conformism of a mass society, can prevent the destruction of the common world.
>
> (Arendt, 1958, pp. 57–58)

4 Michel Misse (2010) reexamined theories on the subject and proposed, for the case of the category "criminal" in Brazil, the theoretical idea of "criminal subjection." This category goes beyond stigmatization and labeling, and also includes the taking on of the label by the person stigmatized, who, therefore, becomes a subject based on imposed limits by external ascriptions.

5 Usually women responsible for giving out blessing and protection through religious practices.

6 Ogum is an orixá, a religious entity in Candomblé and Umbanda. Saint Jorge corresponds to this orixá.

7 A person belonging to the arid regions of Northeastern Brazil who participated in forms of "social banditry" against the government and other prominent landowners in the region.

8 Reference to a song by Jorge Ben Jor, "Charles, Anjo 45."

9 To make this clear might be the biggest merit of another fictional narrative, in this case a dystopia, formulated in the Brazilian film *Bacurau*, de Kléber Mendonça Filho and Juliano Dornelles, which was a success in Brazilian cinemas in 2019 and won the Jury Award at the Cannes Film Festival.

10 This is an issue that Werneck has discussed at length in his work, starting with *A desculpa* (2012).

11

> O que falar desse cara? Esse cara é um personagem, cara... pulou do livro. Imagina o Pinóquio. Imagina o Pinóquio, cara. Boneco de madeira que começa a falar. É esse Guina aí. Talvez se eu tivesse dado o nome real da pessoa que tava envolvida no B.O. da música, não aparecia esse cara. Mas eu dei um nome fictício, e ele... realmente ele... é triste saber que no Brasil muita gente vai na Igreja pra ver o cara, mais por essas ideia [*de ele ser o Guina*] do que pela ideia em si [*religiosa*]. Muita mentira junto, esse cara não existe.
>
> (Brown, 10/12/2016)

References

Almeida, Ronaldo. *A Igreja Universal e seus demônios*. São Paulo: Terceiro Nome, 2009.

Arendt, Hannah. *Human Condition*. Chicago: University of Chicago Press, 1958.

Arendt, Hannah. *Homens em tempos sombrios*. São Paulo: Companhia das Letras, 2008 [1968].

Bertelli, Giordano Barbin, and Gabriel de Santis Feltran (eds.). *Vozes à margem: periferias, estética e política*. São Carlos: EDUFSCar, 2017.

Biondi, Karina, and Adalton Marques. "Memória e historicidade em dois 'comandos' prisionais." *Lua Nova: Revista de Cultura e Política* 79 (2010): 39–70.

Birman, Patricia, and Carly Machado. "A violência dos justos: Evangélicos, mídia e periferias da metropole." *Revista Brasileira de Ciências Sociais* 27, no. 80 (2012): 55–69.

Brown, Mano. "Mano Brown fala do Guina que se diz membro do Racionais nas igrejas." *Rádio Maconheiro* (December 10, 2016). www.youtube.com/watch?v=WsL2J-gRXDo. Accessed on July 1, 2019.

Caldeira, Teresa. "I Came to Sabotage your Reasoning! Violence and Ressignifications of Justice in Brazil." In *Law and Disorder in the Postcolony*, edited by Jean Comaroff and John Comaroff, 102–149. Chicago: University of Chicago Press, 2006.

Caldeira, Teresa. *Cidade de Muros: Crime, Segregação e Cidadania em São Paulo*. São Paulo: Editora 34/ Edusp, 2000.

Cândido, Antônio. *Literatura e sociedade*. São Paulo: Companhia Editora Nacional, 1976.

Côrtes, Mariana. *O bandido que virou pregador: A conversão de criminosos ao pentecostalismo e suas carreiras de pregadores*. São Paulo: Aderaldo & Rothschild, 2007.

Côrtes, Mariana. *Diabo e fluoxetina: Pentecostalismo e psiquiatria na gestão da diferença*. Curitiba: Appris, 2017.

Cozzi, Eugenia, Enrique Font, and María E. Mistura. "Desprotegidos y sobrecrimi nalizados: Interacciones entre jóvenes de sectores populares, policía provincial y una fuerza de seguridad nacional en un barrio de la ciudad de Rosario." *Revista Derechos Humanos* 3, no. 8 (2014), 3.

Cunha, Christina Vital. "'Traficantes evangélicos': Novas formas de experimentação do sagrado em favelas cariocas." *Plural: Revista do Programa de Pós-Graduação em Sociologia da USP* 15 (2008): 13–46.

Drummond de Andrade, Carlos. *Claro enigma*. Rio de Janeiro: Record, 1991.

Durham, Eunice Ribeiro. *A caminho da cidade: A vida rural e a migração para São Paulo*. São Paulo: Ática, 1973.

Feltran, Gabriel de Santis. "A fronteira do direito: Política e violência na periferia de São Paulo." In *Democracia, sociedade civil e participação*, edited by Evelina Dagnino and Luciana Tatagiba, 537–566. Chapecó: Argos, 2007.

Feltran, Gabriel de Santis. "Crime e castigo na cidade: Os repertórios da justiça e a questão do homicídio nas periferias de São Paulo." *Caderno CRH* 23, no. 58 (2010a): 59–73.

Feltran, Gabriel de Santis. "Periferias, direito e diferença: Notas de uma etnografia urbana." *Revista de Antropologia* 53, no. 2 (2010b): 565–611.

Feltran, Gabriel de Santis. "The Management of Violence on the Periphery of São Paulo: A Normative Apparatus Repertoire in the PCC Era." *Vibrant: Virtual Brazilian Anthroplogy* 7, no. 2 (2010c): 109–134.

Feltran, Gabriel de Santis. "Transformações sociais e políticas nas periferias de São Paulo." In *São Paulo: Novos percursos e atores – Sociedade, cultura e política*, edited by Lúcio Kowarick and Eduardo Marques, 360–380. São Paulo: 34/CEM, 2011a.

Feltran, Gabriel de Santis. *Fronteiras de tensão: Política e violência nas periferias de São Paulo*. São Paulo: Editora Unesp/CEM, 2011b.

Feltran, Gabriel de Santis. "Manter a ordem nas periferias de São Paulo: Coexistência de dispositivos normativos na 'era PCC'." In *Ilegalismos, cidade e política*, edited by Christian Azais, Gabriel Kessler, and Vera da Silva Telles, 100–125. Belo Horizonte: Fino Traço, 2012.

Feltran, Gabriel de Santis. "Sobre anjos e irmãos: cinquenta anos de expressão política do 'crime' numa tradição musical das periferias." *Revista do Instituto de Estudos Brasileiros* 56 (2013): 43–72.

Feltran, Gabriel de Santis. "Valor dos pobres: a aposta no dinheiro como mediação para o conflito social contemporâneo." *Caderno CRH* 27, no. 72 (2014): 495–512. www.scielo.br/scielo.php?script=sci_arttext&pid=S0103-49792014000300004 &lng =en&nrm=iso. Accessed on October 1, 2019.

Feltran, Gabriel de Santis. "A categoria como intervalo: A diferença entre essência e desconstrução." *Cadernos Pagu* 51 (2017): 161-197. http://dx.doi.org/10.1590/ 18094449201700 510005. Accessed on November 23, 2019.

Feltran, Gabriel de Santis. *Irmãos: Uma história do PCC*. São Paulo: Companhia das Letras, 2018.

Feltran, Gabriel de Santis. "(Il)licit Economies in Brazil: An Ethnographic Perspective." *Journal of Illicit Economies and Development* 1, no. 2 (2019a): 145–154.

Feltran, Gabriel de Santis. "Homicídios no Brasil: Esboço para um modelo de análise." In *Anuário Brasileiro de Segurança Pública*, edited by Fórum Brasileiro de Segurança Pública, 26–31. São Paulo: Fórum Brasileiro de Segurança Pública, 2019b.

Fiore, Mauricio. "Uso de drogas: Substâncias, sujeitos e eventos," PhD diss., University of Campinas, 2013.

Fridman, Luis Carlos. "Rock and roll, John Lennon e a esfera pública." *Sociologia & Antropologia* 4, no. 2 (2014): 519–541.

Fridman, Luis Carlos. "Imaginação política e um pouco de rock and roll na década de todas as revoltas." *Insight Inteligência* 18, no. 70 (2015): 128–140.

Garcia, Walter. "Elementos para a crítica da estética do Racionais MC'S (1990–2006)." *Ideias* 7 (2013): 81–108.

Garcia, Walter. "Sobre uma cena de 'Fim de semana no Parque', do Racionais MC's." *Estudos Avançados* 25, no. 71 (2011): 221–235.

Garcia, Walter. "Ouvindo Racionais MC's." *Teresa: Revista de Literatura Brasileira* 4–5 (2003): 166–180.

Gimeno, Patrícia Curi. "Poética versão: A construção da periferia no rap," Master's thesis, University of Campinas, 2009.

Goffman, Erving. "Acalmando o otário: Alguns aspectos de adaptação à falha." *Plural: Revista do Programa de Pós-Graduação em Sociologia da USP* 16, no. 1 (2009): 195–211.

Hirata, Daniel Veloso. "Sobreviver na adversidade: Entre o mercado e a vida," PhD diss., University of São Paulo, 2010.

Jackson, Luis "A tradição esquecida: Estudo sobre a sociologia de Antonio Candido." *Revista Brasileira de Ciências Sociais* 16, no. 47 (2011): 127–140.

Kirschbaum, Charles. "Organizational Design for Institutional Change: The Case of MPB Festivals, 1960 to 1968." *BAR: Brazilian Admnistration Review* 3, no. 2 (2006): 57–67.

Kowarick, Lúcio F. F. *Espoliacao Urbana*. Rio de Janeiro: Paz e Terra, 1980.

Magnani, José Guilherme Cantor. "De perto e de dentro: notas para uma etnografia urbana." *Revista brasileira de Ciências Sociais* 17, no. 49 (2002): 11–29.

Marques, Vagner Aparecido. "O irmão que virou irmão: Rupturas e permanências na conversão de membros do PCC ao pentecostalismo na Vila Leste (SP)," Master's thesis, Pontifical Catholic University of São Paulo, 2013.

Marques, Vagner Aparecido. *Fé e crime: Evangélicos e PCC nas periferias de São Paulo*. São Paulo: Fonte, 2015.

Marques, Vagner Aparecido. "As igrejas menores nas quebradas de fé: A construção da hegemonia do pentecostalismo nas periferias de São Paulo (1990–2010)," PhD diss., Pontifical Catholic University of São Paulo, 2019.

Matza, David, and Gresham Sykes. "Delincuencia juvenil y valores subterraneos." *Delito y Sociedad* 2, no. 38 (2016): 119–129.

Misse, Michel. "Malandros, marginais e vagabundo: A acumulação social da violência no Rio de Janeiro," PhD diss., Candido Mendes University's Research Institute of Rio de Janeiro, 1999.

Misse, Michel. "Crime, sujeito e sujeição criminal: aspectos de uma contribuição analítica sobre a categoria 'bandido'." *Lua Nova: Revista de Cultura e Política* 79 (2010): 15–38.

Oliveira, Acauam Silvério. "O evangelho marginal dos Racionais MC's." In *Sobrevivendo no Inferno*, edited by Racionais MC's, 19–41. São Paulo: Companhia das Letras, 2018.

Oliveira, Francisco de. *Crítica à razão dualista*. São Paulo: Vozes, 1981.

Ramalho, José Ricardo. *Mundo do crime: A ordem pelo avesso*. Rio de Janeiro: Centro Edelstein, 2008.

Pardue, Derek. "Uma perspectiva marginal." *Contemporânea: Revista de Sociologia da UFSCar* 3, no. 2 (2013): 447–466.

Pardue, Derek. *Brazilian Hip Hoppers Speak from the Margins*. New York: Palgrave Macmillan, 2011.

Rancière, Jacques. *A partilha do sensível: Estética e política*. São Paulo: EXO/34, 2005.

Sader, Eder. *Quando novos personagens entram em cena – experiências e lutas dos trabalhadores da Grande São Paulo (1970–1980)*. São Paulo: Paz e Terra, 1988.

Simmel, Georg. *Sociology: Inquiries into the Construction of Social Forms, Vol. 1*. Leiden/Boston: Brill, 2009 [1908].

Takahashi, Henrique Yagui. "Evangelho segundo Racionais MC'S: Ressignificações religiosas, políticas e estético-musicais nas narrativas do rap," Master's thesis, Federal University of São Carlos, 2015.

Takahashi, Henrique Yagui. "A mixagem de significações dos Racionais MC's." In *Vozes à margem: Periferias, estética e política*, edited by Giordano Bertelli and Gabriel Feltran, 1–307. São Carlos: EdUFSCar, 2017.

Teixeira, Cesar Pinheiro. "A teia do bandido: Um estudo sociológico sobre bandidos, policiais, evangélicos e agentes sociais," PhD diss., Federal University of Rio de Janeiro, 2014.

Telles, Vera Silva. *A cidade nas fronteiras do legal e ilegal*. Belo Horizonte: ARGVMENTVM, 2010.

Werneck, Alexandre. *A desculpa: As circunstâncias e a moral das relações sociais*. Rio de Janeiro: Civilização Brasileira, 2012.

Wrasse, Dilson. "Afinidades eletivas: Ética religiosa e utopias sociais – Análise psicossocial de uma organização de base comunitária," Master's thesis, Pontifical Catholic University of São Paulo, 2012.

8 Kafka and *lawfare* in Brazil

Maria Ramos's *The Trial*

Stephanie Dennison

Introduction

The director Maria Augusta Ramos (b. 1964) is one of Brazil's most striking contemporary documentary filmmakers. Her films are renowned for their ability to demystify certain Brazilian spaces and processes, through which audiences can nuance their understanding of, for example, the judicial system and how its unweilding nature impacts on the lives of those that pass through it, as in the case of *Justiça* [*Justice* 2004]; the penal system and how its design means it could never successfully serve as either a form of deterrant or a method of individual reform, in the case of *Juízo* [*Behave* 2007], the recent and ultimately failed attempt to "pacify" Rio de Janeiro's notorious slums in *Morro dos Prazeres* [*Hill of Pleasures* 2013], or the impact of what can feel like quite impersonal mass demonstrations on the individual lives of Brazilians from different walks of life, as in *Futuro Junho* [*Future June* 2015]. Ramos's latest film, *O Processo* [*The Trial* 2018], returns to the subject of the law, and specifically the controversial impeachment of Brazilian president Dilma Rousseff in 2016.

The process of impeaching president Dilma Rousseff formally began on 2nd December 2015, the date Eduardo Cunha, then president of Brazil's lower house (the chamber of deputies), accepted an impeachment request, and it ended with a Senate vote on 31 August 2016. The process thus lasted nine months in total, during which time it completely dominated political life and the news in Brazil and brought about a period of stagnation in terms of political and social policy development. Encouraged by friends and colleagues, and clearly driven by a sense of civic duty and deep frustration at the impeachment process, Ramos spent four months and a considerable part of her personal savings in 2016 in her home city of Brasília filming behind the scenes in the Senate Committee Chamber and with Dilma's impeachment defence team as they prepared for the Senate vote. During this time Rousseff had been suspended from office for 180 days, with her Vice Michel Temer acting as interim president.

Ramos's film won post-production funding from the Berlin Film Festival fund: it premiered in Berlin in March 2018 where it was enthusiastically received by a mostly ex-pat audience and it went on to win third place in the Panorama Audience Award at the festival. With its general release in Brazil ahead of the 2018 elections, it contributed to political debates, if not by changing hearts and minds then at least by galvanising support for the Workers Party within sectors of the public used to watching political documentaries in film theatres. It was one of the most watched and most talked about documentaries on theatrical release in Brazil in 2018.

Jay Weissberg writing in *Variety*, the US film industry daily, pulled no punches with regard to his own belief in the injustice of the impeachment process:

> It was always clear to anyone paying attention that the 2016 impeachment of Brazilian president Dilma Rousseff was a diversionary tactic to cover up rampant corruption from across the aisle. Maddeningly, news outlets outside the country spoke more about whether she was qualified for the job – a blatantly misogynistic aspersion generically cast at female politicians – rather than the fact that a rich white male elite had just circumvented Brazilian democracy and staged a coup. The urgent need to clearly narrate these events is behind Maria Augusta Ramos' remarkable *The Trial*, a necessary observational documentary that follows the senate's impeachment hearings to their foregone conclusion. What *The Trial* exposes is the way blatantly unscrupulous politicians desperate to save their own skins against corruption charges made a travesty of justice. (Weissberg 2018)

Not since his scathing review of José Padilha's *Tropa de Elite* [*Elite Squad* 2007] (Weissberg 2008) has a foreign film critic engaged so passionately in a discussion about Brazilian film culture. What is clear from Weissberg's review is the sense he derived from viewing the film of the inevitability of the outcome of the impeachment process, and it is the context of this sense of inevitability that will be discussed in this chapter. I argue that *The Trial* serves as a potent illustration of the use of *lawfare* in contemporary Brazilian politics, and of how we can begin to approach Brazil's far-reaching contemporary legal questions from a cultural studies perspective. In this I acknowledge the importance of a large number of films as key political texts in the Brazilian context and of what Janet Harbord (2002, 100) refers to as "a discursive space for film within an intellectual environment."

Lawfare in Brazil

The portmanteau term *lawfare* (a combination of the words law and warfare) has not yet found its way into the *Oxford English Dictionary*.[1] It has been defined in the Brazilian context by Cristiano Zanin, lawyer to ex-president Luis Inácio Lula da Silva as "the improper use of legal mechanisms as a means for political persecution"[2] (Justificando 2016). The term was discussed in detail by legal expert Rubens R. R. Casara in an article in *Revista Cult*

(2019), in which Casara explains its increasing use as a result of a desire to keep up appearances of democratic normality: it is easier nowadays, he argues, to eliminate political adversaries using the justice system and maintaining a veneer of legitimacy.

Thus, what is implied in the term, which like impeachment is used in its English rendering in Brazil, is not necessarily a disregard for the law *per se*, but a strategic use of existing judicial processes, and specifically to defeat a political adversary. It can also imply taking advantage of the complexity of Brazilian law and reflecting on the seemingly random way it is applied (why are some laws applied in certain situations and others are not? Why are some lawsuits archived and others are handled with uncanny speed?).

One of the results of the use of *lawfare* is the difficulty for the voting public in ascertaining what are false legal claims and what are not, and who is actually guilty of, say, corruption, and who is not. *Lawfare*, then, is increasingly viewed as the taking advantage by one political group of the public's understanding of the neutrality and incorruptability of the third power, the judiciary, in order to seize power. A further dimension to the question of *lawfare* is the issue of the complexity of the language associated with the law (a Brazilian legalese, or *juridiquês*),[3] whose existence and use is frequently cited as an excuse for ruling out popular debate. The Association of Brazilian Magistrates's 2005 campaign to simplify so-called *juridiquês* has arguably had minimal impact on accessibility (Maturana 2012). At the same time, qualified lawyers frequently continue to use archaic titles indicating social distinction (such as *doutor* or Dr), further adding to the sense of distance between those "in the legal know" and everyone else.

Casara (2019) lays out succinctly the challenges presented by this new and increasingly global political phenomenon:

> Against this background, the challenge arises, for all those who are not easily seduced by convenient illegalities, to differentiate between cases of lawfare and legitimate cases against politicians accused of crimes. To do so, three issues need to be considered: firstly, the limits of the term lawfare need to be established. Secondly, the term "corruption" needs to be understood as a mystifying element of discourse that seeks to justify the elimination of political opponents. Finally, we need to understand the role of fundamental rights and guarantees in the legitimation or otherwise of judicial proceedings.[4]

As Casara argues, understanding lawfare and rejecting the myth of the neutrality of the justice system are fundamental for any democratic project.

Kafka in Brazil

The title of Ramos's film is self-explanatory for anyone, regardless of political persuasion, who followed the Kafkaeque process of replacing, with the most wafer-thin veneer of legitimacy imaginable, President Rousseff and her centre-left Worker's Party with her Vice-President of the centre-right MDB party, Michel Temer. The notional grounds for impeaching President Rousseff were as a result of perceived crimes of fiscal responsibility, and specifically *pedaladas* or "fiscal pedalling" in her administration. The Rousseff Administration's budgeting allegedly used these so-called *pedaladas* to improve its fiscal outcomes and make the surplus for the years 2012 to 2014 appear larger. Regardless of what one might think in relation to both her culpability and the need to call for impeachment and thus overthrow a government over the relatively common practice, it is perhaps worth bearing in mind that unlike a huge number of her fellow politicians, no claim has ever been made in relation to Dilma Rousseff, a militant in her youth who was imprisoned and tortured during the military dictatorship, that she used her political position to generate personal wealth. Notwithstanding the fact that such manoeuvres are, like calls for presidential impeachments, very common in Brazilian politics,[5] what becomes clear in the footage of her trail is that her culpability or otherwise is of little importance. What we witness is a kangaroo court in action, but one for which the defence team is still expected to spend a large amount of time and resources in the ultimately pointless preparation of countering claims of illegality. As Maria Ramos put it:

> I was surprised that so few senators were prepared to listen to the arguments of the defence. They had all already made their minds up. In this sense, the trial was Kafkaesque. [...] It was as if the two sides didn't speak the same language.[6]

It is little wonder, then, that many supporters of Dilma and the PT have found the film so distressing to watch.[7]

Few objective observers nowadays deny that the ousting of Dilma in 2016 was tantamount to a parliamentary coup, and watching this documentary certainly leaves very little room for doubt. Where the nation remains divided is over whether her removal was in fact the right thing to do for the long-term good of the country. Some claim that the use of *lawfare* was justifiable in order to rid the nation of what had become a very unpopular leader, in large part as a result of the deep economic recession into which Brazil had been plunged after years of riding the high of a commodities boom. As one *Guardian* commentator dismissively stated, all this happened because the Brazilian Constitution does not provide for a vote of no confidence in the president (Watts 2016).[8] Others argue that Dilma's removal mid-term was part of an ongoing process on the part of Brazil's elites to both halt the progress made in Brazil in terms of social justice, and to scupper the chances of the Workers Party being re-elected in 2018.

The fiercely anti-Rousseff *Folha de S. Paulo* broadsheet, for example, acknowledged early on that Congress president Eduardo Cunha had only accepted the impeachment request (he had previously dismissed over 30 others) as retaliation for corruption charges against him being given the go-ahead in relation to financial improprieties exposed in the Panama Papers. Their editorial line was that, regardless of this, impeachment might be a way out of political stalemate (Pinheiro and Vieira 2018: 159–160). According to the analysis of Pinheiro and Vieira (2018: 160), during the congressional vote *Folha de S. Paulo* made next-to-no reference to the accusations against Rousseff and the voting process itself, and instead criticised her record in government.

At the end of the impeachment process, the editorial line was stated thus:

> The trial took place in strict compliance with the Constitution, with the full right of defence being assured and under the supervision of the impartial supreme court. The accusations of budget fraud, however, while pertinent as a reason for impeachment, *never appeared irrefutable* and sounded to the lay majority as *technically obscure* – and to a significant minority as a pretext for a "parliamentary coup." The top priority of management is now the recovery of an economy on its knees.
>
> (*Folha de S. Paulo*, 2016, my emphasis)[9]

Two years later in May 2018 *Folha de S. Paulo* film critic Marcelo Coelho's review of *The Trial* followed a similar line. While acknowledging the dispassionate and surprisingly politically neutral portrayal of the impeachment process, achieved by the film's refusal in the most part to provide context for the impeachment defence scenes captured in the film, the brief review bizarrely includes a subsection entitled "where are the Workers Party politicians linked to the trial now" (Coelho 2018).[10] The main protagonists of the film, Dilma Rousseff, party president Gleisi Hoffman, Senator Lindberg Farias and defence lawyer José Eduardo Cardozo feature in the subsection, and while Cardozo is sarcastically dismissed as spending most of his time abroad discussing impeachment, references are made to accusations (none proven, and all have since been formally dismissed by the courts) against Rousseff, Hoffman and Farias of financial improprieties. Whether knowingly or not, what this review does is provide further illustration, on this occasion emanating from Brazil's all-powerful print media, of the use of *lawfare* to maintain an image in the minds of readers of corruption being innate to the Workers Party, by drawing attention to the kinds of accusations that are regularly made (and most often dismissed) against Brazilian lawmakers, regardless of party. If anything, the insertion of this material into a broadsheet film review serves to reinforce the Kafkaesque nature of the impeachment process depicted in *The Trial*, and to reaffirm the role of the media in this process. As Lula's lawyers have argued:

> The media is a potent means of creating the conditions for the acceptance and legitimation of legal persecution inherent to lawfare. It stimulates a climate of presumption of culpability of a given enemy.
>
> (Zanin and Martins 2019)[11]

As well as the work of Franz Kafka (and the name *The Trial* was chosen deliberately by Ramos to evoke the sense of absurdity and pointlessness of the trial itself in Kafka's novel of the same name published posthumously in 1925), *The Trial* in its structure and sense of *fait accompli* also evokes Arthur Miller's *The Crucible*, and in particular in the sense of the presentation of rebel-rousing mob behaviour associated with medieval witch-hunts.[12] In *The Trial* the angry mob baying for blood, rather than being outside the courtroom, are to be found inside the chamber of deputies and the Senate. As Weissberg (2018) observes, Ramos presents a relatively neutral portrait of the crowd outside. This is made particularly clear in the first few minutes of the film, with the crowds outside Congress, pro and anti-impeachment, captured high up overhead by drone flanking either side of the *Planalto* or seat of government. Rather than demonising the crowds, they are captured in such a way as to demonstrate how dangerously divisive the political machinations of the impeachment process within the *Planalto* were.

Action shifts quickly from the crowds outside to inside the chamber of deputies and the initial raucous vote on 17 April 2016 which gave rise to the bulk of the action contained in the film. This publicly available footage sets the tone of a witch hunt, whereby the performative elements of the deputies' casting of votes further undermine the significance of the accusations. Later during Rousseff's cross-examination in Senate Ramos is careful to highlight the accused's contrasting demeanour, with its implication of moral fortitude: the camera lingers as Rousseff is seen confidently and defiantly looking around the committee chamber at her accusers, before taking her seat.

The year that never ends

As critic Luciana Veras (2018) has argued, *The Trial* is about "the year that never ends." And here the reference does not just apply to the impact of Dilma's removal from power in terms of the austerity measures quickly put in place by her successor, the deeply unpopular Michel Temer, who according to Jay Weissberg (2018) is "a man who invites credible corruption allegations like rats attract fleas." Temer's measures included a 20-year spending freeze: this constituted "the mother of all austerity plans," according to *The Washington Post* (Sims, 2016) and it was described by the UN special rapporteur on extreme poverty and human rights, Philip Alston, as the most socially regressive austerity package in the world (Sims, 2016). A reference to what happens next, capturing these measures, appears in an intertitle at the end of *The Trial*.

It also is true that 2016 was the year that never ends in the sense that Rousseff's impeachment arguably created the necessary conditions for the election of the deeply controversial Jair Bolsonaro to the presidency in 2018. Rousseff's party, the Workers Party, continued to battle against odds that appear unscrupulously stacked against it in that its chosen presidential candidate, the still very popular two-time Brazilian president Lula, was hurriedly convicted of corruption and barred from standing for election on what looked to many Brazilian and international observers as shaky grounds, begging the question to what extent his imprisonment was part of the same process of *lawfare* that ousted Dilma. At the time of writing, attention is now being drawn to the arbitrary use of the law in relation to *Operação Lava Jato* or the Car Wash grafting scandal linked to Brazil's petroleum company Petrobras, as a result of a series of leaked secret social media messages shared among members of the prosecution team, judges and politicians.[13] The increasing number of right-wing voters and commentators who are now critical of the presidency of Jair Bolsonaro, including two of the three authors of the impeachment request (the third died before Bolsonaro was elected) are particularly chastised for supporting impeachment for its seeming unleashing of anti-democratic forces as represented by the figure of Jair Bolsonaro.

Filming Dilma on trial

One might think that the minimal voiceover and intertitles with explanations and names and roles of participants means that *The Trial* makes no concessions to those who have not been following Brazilian politics closely over the past few years. But in truth Ramos's documentary is shot and edited with such skill that the political persuasion and importance of each individual portrayed is made self-evident. Nevertheless it is perhaps worth singling out a couple of characters that appear in the film.[14] One of the first figures to appear in the documentary, for example, is Eduardo Cunha, then the president of the Chamber of Deputies and for many Dilma Rousseff's nemesis as the mastermind of impeachment. Cunha, within months of Dilma's impeachment, was imprisoned on grounds of corruption and money-laundering, having been named in the Panama Papers and implicated and found guilty in the aforementioned national grafting scandal involving the state petroleum company Petrobras (*Operação Lava Jato*). He is currently serving a 15-year sentence.

Then we have Janaína Paschoal, the high-profile evangelical Christian law professor and co-author of the impeachment submission who perhaps surprisingly granted the filmmaker some access. Paschoal is described by Jay Weissberg (2018) as a "melodramatic shill whose flamboyant performances make one wonder if she's simply lying or truly delusional." Her undoubtedly batty performance in front of the camera stands in contrast to Gleisi Hoffman, Workers Party president and remarkably calm, patient and self-assured under the circumstances. Thus, with the exception of one or two key male Workers Party senators, it is the women, both to the left and the right, and in front of and behind the cameras, that stand out in *The Trial*, in a political world otherwise occupied by unscrupulous, duplicitous and in many cases misogynistic men.

It is interesting to note that two other high-profile women filmmakers, Petra Costa and Anna Muylaert have been involved in their own documentation of the impeachment process. Petra Costa, together with her editor Jordana Berg, made the Netflix-distributed feature-length documentary *Democracia em*

Vertigem [*The Edge of Democracy*, 2019]. In this they received support from Sundance (documentary edit and story lab) and the Venice Film Festival, and a nomination for best documentary feature at the Academy Awards in 2020. Anna Muylaert, together with Lô Politi, is also working on a similar project, again without recourse to public or party funding.[15] The number of women filmmakers drawn to the subject of impeachment lends weight to the view that what happened to Rousseff, regardless of what one might think of her political ability, was regarded as an assault on all women in positions of power and influence, and was felt particularly strongly within increasingly well organised and politicised women's filmmaking circles.

Typical courtroom dramas, from *Perry Mason* to *Law and Order*, tend to end on a positive, whereby justice is seen to be done and the defendant is proven innocent, either by the last-minute revelation of a vital piece of evidence, or by a brilliant, convincing defence summing up. What is made patently clear throughout *The Trial* is that there is absolutely nothing that the defence team can say or do within the limits of Brazilian law that will prevent Rousseff's impeachment, because of the use of *lawfare* on the part of her numerous adversaries. However *The Trial* does end with a victory, even if it is only a rhetorical, moral one.

The last "witness" to take the floor in the Senate hearing is impeachment co-author Janaína Pascoal. In the sequence of her speech included in *The Trial*, Pascoal acknowledges that the impeachment request is about much more than "accounting issues," and if it were solely about accounting issues, then yes, it would be a coup. On the contrary, Rousseff, according to Pascoal, was being removed from the presidency as a result of the dishonesty of the Workers Party.

Having acknowledged, then, that *lawfare* is indeed at play, Pascoal goes on to declare that even though she is convinced that she is right, she is aware that her actions will affect others. She apologises to Rousseff and, seemingly overcome with emotion, she states that she brought the impeachment accusation for the sake of Rousseff's children and grandchildren. At the end of her pronouncement a tearful Pascoal is embraced by a number of pro-impeachment politicians in what is understood to be a congratulatory gesture but which has the effect of reducing Pascoal to a mere pawn in a complex political game.

Rousseff's attorney José Eduardo Cardozo then takes the floor. He starts by referencing the three years that a young Dilma Rousseff was imprisoned during the dictatorship, during which time she was brutally tortured, her dignity attacked and her political rights suspended. He continues:

> It is possible that some of her accusers, overcome by a fit of sentimentality, said to her: "Girl, we are arresting and torturing you for the sake of the country, for the sake of your kids and grandkids [...]" Sometimes that happens to an accuser. They suddenly grow a conscience. But they cannot eliminate the injustice of the accusation.[16]

The narrative of *The Trial* thus ends with a comparison being drawn between the impeachment process and the most recent period of dictatorship in Brazil (1964–1984) and with Pascoal's emotive speech being deconstructed and thus ridiculed by Rousseff's defence team.

Conclusion

Since the days when cameras have been allowed into Brazilian political spaces, from local councils to the Senate, they have been the site of self-promotional histrionics. In Ramos's film there is a clear division drawn between those who voted against her impeachment, and those who did not, and who are portrayed as speciously and melodramatically performing their impeachment calls for the camera, producing a kind of theatre of the absurd (Sobrinho 2018). By all accounts viewing such histrionic scenes had a cathartic impact on audiences: the angry reaction to Rousseff's many enemies who are captured in *The Trial*, including the then federal deputy Jair Bolsonaro who dedicated his pro-impeachment vote to Brilhante Ustra, the general who tortured a young Dilma Rousseff during the dictatorship, was extremely vocal at screenings.[17]

Lula's lawyers, the husband-and-wife team of Cristiano Zanin and Valeska Martins, together with Rafael Valim have recently sought to capitalise on the potential of the term *lawfare* to help argue for Lula's release by setting up the Lawfare Institute. An English-language website which was launched in the United Kingdom in 2017 in association with the student law society of SOAS, University of London, it purports to offer the opportunity for visitors to the site to denounce instances of lawfare across the world.[18] The website defines the potential of lawfare thus:

> To destroy someone, lawfare is using [*sic*] the following tactics: abuse existing laws to delegitimize and harm the adversary's public image; use of legal procedures to restrain their freedom, to intimidate them; to silence them; influence public opinion negatively to anticipate judgments and curtail their right to an unbiased defense; constrain public agents and bring retaliations against the politicians to hamper legal defense mechanisms; tactical manipulation of a false cause and attempt to harass and embarrass defense lawyers.

The term is slowly gaining traction elsewhere, with the number of articles dedicated to the subject increasing steadily throughout 2019. Take, for example, the interview published in *Jacobin* magazine (2019) (and translated and republished in the Brazilian edition of the magazine) with the former president of Ecuador, Rafael Correa and former French presidential candidate Jean-Luc Mélenchon. Both politicians claim to be the victim of lawfare through a sustained "legal harassment of the left" (Rogatyuk and Bell 2019) and both cite the imprisonment of Lula as the most obvious example of this tendency.

Further illustration of precisely what the Lawfare Institute and others argue exists in the current political landscape in Brazil was recently provided by the conviction handed down to ex-presidential candidate Fernando Haddad. The former Workers Party mayor of São Paulo, in his own words (2019) has spent four years defending himself in the press and providing evidence to counter an accusation of financial irregularities made via plea bargain, only for a judge to convict him of something he had not been accused of. *Folha de S. Paulo* correspondent Mônica Bergamo (2019) drew attention to the fact that the judge at the centre of the farcical conviction delivered his verdict in a whopping 500 pages of pure legalese.

Anti-PT/pro-Bolsonaro news and fake news sites and meme-makers have actively reported Haddad's conviction, unsurprisingly leaving out the details that the conviction is expected to be promptly overturned on the basis laid out above. The number of shares and comments of approbium prove the old adage that if enough mud is thrown, some (or in this case, a great deal) will eventually stick. With this I do not wish to suggest that the PT is beyond suspicion: a number of high-profile members are currently serving prison sentences for corruption without the party proclaiming their innocence and demanding their release. What I am arguing, and what current discussions of *lawfare* in Brazil demonstrate, is that a large part of the news media and opposition have created the wholly unjustified sense that there were and continue to be a greater number of politicians belonging to the Brazilian Workers Party (PT) embroiled in corruption than in other political parties. *The Trial*, with its behind-the-scenes footage of the defence team fighting a losing battle during Rousseff's impeachment, illustrates just one in many ways that the PT are portrayed to be permanently "in the dock," with little or no importance being given to whether they deserve to be there.

As we go to press (February 2020), Maria Ramos is working on a follow-up to both *The Trial* and her other award-winning legal-based documentaries, with a study that specifically examines the trial and imprisonment of Lula, and the *Vaza Jato* revelations mentioned above that seek to uncover the extent to which lawfare has been at play in Brazilian politics in the twenty-first century. In an interview with *Globo* newspaper in February 2018, before Lula's imprisonment and the successful presidential campaign of Jair Bolsonaro was fully underway, Maria Ramos reflected on the current and likely future state of political affairs in Brazil, with bleak observations that could prove prophetic:

> The future of the country, as far as I can tell, is dark. I don't know how this film will go down in Brazil, but I hope that it serves to encourage people to reflect on what happened, to reevaluate their positions and to act in a less irrational and angry way in relation to politics. The polarization that we are witnessing could destroy our country.
>
> (in Heli de Almeida 2018)[19]

Notes

1 New entries in 2018 included the portmanteau term lumbersexual and chanchada, the latter a seemingly obscure reference to popular Brazilian comedy films of the 1930s–50s.

2 "o uso indevido dos recursos jurídicos para fins de perseguição política." All translations are by the author unless otherwise stated.

3 For a definition of *juridiquês*, see Schwirkowsky 2014. Also in relation to language, in a critical discourse analysis of the Bill of Indictment of Rousseff, Georg Wink (2017) draws attention to the use of political (and therefore exaggeratedly persuasive) rhetoric in the formulation of the Indictment, illustrating what he refers to as the "politicization of Justice" in contemporary Brazil.

4

> Diante desse quadro, surge o desafio, para todos aqueles que não se deixaram seduzir por ilegalidades convenientes, de diferenciar os casos de lawfare dos processos legítimos contra políticos acusados de crimes. Para tanto, três questões precisam ser objeto de reflexão: em primeiro lugar, é preciso delimitar o conceito de lawfare. Depois, desvelar a utilização do significante "corrupção" como principal elemento mistificador do discurso que busca justificar a eliminação de adversários políticos. Por fim, compreender a função dos direitos e garantias fundamentais na legitimação, ou não, dos processos judiciais.

5

> In ruling that the budgetary manoeuvres for which Dilma was removed was a crime of responsibility worthy of removal from office, Congress ignored a history of permissiveness with regard to the budget by executive branch leaders in Brazil that includes former presidents, state governors, and mayors.
>
> (Garmany and Pereira 2019, 38)

6

> Fiquei surpresa com o fato de que houvesse poucos senadores abertos a ouvir os argumentos da defesa. Todos já tinham tomado suas decisões. Nesse sentido, foi um processo kafkiano. [...] Era como se os dois lados não falassem a mesma língua.
>
> (in Heli de Almeida 2018)

7 Film critic Pablo Villaça (2018) likens the experience of viewing the film to reliving a nightmare.

8 In fact no presidential system does: the legislative cannot recall an executive directly elected by the people. But the Brazilian impeachment Law of 1950 is so encompassing that it practically allows for impeaching any president for whatever reason, as long as the two gatekeepers (presidents of chamber and senate) accept it. I am grateful to Georg Wink for this information.

9

> O processo decorreu em estrita obediência à Constituição, assegurado o amplo direito de defesa e sob supervisão de suprema corte insuspeita. As acusações de fraude orçamentária, porém, embora pertinentes enquanto motivo para o impeachment, nunca se mostraram irrefutáveis e soaram, para a maioria leiga, como tecnicamente obscura – e, para uma minoria expressiva, como pretexto de um "golpe parlamentar". A prioridade máxima

da administração agora confirmada é a recuperação de uma economia em frangalhos.

10 "Onde estão os petistas ligados ao processo."
11 "A mídia é um meio potente para criar um ambiente propício para a aceitação e legitimação da perseguição jurídica inerente ao *lawfare*. Ela estimula o clima da presunção de culpabilidade do inimigo eleito."
12 In truth a large part of the Brazilian media had already conducted its own witch hunt in relation to Dilma: for more information see Dennison (2020).
13 The so-called *Vaza Jato* (the Car Wash leaks) secret messages have incriminated in particular the current head of the Carwash operation, Deltan Dallagnol and the ex-judge and now Justice Minister Sérgio Moro. They were first shared (in drip-feed fashion) by Glenn Greenwald's *The Intercept Brasil* online newspaper, and later in conjunction with the *Folha de S. Paulo* and the even more right-wing *Veja* magazine and journalist Reinaldo Azevedo's blog. See Milz 2019. *Vaza Jato* has also seen a notable increase in commentators using the term *lawfare* in their analyses: see, for example, Proner and Neuenschwander (2019) and Fortes (2019).
14 It is worth noting that Rousseff's participation in the behind-the-scenes filming is minimal: the only footage we see of her that is not public access footage is of a meeting with foreign correspondents. Writing about Rousseff in May 2016, *Guardian* correspondent Jonathan Watts (2016) commented "in the past month she may well have given more interviews to overseas journalists than in the previous six years." Rousseff makes a more substantial appearance in Petra Costa's *Democracia em Vertigem* (The Edge of Democracy, 2019), whose focus is likewise the impeachment process, but even here her contributions are hardly revelatory.
15 The male filmmaker Adirley Queirós released in 2017 *Era uma vez Brasília*, enthusiastically received at the Locarno Film Festival, about the impact on impeachment proceedings on the lives of ordinary people in Brasília and the satellite town Ceilândia. Another male director, Douglas Duarte, released *Excelentíssimos* in late 2018: the film, whose original remit was to depict the Brazilian legislature and executive in action, focuses on the time of impeachment and beyond. For more information on the raft of female-led film productions dealing with the current political climate in Brazil, see Meira do Amaral 2019.
16

É possível naquele momento que alguns dos seus acusadores, tomados de uma crise de sentimentalismo, teria lhe dito: "Menina, estamos te prendendo e te torturando pelo bem do país, nós estamos pensando nos seus filhos, nos seus netos [...]". Às vezes acontece assim com os acusadores. Subitamente tem uma crise de consciência. Mas não conseguem com ela eliminar a injustiça do seu golpe.

17 Information imparted to author by the film's director, Maria Augusta Ramos.
18 Although the website has been up and running for some time, I could find no trace of the reported publications of the group, such as the weekly *The Lawfare Journal*. Google searches of both *The Lawfare Journal* and Lawfare Institute bring up the established and respected US-based Lawfare website, sponsored by Brookings think-tank. While there is no link between the Brazilian and US lawfare websites, there is also seemingly no effort made to avoid confusion, with at least one Brazilian news article reporting that the Brazilian website was sponsored by Brookings.

19

> O futuro do país, até onde sei, é obscuro. Não sei como esse filme será recebido no Brasil, mas espero que ele sirva para que as pessoas reflitam sobre os acontecimentos, reavaliem posições e ajam de forma menos irracional e raivosa em relação à política. A polarização que estamos testemunhando pode acabar com o país.

References

Bergamo, Mônica. "Juiz usou 500 páginas e fórmulas de linguística em sentença que condenou Haddad." *Folha de S. Paulo*, August 22, 2019. https://www1.folha.uol.com.br/colunas/monicabergamo/2019/08/juiz-usou-500-paginas-e-formulas-de-linguistica-em-sentenca-que-condenou-haddad.shtml. Accessed on October 23, 2019.

Casara, Rubens R. R. "Breve roteiro para identificar perseguições políticas através do Sistema de Justiça." *Revista Cult*, October 7, 2019. https://revistacult.uol.com.br/home/lawfare-sistema-de-justica. Accessed on October 23, 2019.

Coelho, Marcelo. " 'O Processo' apresenta versão desapaixonada do impeachment." *Folha de S. Paulo.* May 17, 2018. https://www1.folha.uol.com.br/ilustrada/2018/05/o-processo-apresenta-versao-desapaixonada-do-impeachment.shtml. Accessed on October 23, 2019.

Dennison, Stephanie. *Remapping Brazilian Film Culture in the Twenty-First Century.* London and New York: Routledge, 2020.

Folha de S. Paulo. "Governo Novo." Sept 1, 2016. http://acervo.folha.uol.com.br/fsp/2016/ 09/01/2/#. Accessed on October 23, 2019.

Fortes, Alexandre. "Lawfare Unmasked in Brazil." *Nacla.* July 1, 2019. https://nacla.org/news/2019/07/01/lawfare-unmasked-brazil. Accessed on October 23, 2019.

Garmany, Jeff, and Anthony W. Pereira (eds). *Understanding Contemporary Brazil.* London and New York: Routledge, 2019.

Haddad, Fernando. "Fernando Haddad: Condenação." Partido dos Trabalhadores website, August 24, 2019. https://pt.org.br/fernando-haddad-condenacao. Accessed on October 23, 2019.

Harbord, Janet. *Film Cultures.* London: Sage, 2002.

Heli de Almeida, Carlos. " 'Um filme-denúncia teria sido muito mais fácil', diz diretora de doc sobre impeachment." *O Globo.* February 23, 2018. https://oglobo.globo.com/ cultura/filmes/um-filme-denuncia-teria-sido-muito-mais-facil-diz-diretora-de-doc-sobre-impeachment-22423985. Accessed on October 23, 2019.

Justificando. "Lawfare representa o uso indevido dos recursos jurídicos para fins de perseguição política." *Justificando*, November 17, 2016. www.justificando.com/2016/11/17/lawfare-representa-o-uso-indevido-dos-recursos-juridicos-para-fins-de-perseguicao-politica. Accessed on October 23, 2019.

Maturana, Márcio. "Guerra contra o 'juridiquês' pode levar a mudanças em projetos de lei." *Senado Federal*, June 27, 2012. https://www12.senado.leg.br/noticias/materias/2012/ 06/27/guerra-contra-o-2018juridiques2019-pode-levar-a-mudancas-em-projetos-de-lei. Accessed on October 23, 2019.

Meira do Amaral, Denise. "A politica pelas lentes do feminino." *Revista Trip*, May 23, 2019. https://revistatrip.uol.com.br/tpm/anna-muylaert-petra-costa-carolina-jabor-sandra-kogut-e-tata-amaral-lancam-filmes-politicos. Accessed on October 23, 2019.

Milz, Thomas. "Brazil's Anti-Graft Operation Lava Jato in Hot Water." *DW*, July 24, 2019. www.dw.com/en/about-dw/profile/s-30688. Accessed on October 23, 2019.

Pinheiro, Tiago Roberto, and José Carlos Vieira. "A mídia brasileira no impeachment de Dilma Rousseff." *Caderno da Escola Superior de Gestão Pública, Política, Jurídica e Segurança* 1, no. 2 (2018): 151–180.

Proner, Carol, and Juliana Neuenschwander. "Informações reveladas provam o 'lawfare' como arma política no Brasil." *Carta Maior*, June 17, 2019. www.cartamaior. com.br/?/Editoria/Que-Justica-e-essa-/Informacoes-reveladas-provam-o-lawfare-como-arma-politica-no-Brasil/62/44371. Accessed on October 23, 2019.

Rogatyuk, Denis, and Patricio Mery Bell. "Lawfare: The Technocrats' War on Democracy." *Jacobin*. September 20, 2019. www.jacobinmag.com/2019/09/rafael-correa-jean-luc-melenchon-lawfare-ecaudor-france-insoumise. Accessed on October 23, 2019.

Schwirkowsky, Vanessa. "Linguagem x Juridiquês." *JUS*, May 2014. https://jus.com.br/ artigos/28441/linguagem-x-juridiques. Accessed on October 23, 2019.

Sims, Shannon. "Brazil Passes the Mother of All Austerity Plans." *The Washington Post*, December 16, 2016. www.washingtonpost.com/news/worldviews/wp/2016/12/16/brazil-passes-the-mother-of-all-austerity-plans/?noredirect=on. Accessed on October 23, 2019.

Sobrinho, Gilberto Alexandre. "*O Processo* ou as imagens e os sons que nos dominam." *Carta Maior*, June 6, 2018. www.cartamaior.com.br/?/Editoria/Cinema/O-Processo-ou-as-imagens-e-os-sons-que-nos-dominam/59/40513. Accessed on October 23, 2019.

Veras, Luciana. "*O Processo*: 2016, Ano que Não Tem Fim." *Revista Continente*, May 22, 2018. https://revistacontinente.com.br/secoes/entrevista/-o-processo---2016--ano-que-nao-tem-fim. Accessed on October 23, 2019.

Villaça, Pablo. "O Processo." *Cinema em Cena*, February 22, 2018. http://cinemaemcena.cartacapital.com.br/critica/filme/8450/o-processo. Accessed on October 23, 2019.

Watts, Jonathan. "Dilma Rousseff Impeachment: What You Need to Know – the Guardian Briefing." *The Guardian*, August 31, 2016. www.theguardian.com/news/2016/aug/31/dilma-rousseff-impeachment-brazil-what-you-need-to-know. Accessed on October 23, 2019.

Weissberg, Jay. "The Elite Squad." *Variety*. February 11, 2008. https://variety.com/2008/film/markets-festivals/the-elite-squad-1200548140. Accessed on October 23, 2019.

Weissberg, Jay. "Berlin Film Review: *The Trial*." *Variety*. March 13, 2018. https://variety.com/2018/film/reviews/the-trial-review-1202725767. Accessed on October 23, 2019.

Wink, Georg. "Judicialização da política ou politização da justiça? Uma Análise Crítica do Discurso do Libelo Acusatório contra a presidenta Dilma Rousseff no processo de impeachment." *Moara* 47 (2017): 152–173.

Zanin, Cristiano, and Valeska Martins. "Lawfare, o uso do sistema como arma de guerra política e econômica." *Carta Capital*, August 17, 2019. www.cartacapital.com.br/opiniao/lawfare-o-uso-do-sistema-como-arma-de-guerra-politica-e-economica. Accessed on October 23, 2019.

9 Night trespassing in contemporary Brazilian cinema

Unveiling (il)legalities in *Neighbouring Sounds*

Sara Brandellero

"Cities, like cats, will reveal themselves at night", the poet Rupert Brooke famously wrote in his literary musings on the city of New York (Brooke 2013 [1916], 88). Following in Brooke's exploration of often neglected aspects of city life that reveal themselves after dark, this chapter discusses the significance of nightscapes of the Brazilian North-Eastern city of Recife, capital city of the state of Pernambuco, in director Kleber Mendonça Filho's film *Neighbouring Sounds* [*O som ao redor*] (2012). It contends that representations of the nocturnal city constitute a key narrative device in the film's probing of unspoken social dynamics in their historical connections and in the slippages between legality and illegality. I will take the figure of the trespasser as entry point in this analysis, understanding trespassing in its multifaceted dimensions, as defined in the *Oxford English Dictionary* (2000):

> to enter unlawfully on the land of another, or on that which is the property or right of another [...]; to commit a transgression or offense [...]; to make an improper or uninvited inroad on (a person's time, attention, patience, etc.); to intrude on or upon the rights or domain of; to encroach on, infringe.

The multidimensionality of the trespasser, as one who disregards boundaries in one way or another, mirrors the nocturnal iterations of a number of key characters in the film. In this way, as it leads the viewer under the cover of night, the film actually exposes many of the limitations of life in Brazil's contemporary cities.

Neighbouring Sounds was awarded the FIPRESCI Prize in the Tiger competition at the Rotterdam Film Festival, "for evoking an atmosphere of paranoia and menace through a highly ambitious use of sound and cinematography" (in Marsh 2015, 140). First feature-length film of journalist and film critic and programmer Kleber Mendonça Filho, it revolves around the largely mundane daily business of the inhabitants of a non-descript middle-class street in Recife (which we know to be Mendonça Filho's own neighbourhood of Setúbal). Much of the action takes place after dark, as middle-class inhabitants strive to protect themselves from the perceived menace of what lurks beyond the barred doors and windows of their domestic spaces. Prominent in the storyline is elderly patriarch Seu Francisco (W. J. Solha), owner of much of the real estate in the neighbourhood, now managed by his grandson João (Gustavo Jahn), and whose power in the contemporary city stems from the family's historic wealth in the rural interior. In some of the most striking sequences of the film, the storyline takes us to the rural property that is still in family hands, contextualising contemporary urban issues against Brazil's historical rural, slave-based economy and the unfettered violence and crimes committed therein, a link that turns out to be pivotal in the film's dramatic nocturnal dénouement.

Thus, if place, understood as space "invested with meaning" (Cresswell 2004, 10), is a central concept in this discussion, I wish to focus on the significance of daily thresholds in engaging with the city after nightfall. The "after hours" city is the most evidently impacted by interpretations of law and order along class and racial fault-lines that determine who can go where and when. Indeed, in the nightscapes that Mendonça Filho's film constructs, social contradictions appear magnified and yet they are also where the contemporary landscape is most poignantly disturbed by spectral interventions of characters trespassing spatial and temporal boundaries.

Although night is a phenomenon that occurs naturally, night spaces are "socially mediated" (Williams 2008, 514). This has entailed the authorities' traditional suspicion of the night and measures taken to control it, while at the other end of the spectrum are the enhanced transgressive, "deterritorializing possibilities of darkness", with which Williams (2008, 520) understands the counter-hegemonic spatial practices that can range from transgression to all-out illegality. The tension between control and transgression, and their connection with issues of legality and illegality, will form the crux of the discussion of this chapter. To this end, I draw on Matthew Beaumont's considerations of the Nightwalker in early modern London "as dramatizing the dialectics of alienation and disalienation in modernity" (2015, 49) to discuss how images of nocturnal mobility in *Neighbouring Sounds* articulate a tension between guilt and retribution in a deeply fractured society, in which justice is uncertain.

Studies on Mendonça Filho's acclaimed film have homed in on its stark representation of contemporary urban living, imbued with a pervasive sense of fear of violence and criminality, but no study has so far acknowledged the night as a significant chronotope for understanding the vision of Brazil that the film articulates. In fact, the film actually ascribes considerable narrative weight to how night spaces are imagined and experienced, and the night acquires an increasing metaphorical dimension with the film's narrative development. As *Neighbouring Sounds* moves towards its conclusion, the threshold between day and night becomes increasingly blurred, reflecting the fuzzy boundaries between the past and the present (into which the past "trespasses"), where old crimes have gone unchallenged and where, consequently, the present becomes the stuff of nightmares. Thus, I consider how nighttime mobilities are cast as instances of trespassing in which guilt and retribution are dramatised, to project the city as a haunting and haunted space: "simultaneously living and spectral, containing the experience of the actual moment as well as the many times that have already transpired and become silent – though not necessarily imperceptible – to the present" (Blanco and Pereen 2013, 395).

City spaces

The construction of landscapes and spaces in Brazilian cinema has provided an instigating focus for scholarship, and much of the attention has been directed at the recurring *topoi* competing for the camera lens – the urban sprawls and particularly the cities' shantytowns, or *favelas*, on the one hand, and the rural outback of North-East Brazil, known as the *sertão*, on the other. Critic Ivana Bentes' now classic chapter "The *sertão* and the *favela* in contemporary Brazilian film" reminds us how they have "always been 'the other side' of modern and positivist Brazil" (Bentes 2005, 121). By his own admission, Mendonça Filho aimed "to break the mold" in bringing onto the screen a middle-class neighbourhood, while still aiming to provide an insight into pressing historical social concerns (in Draper 2016, 134). Indeed, *Neighbouring Sounds* reflects a contemporary trend of films, such as *The second mother* ([*Que horas ela volta?*], dir. Ana Muylaert, 2015); or, more recently *Loveling* ([*Benzinho*], dir. Gustavo Pizzi, 2018), that focus on middle-class neighbourhoods, dramas and class conflicts, providing a notable departure from the landscapes of the Brazilian favelas that had featured prominently in contemporary productions, particularly in the wake of the international acclaim of Fernando Meirelles and Kátia Lund's *City of God* ([*Cidade de Deus*], 2003). Against the background of significant societal shifts in the last decades, with economic prosperity and policies aimed at redressing Brazil's historic income and privilege inequality being implemented under the govenments of former presidents Lula (2003–2010) and Rousseff (2011–2016) and the rise of approximately 30 million people into the middle-class in Brazil, these films hone in on unprecedented social repositions often played out within the domestic sphere (De Luca 2017, 204–205).[1]

In the case of *Neighbouring Sounds*, the film contextualises the simmering tensions between the (high) middle classes and their domestic servants within a history of colonial relations with which contemporary social and class dynamics are impregnated (Salles 2019; Rabello 2016; Bras 2017). As Lúcia Nagib (2013) has noted, the film articulates a postcolonial dystopian vision of Brazil precisely by choosing not to showcase landscapes that might hark back to celebratory colonial visions of the "New World" and compressing much of the action into one non-descript urban street. Moreover, significant debunking of colonial imaginaries is achieved thanks to the deployment of stylistic conventions of the horror genre, deployed to convey the climate of paranoia that envelops the middle classes in their prejudices and presumptions of lower-class criminality (Draper 2016).

Rabello has argued that public spaces are notably devoid of living presence (Rabello 2015, 158). Yet, a ghostly presence occupies these city streets, which are imprinted with real, borderline or suspected infringements of the law that re-enact deep-seated associations between the night and cultures of illegality (real or imagined), as will be discussed further in the following section.

Stepping into the night

Matthew Beaumont (2015, 31) recalls how, in a 1927 essay entitled "Street Haunting", Virginia Woolf describes the feeling of liberation upon stepping out into the city streets after dark when, she tells us, we cease to be quite ourselves, thanks to the "irresponsibility that darkness and lamplight bestow" (Woolf 2008 [1930], 177). Any excuse will do for indulging in this "greatest pleasure" of city life, as Woolf puts it in her fictionalised account of a winter's evening ramble across London, taken with the pretext of buying a pencil (Woolf 2008 [1930], 2). Rebecca Solnit draws attention to the implications for constructions of identity that Woolf's nighttime perambulation entails, as "an excuse to explore darkness, wandering, invention, the annihilation of identity, the enormous adventure that transpires in the mind while the body travels a quotidian course" (Solnit 2014). In Woolf's account, the element of "irresponsibility" implied in the act of nightwalking enables a temporary release from restrictions traditionally imposed on women's mobility, and throws into focus the possibilities as well as the challenges that come with the cover of darkness.

Picking up on the multifarious significance of the act of nightwalking captured by Woolf's title, Beaumont, in his cultural history of nighttime in London, notes that:

> if to 'haunt' a place, a verb derived from the French, originally meant to visit a place habitually, perhaps obsessively, then those who walk at night inhabit the city both in this older sense and in the more persistent, colloquial sense of disturbing it like a spectre.
>
> (Beaumont 2015, 18)

The spectrality associated with the act of being out after nightfall, to which Beaumont refers, and which I will explore further in this chapter, connects to a long history of suspicion surrounding those who step into the shadows of the night. As Brian Palmer has noted, "the night has always been the time for daylight's dispossessed" (in Beaumont 2015, 32), and the mistrust as to their toing and froing under cover of darkness has entailed being caught up, in fact, in a long history of criminalisation. Indeed, the tendency to criminalise the night and those who frequent it goes back thousands of years and is encoded in the earliest legal traditions. In the very origins of the English justice system, for example, the Statute of Winchester of 1285 criminalised the so-called "common nightwalker" who disregarded the medieval city's curfews, and authorised the apprehension of individuals out at night who failed to carry lanterns (who failed to make themselves visible), essentially meaning the poor (Beaumont 2015, 29 and 61).

Historical similarities are found elsewhere, including in Brazil, the focus of this essay, where, Chazkel recalls, the "inability to see a person's face" lay at the heart of a series of draconian legal measures that in the nineteenth century, and for an uninterrupted period of 53 years from 1825 to 1878, led to the introduction of a curfew – known as Toque do Aragão – in the city of Rio de Janeiro, where the night became a chronotope shaped by the normalisation of civil and political rights violations that in turn enabled the normalisation of police violence (Chazkel 2017). In a city like Rio de Janeiro, then the busiest slave port in the South Atlantic, 46% of whose population was made up of enslaved people, legislation controlled movement and social gatherings of specific groups, fundamentally criminalising its Afro-Brazilian population and the poor and explicitly sparing people of high profile and of perceived integrity (Chazkel 2013, 40). Studies highlight how legal history has specifically differentiated the night – when supposed crimes were deemed to warrant more severe punishments (Beaumont 2015). Repressive nighttime legislation towards particular social groups (enslaved; the poor), such as making it illegal to whistle in the streets or engage in other activity that could be interpreted as a signal, ended up normalising and legitimising repression against them at other times of day (Chazkel 2013); and similar practices were in place around that time throughout Brazil, including in Pernambuco (Maia 1996), where Mendonça Filho's film is set.

Echoes of this historical normalisation of racial and class criminalisation through nighttime policing and law enforcement still reverberate today. For instance, despite ongoing controversy and attempts to do away with it, article 59 of the Penal Contravention Law, the so-called "Lei da Vadiagem" [Law of Vagrancy],[2] originally instituted in 1941 during the dictatorship of Getúlio Vargas, criminalises the most disenfranchised sections of society to this day. It determines a possible sentence of between two weeks and three months' imprisonment for anyone found to "indulge in idleness, despite being fit to work, without having enough means to ensure their subsistence, or found to provide for their subsistence by way of an illicit occupation".[3]

The recent polemic surrounding curfews for under 18-year-olds in some municipalities in Brazil, widely covered in the press, testifies to the perceived societal impact of nighttime mobilities – something that is also key to the contemporary Brazilian city featured in *Neighbouring Sounds*.[4] Indeed, what happens there while the city "sleeps" provides a foray into the complex web of social relations that determine who can be where and when and how guilt and responsibility are apportioned.

Nocturnal intrusions

The film's opening, made up of a montage of old black and white photographs set in Brazil's rural interior, accompanied by the sounds of country wildlife, then a tractor and eventually drum beats, initially seems disjointed from the polished, sleek survey of contemporary urban life that follows. Yet, it provides some clues to the historical context that underpins many of the urban relationships and tensions we will witness later on in the film and that have their roots in Brazil's history of violence on the land. Together with the still photo montage, a series of vignettes set in present-day Recife form a preamble to the subsequent three-part narrative (all revolving around the theme of private security) in which contemporary living comes under scrutiny.

Suspicion, paranoia, fear of violence, frustration, surveillance and isolation scar the daily existence of those living behind barred windows in the high-rise contemporary city. Extreme low and high-angle shots in the opening vignettes seem to critique the vertiginously swift verticalisation of city living, concurrently suggesting the film's deliberate defamiliarisation of this otherwise mundane urban setting. The car crash that takes place in this same quiet and unassuming neighbourhood, in the closing vignette, thus becomes the metaphor for the film's questioning of "normality". A subsequent cut to a nighttime view of the same street signals the start of the narrative proper, with part I entitled "Guard Dogs".

Following an establishing shot of the deserted nighttime street, we are taken to the home of Bia (Maeve Jinkings), a frustrated middle-class housewife who is kept awake by the neighbour's barking guard dog. Bia is sitting alone at the kitchen table, when her son appears to fetch a glass of water and suggests she take her usual sleeping tablets. This brief exchange and her subsequent ploy to disguise a sleeping pill into a piece of meat thrown over the boundary wall establishes the night as a time of insomnia, of anxiety and of scheming, when the barriers between private and public spaces, inside and out appear most porous. Mendonça Filho's use of the horror aesthetic as he films Bia plunging the knife into the piece of meat she will feed to the dog suggests the intensity of her anger towards the uncontrollable "nuisance" that lies beyond the barred windows but cannot be kept out. Borrowing from the crime/horror genre aesthetic in portraying Bia also serves to complexify the legal status of her actions, for which she will never be duly reprimanded.

The allusion to the hapless canine implied in the subtitle "Guard Dogs" is clear, but a connection is also implied with the group of security guards, led by Clodoaldo (Irandhir Santos), who later on in the film set up business promising nighttime security to a neighbourhood feeling increasingly under siege from perceived external dangers. Poignantly, the opening night scene establishes the paradox implicit throughout the film that those tasked with providing protection are at once the underdog and a perceived trespassing menace. It also sets the tone for the film's exploration of the unspoken violence and impunity that run along the racial and class fault-lines.

Thus, in the "morning after" sequence, the scene shifts to a high-rise apartment, home to João, the oldest grandson of the local real estate magnate, Seu Francisco, and serves to underline exactly where criminality is actually to be found. In the scene that introduces the contemporary high-rise setting, we see the family's long-serving black maid, Maria (Mauricéia Conceição), entering by the back door of the apartment, the so-called "área de serviço" [i.e. the servants quarters] – in traditional Brazilian home layout this includes the kitchen and laundry areas, the maid's miniscule bedroom and bathroom. The camera captures Maria hovering behind the partition wall separating the kitchen from the plush sitting room, as João and his new girlfriend, Sofia (Irma Brown), scuttle naked into the bedroom, having spent the night partying. Maria is clearly aware of the unspoken demarcation of spaces within the home, and the fact that her work-shift begins as her wealthy boss recovers from a night of indulgence is also subtly made.[5] A visual rhyme seems to comment on the vacuous living enjoyed by the affluent classes when a play on scale is made between the window view of high-rise buildings outside and the clutter of empty bottles scattered on the table.

At breakfast, talk soon turns to overnight events and mention of criminal activity is soon to follow. Yet, crucially, the only crime of which there is news as day breaks is one committed by a member of the upper class, Dinho (Yuri Holanda), the small-time criminal grandson of Seu Francisco, and João's cousin. Suspicion is rife amongst the street inhabitants that Dinho is the person responsible for breaking into Sofia's car and making off with her car radio, but a wall of silence falls whenever witnesses are asked to come forward, ensuring that the impunity he enjoys remains unthreatened. A police patrol vehicle is filmed driving by just as the night porters uneasily refuse to incriminate Dinho, underlining just who is above the law. A counterpoint to Dinho is provided by the character of Sidiclei (Alex Britto), the maid Maria's nephew, who struggles to make ends meet despite working gruelling night shifts as cashier at a local supermarket.

Notwithstanding the lack of evidence of widespread nighttime lawlessness and despite actual evidence of criminality perpetrated by the most comfortably off in the neighbourhood, a team of nighttime security men is contracted to keep watch from 7 PM. Part II, entitled "Night Guards", opens with Bia's family sitting round the dinner table commenting on the new private security firm recently contracted to keep them safe. The howling of the next-door guard dog we hear intruding into the family's conversation works as a haunting reminder of Bia's guilt from the earlier sleepless nighttime scene as well as of the impossibility of shutting the outside world out completely from the comfort of her home.

If part I introduces the motif of the night as chronotope of magnified social inequality and misplaced criminalisation of the poor, perceived as "strangers" and "inner enemies" (Simmel 1908), part II of the film is almost entirely set at night and endows the motif with a historical dimension. Two scenes portraying instances of nightwalking (or we could define them trespassing) happening under the watch of the new security guards are particularly revealing of this, and I will discuss them in some detail.

The first of these scenes is again focused on Bia, who is again unable to sleep, this time disturbed by her husband's snoring. She gets up, and the camera follows her up the stairs as she she makes her way to the apartment's terrace overlooking the city's night skyline. A dissolve transition between shots creates a ghostly atmosphere of insomnia. As she leans onto the parapet, the extra diegetic sound of a helicopter hovering above suggests her character is deep in thought and disconnected from her surroundings. This is the same disturbing sound commentary that is introduced in the opening scene of the film as the camera captures a man working on metal bars protecting a window overlooking a children's playground – suggesting her thoughts are drawn to issues of security. It is as she looks distractedly out into the night that the camera suddenly captures a dark-skinned trespasser crawling along the rooftop of the building opposite. Always on all fours, something quite animal-like is invoked by the moving silhouette slithering along the rooftop. His features are not clearly distinguishable under the cover of darkness, but the muscular figure we see with a bare torso and light-coloured shorts harks back to stereotypical images of black male bodies from classic colonial iconography. The abrupt interruption of the sound commentary and the fact that we are not given a follow-up glimpse into the wanderings of the intruder underscores the possibility of it being a figment of the imagination (or fears) rather than a real intruder.

This scene cuts to Seu Francisco, whom we see leave his heavily guarded high-rise apartment block to take a dip in the sea. Elliptical editing of his movements from leaving the house to the beach suggests his freedom to elude surveillance and his real power to negotiate geographical and temporal boundaries. A dissolve transition capturing Seu Francisco's figure heading down the street adds a spectral quality to his characterisation. The camera is careful to pick up the sign warning against swimming due to the shark-infested waters, something that Seu Francisco ignores in his assertion of seemingly unquestioned power and disregard for others' authority. The foundational sea repeatedly referenced and critiqued in Brazilian cinema (Nagib 2007) appears to be referenced here, too, represented as a space at the city's edge where historic power and rigid social structures are reaffirmed in present-day Brazil through the character of Seu Francisco, who appears to have metaphorical ownership of it. If, as Beaumont states, "to walk at night is to yield to, or embrace, an outlaw status" (Beaumont 2013, 120), Seu Francisco's purposeful city nightwalk is rather a reassertion of his perceived position above the law. The confrontation that takes place that same night between the similarly disreputable characters of Clodoaldo and Dinho, when the latter warns the former that the road belongs to "gente grande" [important people], reinforces the point that the right to occupy nocturnal city spaces is demarcated along historical class lines. The fact that Bia is only visualised inside the domestic space after dark adds a gender dimension to how disjunctions in the right to the nocturnal city are portrayed. The cover of darkness does not provide scope for a geography of resistance, that is "to create alternative spatialities" (Pile and Keith 1997, 3) to those shaped by the dominant white, patriarchal order.

The "aesthetic of layers", to which Marsh (2015, 141) refers, conveyed through recurring shots of images of confinement such as barred windows and gates, also translates on a narrative level to "coexisting narrative lines" that suggest the proximity and threat of the other (Marsh 2015, 141). Yet, these layers are also evoked metaphorically in the spectrality of past violence glimpsed in the contemporary streets of Recife.

Temporal trespassing

The spectrality of the night introduced in part II is further developed in part III, entitled "Body Guards", which entails the final showdown for Seu Francisco. As the film moves towards its conclusion, the transitions between daytime and nighttime scenes become more fluid, edging towards the final nocturnal scenes, where the present and the past violently collide. Contributing to this motif is the tension created through two nightmare scenes that produce an atmosphere of fractured temporality.

The first involves the nightmare experienced by Bia's daughter, Fernanda (Clara de Oliveira), in which she dreams of her home being invaded by scores of anonymous black male figures. Visions of these trespassers jumping over the garden wall convey her terror alongside images of their black silhouettes crowded into a narrow, cell-like space – which, as Marsh suggests "exposes the psychosocial process that naturalises the criminalisation of the young, black, male body" (2015, 155). Thus, in part III, the fear of the night (and of what lurks in the darkness) intensifies to terrifying nightmares, while daytime coincides with the disturbed sleep of the privileged while others work. In fact, in one of the film's most striking scenes, João recalls a trip to his grandfather's *fazenda* [farm] and visualises himself under a blood-red waterfall. The connection between historic racial violence and exploitation on the land and the reality of contemporary urban Brazil is made when the shot of bloodied waters cuts to João lying in bed back in his Recife flat. It is broad daylight, and he wakes up and opens his eyes to see the maid's young black granddaughter laughing at him as she recites the well-known nursery rhyme that is actually intended to frighten children into submission – "Boi da cara preta" [Bull with the black face], which is ironically goading him to go to sleep. The child's laughter implies that sleep will elude him, and that his family's past will haunt him into a living nightmare.[6]

The night as metaphor for fractured temporalities, of spectral incursions where past and present collide, chrystallises in the penultimate scene of the film. Here, we learn that one of Seu Francisco's loyal henchmen, Reginaldo, who had given him protection and guarded his interests in the interior over many years, has been killed. Francisco suspects this to be a revenge killing and attempts to contact Clodoaldo to discuss concerns about this, yet Clodoaldo does not return his calls. They finally meet in the street just as Seu Francisco is returning home from a nighttime family birthday close by, when he summons Clodoaldo back to his house with a view (as we will soon discover) to discuss a special request regarding his personal protection. Clodoaldo turns up at Seu Francisco's accompanied by his brother Claudio (Sebastião Formiga), who arrives uninvited. Tension builds as Clodoaldo and Claudio reveal to Seu Francisco that they were in fact implicated in Reginaldo's murder, as they concurrently reveal their true identity to him: they are the sons of Seu Antônio, who, Clodoaldo reminds Seu Francisco, was murdered under his orders by his own henchman Reginaldo over a land dispute – "por causa de uma cerca" [because of a boundary fence].

Clodoaldo refreshes a clearly oblivious Seu Francisco's memory of the date of the assassination – it was the year of 1984, coinciding with Brazil's gradual (as we know now, all too fragile) emergence into democratic rule that would end 21 years of dictatorship. This provides a poignant comment on the limitations of Brazil's difficult transition to democratic rule and the shortfalls in attempts to address past injustice.

The night here is when the nightwalker as trespasser, that is Clodoaldo, is able to transpose the boundary of Seu Francisco's safe house (under false pretences). As Marsh (2015) points out, the film carefully elides any visual reference to Seu Francisco's murder by the two body guards in his own home, but this is, however, implied through the sound of popping fireworks being let off outside – a sound commentary and metaphor for the invisibility of violence that is, nonetheless, pervasive.

According to Palmer:

> The night can be grasped historically as both a figment of power's imaginative fears, a dark designation illuminating the historical traumas of hegemonic regimes, and as an actual place and space in which the ubiquitous contestations of everyday life were fought out on a terrain that afforded slightly more opportunity for engagement by the oppressed and the exploited.
>
> (Palmer 2000, 454)

If, as Williams argues, the night has traditionally provided more opportunities for deterritorialisation, that "in everyday practices … in different ways, empower, parody, derail, or subvert state agendas" (Williams 2008, 167), against oppression and injustice, Mendonça Filho's film deliberately focuses on the limitations that even the potentiality of darkness affords.

Thus, to conclude, in *Neighbouring Sounds*, the cover of darkness allows old scores to be settled, but the film also exposes the limitations of dealings not carried out "às claras" – in the open – given that we do not see Seu Francisco's actual murder, nor him being brought to justice for having blood on his hands. In this sense, the figure of the nocturnal trespasser that is implied to have the upper hand in the end dramatises the interplay of guilt and retribution against the background of a history of slavery and authoritarian rule in Brazil, still unresolved.

In dramatising this interplay, the city at night becomes a key chronotope that exposes the fragile foundations of law and order and the slippages between legality and illegality that come into play behind the veneer of respectability of "normals", everyday life. Recalling Rupert Brooke's nocturnal city, Mendonça Filho's home city of Recife seems indeed to reveal itself most eloquently at night.

In actual and metaphorical terms, the night is a chronotope of potential transgression, but where justice is rarely to be found. As the nightmare scenes that accentuate the film's closing section suggest, the night crystallises most powerfully the experience of spatial and temporal trespassing: seen either in the anger directed at, and fear of, those traditionally denied their rightful place in society or in the past that returns to haunt the present. The camera itself, whose point of view we share, often positions itself as an unnoticed intruder, spying onto the life of a seemingly unassuming urban street. In so doing, it invites us to peer under the cover of darkness and, thus, into the murky boundary between legality and illegality that has shaped the past, shapes the present and points to an uncertain future.

Notes

1 On this issue, see also Marsh, Leslie, and Hongmei Li, *The Middle Class in Emerging Societies: Consumers, Lifestyles and Markets*. London and New York: Routledge, 2015.

2 All translations are mine, unless otherwise stated.

3 "Entregar-se alguém habitualmente à ociosidade, sendo válido para o trabalho, sem ter renda que lhe assegure meios bastantes de subsistência, ou prover à própria subsistência mediante ocupação ilícita." See www.jusbrasil.com.br/topicos/11736424/artigo-59-do-decreto-lei-n-3688-de-03-de-outubro-de-1941. A Member of Parliament for the Workers Party attempted to revoke the legislation in 2004, but this motion was shelved by Senate in 2019. See Brazilian Chamber of Deputies records at www.camara.leg.br/proposicoesWeb/fichadetramitacao?idProposicao=273651.

4 For coverage of the issue of curfew for unaccompanied minors, see, for example, the 2009 Correio Braziliense editorial "Toque de recolher para menores", www.correiobraziliense.com.br/app/noticia/brasil/2009/08/20/interna-brasil,136513/toque-de-recolher-para-menores.shtml.

5 The fact that the second maid we meet later in the film (we are told Maria is about to retire) shares the same moniker with the earlier character emphasizes the continuity of this domestic setup in Brazilian society. The second, younger maid (now a *diarista*, i.e. employed on a daily basis and no longer a full-time domestic servant for a single household) is notably more laconic and seemingly more resentful of her marginal role within the home, suggesting gradual change in domestic labour dynamics and possibly the improved expectations for young black Brazilian women that labour, social policies being developed at the time facilitated. This reflects the film's structure of disjunctures and continuities.

6 The nursery rhyme belongs to Brazilian folklore and it references a legendary black-faced bull, invoked to capture a terrified child. The racial prejudice implied in the rhyme is evident, as these lines suggest: "Boi, boi, boi / boi da cara preta / pega essa menina / que tem medo de careta [...] Pega esse menino / que não gosta de dormir" [Bull, bull, bull / bull of the black face / catch this girl / who is frightened of your

scary face [...] Catch this boy / who does not like to sleep]. The fact that the rhyme is sung to João by a black child suggests this is a time of postcolonial reckoning, a nightmare from which he (and the class he represents) cannot easily escape until justice has rightfully taken its course.

References

Anon. *Oxford English Dictionary*. Oxford: Oxford University Press, 2000. [Online].

Beaumont, Matthew. "The Mystery of Master Humphrey: Dickens, Nightwalking and the Old Curiosity Shop." *The Review of English Studies*, New Series, 65, no. 268 (2013): 118–136.

Beaumont, Matthew. *Nightwalking: A Nocturnal History of London Chaucer to Dickens*. London: Verso, 2015.

Bentes, Ivana. "The sertão and the favela in Contemporary Brazilian Cinema." in *The New Brazilian Cinema*, edited by Lúcia Nagib, 130–156. Oxford/New York: I. B. Tauris, 2005.

Blanco, Maria Pilar Blanco, and Esther Peeren (eds). *The Spectralities Reader: Ghosts and Haunting in Contemporary Cultural Theory*. New York: Bloomsbury Academic, 2013. E-book.

Brás, Patricia Sequeira, "O Som Ao Redor: Aural Space, Surveillance, and Class Struggle." In *Space and Subjectivity in Contemporary Brazilian Cinema*, edited by Antônio Márcio Da Silva, and Mariana Cunha, 221–233. Cham: Palgrave, 2017.

Brooke, Rupert. *Letters from America: Preface by Henry James*. The Project Gutenberg, 2013 [1916]. Online.

Chazkel, Amy. "O lado escuro do poder municipal: A mão de obra forçada e o Toque de Recolher no Rio de Janeiro Oitocentista." *Revista Mundos do Trabalho* 5, no. 9 (2013): 31–48.

Chazkel, Amy. "The Invention of Night: Visibility and Violence after Dark in Rio de Janeiro." In *Violence and Crime in Latin America: Representations and Politics*, edited by Gema Santamaría, and David Carey, 143–158. Norman: University of Oklahoma Press, 2017.

Cresswell, Timothy. "Night Discourse: Producing/Consuming Meaning on the Street." In *Images of the city: Identity and control in public space*, edited by N. R. Fyfe, 268–279. London: Routledge, 1998.

Cresswell, Timothy. *Place: An Introduction*. Oxford: Blackwell, 2004.

De Certeau, Michel. *The Practice of Everyday Life*. Translate by S. Rendall. Berkeley: University of California Press, 1984.

De Luca, Thiago. "'Casa Grande & Senzala': Domestic Space and Class Conflict in *Casa Grande* and *Que horas ela volta*?" In *Space and Subjectivity in Contemporary Brazilian Cinema*, edited by Antônio Márcio Da Silva, and Mariana Cunha, 203–219. Cham: Palgrave, 2017.

Draper, Jack. "'Materialist Horror' and the Portrayal of Middle-Class in Recent Brazilian Film Drama: *Adrift* (2009) and *Neighbouring Sounds* (2012)." *Studies in Spanish and Latin American Cinema* 13, no. 12 (2016): 119–135.

Editorial. "Toque de recolher para menores." *Correio Braziliense*, August 20, 2009. www.correiobraziliense.com.br/app/noticia/brasil/2009/08/20/interna-brasil,136513/ toque-de-recolher-para-menores.shtml. Accessed on November 20, 2019.

Harvey, David. *Spaces of Hope*. Berkeley: University of California Press, 2000.

Holston, James. "Spaces of Insurgent Citizenship." In *Cities and Citizenship*, edited by James Holston, 155–173. London and Durham, NC: Duke University Press, 1999.

Lefebvre, Henri. *The Production of Space.* Translated by D. Nicholson-Smith. Oxford, UK: Basil Blackwell, 1991 [1974].

Maia, Clarissa Nunes. "Samba, batuques, vozerias e farsas públicas: O controle social sobre os escravos em Pernambuco (1850–1888)." *CLIO: Revista de pesquisa histórica* 1, no. 16 (1996): 65–73.

Marsh, Leslie. "Reordering (Social) Sensibilities: Balancing Realisms in Neighbouring Sounds." *Studies in Spanish & Latin American Cinemas* 12, no. 2 (2015): 139–157.

Marsh, Leslie, and Hongmei Li. *The Middle Class in Emerging Societies: Consumers, Lifestyles and Markets*. London and New York: Routledge, 2015.

Massey, Doreen. *Space, Place, and Gender*. Minneapolis: University of Minnesota Press, 1994.

Melbin, Murray. "Night as Frontier." *American Sociological Review* 43 (1978): 3–22.

Nagib, Lúcia. *Brazil on Screen: Cinema Novo, New Cinema, Utopia.* New York: I. B. Tauris, 2007.

Nagib, Lúcia. "Em *O som ao redor* todos temem a própria sombra." *Folha Ilustríssima* (February 17, 2013). https://www1.folha.uol.com.br/ilustrissima/2013/02/1231435-em-o-som-ao-redor-todos-temem-a-propria-sombra.shtml. Accessed on November 15, 2019.

Palmer, Brian. *Cultures of Darkness: Night Travels in the Histories of Transgression (from Medieval to Modern)*. New York: Monthly Review Press, 2000.

Penal Contravention Law. Article 59. www.jusbrasil.com.br/topicos/11736424/artigo-59-do-decreto-lei-n-3688-de-03-de-outubro-de-1941. Accessed on November 20, 2019.

Pile, Steve, and Michael Keith (eds.). *Geographies of Resistance*. London: Routledge, 1997.

Rabello, Ivone Daré. "O Som ao Redor: Sem futuro, só revanche?" *Novos estudos CEBRAP* 1, no. 101 (2015): 157–173.

Salles, Michelle. "Pós-colonialismo(s) e o cinema brasileiro: A retomada." *Buala* (February 19, 2019). www.buala.org/pt/afroscreen/pos-colonialismos-e-o-cinema-brasileiro-a-retomada. Accessed on August 25, 2019.

Simmel, Georg. "The Stranger." In *The Sociology of Georg Simmel*, edited and translated by Kurt Wolff, 402–408. London: Free Press, 1950 [1908].

Solnit, Rebecca. "Woolf's Darkness: Embracing the Inexplicable." *New Yorker* (April 24, 2014). www.newyorker.com/books/page-turner/woolfs-darkness-embracing-the-inexplicable. Accessed on October 1, 2018.

Williams, Robert. "Night Spaces: Darkness, Deterritorialization, and Social Control." *Space and Culture* 11, no. 4 (2008): 514–532.

Woolf, Virginia. "Street Haunting." In *Selected Essays*, edited by David Bradshaw, 177–187. Oxford: Oxford University Press, 2008.

10 Something to declare

Illegal immigrants in contemporary Brazilian literature

Claire Williams

In a 2015 article entitled "Espaços *na* e *da* clandestinidade" [Spaces in and of the Clandestine] Leonardo Tonus describes the conundrum of how, despite the continual and increasing phenomenon of migration *away from* Brazil, and in spite of the growing number of Brazilian novels set *outside* the country of origin, and, in contrast to the numerous literary representations of migration *to* Brazil from all around the world, "o clandestino [...] permanence relativamente ausente" [the illegal immigrant is relatively absent] (Tonus 2015, 139).[1] Certainly, representations of this particular group are rare in literary form, although there are a number of studies on and interviews with legal and illegal Brazilian migrants in ethnographic research and reports by social scientists.[2] In fact, a Report from 2011 (Kubal, Bakewell and de Haas, 6) found that unlike the other countries (Morocco and Ukraine) studied by the authors, who were able to access "an almost complete series of quantitative data" to help "cast some light on the past trends and types of migration", they could find "no written evidence on the history of Brazilian migration to the UK",[3] echoing Maxine Margolis's description of an "invisible minority" of Brazilians in New York (2009).[4] Nevertheless, a small number of novels, memoirs and films[5] made over the last 30 years, do portray illegal Brazilian migrants' lives abroad and in this chapter I will focus on one set in London and two in Lisbon.[6]

The three narratives under analysis highlight challenges that are also identified by participants in scientific surveys and reports mentioned earlier and in my footnotes. The first, Regina Rheda's *Pau-de-Arara: Classe Turística* [Parrot's Perch: Economy Class] (1996), is a transnational comedy of errors set in London in the mid-1990s, which identifies and critiques differences between Brazilian and British culture.[7] The second, Cláudia Canto's *Morte Às Vassouras* [Death to the Brooms] (2002), is the diary of a journalist from a peripheral neighbourhood in São Paulo who decides to try her luck working in Lisbon for six months (August 2002–February 2003).[8] She finds a job as a maid in the house of an elderly aristocratic couple, but she is shocked at their imperious treatment of her and their outdated, prejudicial ideas. This sort of refusal to believe that Brazil is no longer part of the Portuguese empire resurfaces in Luiz Ruffato's *Estive em Lisboa e Lembrei de Você* [I Went to

Lisbon and Thought of You] (2009).[9] The novel claims to be the transcription of interviews with a real migrant, Serginho, stuck in Lisbon for six and a half years. Serginho adapts in many ways (linguistically, geographically), but learns about other cultural differences the hard way.

All three novels are set in what Gustavo Dias and Angelo Martins Junior call the first wave of Brazilian migration, which took place in the late 1990s and early 2000s, before the Worker's Party reforms could shape society (2018, 117). Aware of their illegal status, the protagonists have to undergo humiliations and devise survival strategies, ultimately accepting defeat. The novels follow a chronological structure, starting with disenchantment with their lives in Brazil (the main motivation for emigration) and dreams of success and romance abroad. The diversity in the protagonists' social class (and education), gender and, in Canto's case, race, lead to differences in the ways they experience the host culture, but, at the same time, their stories are all told defiantly, making them picaresque heroes, overcoming obstacles and outwitting their enemies.

Brazil is better known as a country that receives migrants, rather than losing citizens. As Fernando Arenas puts it "successive waves of forced African and voluntary European migration (as well as that from East Asia and the Middle East) constitute the foundation of the modern [Brazilian] state, alongside the native Amerindian population" (2017, 144). However, in the 1980s and 1990s, the spread of neoliberalism, economic crisis and increasing social inequality led to a growth in migration. These migrants intended to work abroad temporarily, send remittances home and eventually return themselves, once the crisis had abated. In the early 1990s, migrants tended to be students or young people (usually white and middle class) planning to learn English and improve their cultural capital (Dias and Martins Junior 2018, 117). Many of them settled and constructed communities into which subsequent migrants could integrate. Empirical analysis suggests that the "second wave" of migration to the United Kingdom (from the late 1990s onwards) became more diverse (in terms of gender, social class and regional origin), enabled by economic, social and political changes in Brazil, including the popularisation of international travel (Dias and Martins Junior 2018, 115, 127).

As for how they entered the country, research has shown that "the major legal channels of entry have remained student and tourist visas", but a mapping study from 2007 found that over half of the immigrants interviewed admitted their "visa expired" status (Kubal, Bakewell and de Haas 2011, 8, 3).[10] Another factor involved in the increase of Brazilian immigration to Europe in the 2000s, rather than the more "traditional" destination of the United States, had to do with increasing restrictions in US immigration policy after 9/11, leading to the criminalisation of "illegal" immigrants (Kubal, Bakewell and de Haas 2011, 6–7).[11]

At the same time, at the turn of the new millennium, there was a modernisation and expansion of the Portuguese economy that attracted migrants from the former colonies and further afield, particularly Eastern Europe. As an effect of the global economic downturn and the fact that Portugal has been one of the hardest hit European countries, migration from Brazil slowed down (and some migrants returned home),[12] although the United Kingdom, and London in particular, has seen a steady influx (Dias and Martins Junior 2018, 131). Insecurity about the current government seems to have provoked a new wave of migrants to Portugal, according to the President of the Casa do Brasil (a non-profit organisation which assists migrants) in Lisbon (Agência Lusa 2019). Of course, official figures represent an undercount of the actual size of the Brazilian population residing and working in other countries.[13]

In the opening paragraphs of *Pau-de-Arara*, Regina Rheda (1996, translation into English in 2005) presents a pseudo-historical account of the situation facing young Brazilian graduates at the turn of the millennium, laying the blame squarely at the feet of politicians:

> Nas décadas finais do século XX, o Brasil viveu um fenômeno inédito em seus quinhentos anos de história. Um grande número de jovens brasileiros de classe média decidiu trocar o diploma pelo esfregão, a roupa de grife pelo avental, o volante pela pia, a prosperidade pela gorjeta e o Brasil pelo Primeiro Mundo. Nossa pátria, mãe ausente, submissa e ignorante, dilapidada por uma sucessão invencível de governantes parasitas, deserdou mais de uma geração de universitários e profissionais liberais. [...] Jovens que jamais se empregariam como lavadores de pratos em seu país foram fazê-lo no exterior, onde a remuneração pelo serviço suplantava os salários que os professores brasileiros recebiam na sua própria terra.
>
> (7–8)

> In the late twentieth century, Brazil experienced a phenomenon quite unprecedented in its five-hundred-year history. Many young middle-class Brazilians decided to swap their university diplomas for mops, their designer clothes for aprons, their cars for kitchen sinks, their prosperity for tips, and Brazil for the First World. Our country, ruined by an unbroken succession of parasitic politicians, disowned, like a negligent, submissive and ignorant mother, more than one generation of university graduates and liberal professionals. [...] Young people who would never have dreamed of washing dishes in their own country went off to do just that overseas, where their wages surpassed the salaries of teachers back in Brazil.
>
> (89)

She sets up a series of contrasts between 'us' and 'them', 'here' and 'there', emphasising the way her generation has been cheated out of their qualifications, earnings, freedom ("o volante" [steering wheel]), and their rightful inheritance ("desherdou" [disinherited]), in under-developed Brazil. Migration to Europe becomes a valid option, despite the realisation that it may imply working in cleaning or catering ("esfregão" [mop], "avental" [apron], "pia" [sink], "gorjeta" [tips]), employment considered by her to be degrading manual labour. She provides further illustrations of downward mobility: actresses become night-club dancers, teachers become waiters, psychologists become cleaners, sociologists become manicurists (89).[14]

This is the justification for 30-year-old Rita Setemiglia's trip to Europe in search of romance, great sex, and her fortune, all of which she believes she can achieve if she can prove her Italian heritage and obtain dual citizenship. She spends six months in London on a tourist visa; making up three-quarters of the text. The opening paragraphs are a good example of Rheda's satirical tone.[15] They pave the way for this inverted fairy tale, in which the protagonist is unlucky in her search for an Italian passport, a successful career and true love.

The title is revealing: "pau-de-arara" [parrot's perch] is the name used to refer to the means of transport used by the poorest migrants from Northeastern Brazil to travel to the affluent southeast in the backs of trucks, leaning, or perching like parrots, on the metal supports around the edges.[16] "Classe turística" is the equivalent of economy class, so the title as a whole evokes economic migration at the lowest price. The title of the published English translation, *First World, Third Class*, brings out the theme of opposing contrasts that dominates migrant literature: home versus abroad, and the inferiority complex she points to in the opening paragraphs: those affected feel "inferiorizados pelo destino" (8) [resentful of their fate] (89). At different points, either location can be associated with heaven, or hell, according to Antonio Luciano de Andrade Tosta (2005) in his analysis of what he denotes Brazuca literature. For Rita, London is both a cultural heaven, paved with opportunities just out of her reach, and hell because she feels undervalued and exploited, as well as under the threat of being exposed as an illegal worker.

Rita feels entitled to a better life than the one she had in São Paulo, but she is unable to find one in London, where her talents go unrewarded and her physical attractions unnoticed. It seems unfair to her that a prizewinning film director should be limited to childcare and household tasks, and she is aware of the extra humiliation involved in working for a Portuguese woman:

> Algumas décadas atrás, em São Paulo, o português era o semi-analfabeto da padaria da esquina. Rita, ela própria, quando menina, tivera uma empregada portuguesa. Hoje, uma brasileira de formação universitária investe todas as suas economias em se mudar para Europa para ser o quê? Para ser criada de uma portuguesa psicopata.
>
> (73)

> In São Paulo until a few decades ago your average Portuguese person was just a semi-literate who ran the corner bakery. Rita herself had had a Portuguese maid as a child. And today a university-educated Brazilian sinks all her savings into a move to Europe – and for what? To be housemaid to a psychopathic Portuguese woman.
>
> (2005, 134)

This quotation shows Rita's tendency towards cultural pigeonholing and caricature, via the common Brazilian stereotype of the Portuguese shopkeeper/

baker, as well as swerves in flows of migration. In the late nineteenth century, southern Europeans emigrated to the Americas in droves and in the mid-twentieth century many Portuguese fled to Brazil from the oppressive Estado Novo dictatorship. Rita's current economic dependency on the Portuguese woman also brings to light uncomfortable echoes of colonialism.[17]

Rita's hunt for a British boyfriend leads her from concerts and exhibitions to a series of insalubrious pubs and clubs, but her most persistent suitor is, the nerdy immigration official who interviewed her, aggressively, when she first arrived at Heathrow airport. He tracks her down to various addresses and threatens to denounce her to the authorities for working illegally unless she will go out with him. This act of stalking, can perhaps be seen as a metaphor for the lawbreaking migrant's constant fear of being discovered.[18] Indeed, as in other narratives about migration, the immigration interview and related legal procedures are foregrounded as traumatic experiences that taint the first impressions of arriving in a new country.[19]

The novel counters the protagonist's fears with a comic portrayal of British life. It is full of common complaints levelled by visitors to the country, succinctly summarised as "o trinomio solidão-frio-comida" (33) [the triad: cold-food-solitude] (105), but also revelations about cultural differences such as the European way of washing up, and how a woman can refuse a man's advances effectively.[20] These most often take the form of gossip to friends, in Rita's letters home, and disclose a variety of observations and judgements that establish her own moral, social and physical superiority, to counterbalance her vulnerable legal status. She considers British homes to be unhygienic, and washing of both bodies and clothes inadequate.[21] Her attempts to ingratiate herself with her first hosts, including cleaning the house, prove disastrous, and set the tone for the rest of her awkward encounters with British families and households.

Rita gleefully reports all sorts of sexual proclivities denied or masked by hypocritical Brits, despite herself seducing a twelve-year-old boy in her charge and framing the affair as an illicit but requited and consensual love story. Against the background of chaotic culture clashes, she finds solace in her own sense of self-worth and moral superiority, as well as in other foreigners, including Brazilians. At the same time as it confirms (and debunks) some stereotypes, the novel laughs as much at Brazilians as does the British. Rita considers Zeca, the only male Brazilian character in the novel (another middle-class migrant, on a student visa), to have become domesticated by his British girlfriend. He is shown on more than one occasion wearing an apron, he is training to be a nurse not a doctor and he has accepted that moving to the United Kingdom and marrying a British citizen will entail compromise and sacrifice. All of this seems like emasculation to Rita who he describes as still being "muito caipira" (29) [a bit of a hick] (102) in her attitudes.

Lastly, Estella Maris, aka Baiana, a *sambista*, who immediately identifies Rita as a compatriot among the tourists in Covent Garden and approaches her smiling with "a cordialidade meiga exclusiva dos brasileiros" (69) [the sweet cordiality exclusive to Brazilians] (131), saying "A gente que é brasileira se reconhece. É alguma coisa no jeito, no andar, no astral, sei lá!" (69–70) [One Brazilian can always spot another. It's just something about us, in the walk, in the way we are, who knows?] (131).[22] Baiana is also working illegally, but living in a squat and doing lots of extra jobs, "bicos" (71) to get by. She lives by her wits, exploiting the ways she conforms physically to the stereotypical European idea of a Brazilian woman: an exuberant, dark-skinned dancer.[23]

> Baiana não sabia inglês. Não sabia língua nenhuma. A bem de verdade, tinha desistido do curso secundário para viajar. Mas se virava muito bem. [...] com apenas um mês em Londres já lecionava ['ritmos brasileiros'] no Gateway Community Center, em Balham. (O modo como ela pronunciou Gateway Community Center atestou a Rita a sua ignorância da língua.)
> (71)

> Baiana couldn't speak English. She couldn't really speak any language at all. In fact she had dropped out of high school to travel. But she was doing all right. [...] she had begun teaching at the Gateway Community Center in Balham almost at once. (The way she pronounced *Gateway Community Center* proved to Rita that she didn't know the language.)
> (2005, 132)

Despite her lack of qualifications, she always falls on her feet and gets her man. Rita is jealous, calling her compatriot a *malandra* and a *trambiqueira* [hustler], but they make friends, and Baiana is able to help her out later in the story. Nevertheless, Rita's attempts to make her mark in the "First World" are in vain. She simply does not fit in and eventually, after a number of Quixotic escapades, has to give up and go back to where she started.

Another failed, and traumatic experience of migration is narrated by Cláudia Canto in *Morte às vassouras* (2002). This is the bitter title of a "diário de uma jornalista que se tornou empregada doméstica" [the diary of a journalist who became a maid] (11) in Lisbon between August 2002 and February 2003. Cláudia set off with high hopes of adventure, disregarding advice about the dubious legality of her plans: "Leis contra imigrantes!? Não era problema ou melhor, não tocávamos no assunto, driblávamos estes pormenores, ceifávamos tudo com muito otimismo"[Laws against immigrants!? They weren't a problem, or rather, we didn't even touch upon the subject, we skated round those details, we mowed through it all full of optimism] (20). This conscious breaking of the rules highlights the themes of *malandragem* and *jeitinho* which run through these texts, which I will discuss shortly.[24] The characters seem to revel in outwitting the authorities, but such outlaw practices are perhaps easier to describe in retrospect, once back in Brazil.

The jobs Cláudia found, however, were not what she was expecting. The first was *au pair* in a house where she was propositioned by her boss's son, in what she sees as an echo of the role of sexual initiator commonly expected of the slave or maidservant in pre-Abolition Brazil, alluded to by the character

Monique in *Pau-de-arara*.[25] Then she became housemaid to an elderly aristocratic couple living in an enormous house, where she was treated like a servant and expected to behave in ways she found completely dehumanising and anachronistic:

> Aprendi logo o meu trabalho. Os rituais, como colocar uma mesa, a postura ao servir, o pouco falar, o uniforme impecável, me tornar invisível, a submissão, a subserviência, o preconceito, o movimentar constante para não parecer uma hóspede, as manias, as chatices, os poucos elogios, a falta de privacidade. (27)
>
> I learned what my job was straight away. The rituals, like laying the table, posture when serving, hardly speaking, a spotless uniform, making myself invisible, submission, subservience, preconceptions, moving around constantly so as not to appear to be a guest, the obsessions, the hassles, almost inexistent praise, the lack of privacy.

She uses the metaphor of entrapment to convey her feelings of alienation and impotence: her elderly employers are "algozes" [torturers] (57), she is an "anima[l] enjaulad[o]" [caged animal], a "presidiária" [prisoner] (28), a "robô" [robot] (57), "detenta" [detainee] (67). She considers her employers' patronising behaviour and assumptions about her class and status to be highly offensive, but is determined not to be broken by them. She vents her frustrations and takes her revenge through writing and publishing this "livro-desabafo" [letting-off-steam book], which she has also adapted for performance, though she refrains from naming her employers (Maio 2009, 6).

Cláudia's description of fear of discovery by the authorities is very compelling:

> Ando na rua como se estivesse caminhando por sobre ovos.
>
> Um toque no ombro para uma simples informação, é o suficiente para ter meus nervos escandalizados. O medo de ser descoberta é uma constante.
>
> Decididamente me sinto como uma detenta, tanto aqui trancada dia e noite, como na rua.
>
> Sou como uma assaltante em fuga. Falo baixo, sorrio discretamente, me exponho pouco.
>
> (64)
>
> I walk along the street as if on eggshells.
>
> A mere tap on the shoulder and simple request for information is enough to rattle my nerves.
>
> The fear of being discovered is constant.
>
> I feel completely like a detainee, whether I'm locked up here day and night, or in the street.
>
> I'm like a criminal on the run. I keep my voice low, smile discreetly, don't go out much.

Like Rita, she is humiliated by the lack of recognition of her intelligence and professional qualifications, and like Serginho she realises that the Portuguese do not consider Brazilians to be their equals: "Eu aqui neste país sou somente mãos, braços e pernas" [Here in this country all I am is hands, arms and legs] (102). By the time her tourist visa has run out and it is time to return home, she has realised something about herself "não será o fim, nunca vivirei em paz, nada é definitivo, as coisas estão sempre mudando" [this is not the end of it, I will never live in peace, nothing is final, things are always changing] (157). She is resistant to change, not a natural migrant, nor likely to accept working in the service industry again.

Luiz Ruffato's *Estive em Lisboa e Lembrei de Você* (2009) claims to be the "depoimento" [testimony] of one Sérgio de Souza Sampaio (born 1969), following four interviews with the author in July 2005.[26] A mere 85 pages long, Sérgio's story covers the six years he has spent in Lisbon, from his initial decision to leave his home town of Cataguases to the present. Ruffato's novel continues many of the themes covered in his four-part series *Inferno Provisório*, which charts the development over time of Brazil's working class, from the experiences of Italian migrant forebears, through migration from the countryside to the city, and, in *Estive em Lisboa*, to the former colonial power.

There is a considerable emphasis (roughly half the text) on what prompted the humble factory worker to set off to the other side of the Atlantic. He goes (a) because of the financial demands of his estranged family, (b) because he has lost his parents and his job, (c) because he wishes he could have access to imported goods like cigarettes and whisky, and (d) because he convinces himself that he will make his fortune and be able to return to a life of leisure and ease, of which others will be jealous. He wants to make his fortune and "vir agente importante" [become a big shot] (57). He believes that with hard work and a bit of luck, such a transformation is achievable, that "desespero" [despair] can be turned into "desafio" [a challenge] (76). He describes himself as a "*colosso* de conquistador" [colossus of a conqueror] (33) (author's emphasis), who performs "hercúleos esforços" [herculean tasks] (44), imagines having thousands of fans, and enjoys the town's attention and professions of pride in him. These come at a cost, though: he has promised to bring back a whole list of requested items. Nonetheless, Sérgio is always thinking about what the people back home will think of how he behaves and what he achieves, how to gain their approval and impress them, how not to fail them.

The title of the novel uses the preterite tense of the verbs *estar* [to be] and *lembrar* [to remember], as if to show that Sérgio will never achieve social mobility, or escape his past and roots, even if he travels across the world. He cannot "be" or "go" without "remembering" a generic "you"/*você*. The temporal link between *estive* [I went] and *lembrei* [I remembered] also suggests contemporaneity (the acts happened at the same time) and causality. It references a slogan associated inextricably with tourism, memory, consumerism and the inevitable return, inscribed on T-shirts, fridge magnets and other such souvenirs: "I went to (insert name of tourist destination) and thought of you". Tourists are glimpsed in the novel, in the restaurant where he works as a waiter, at the monuments, lumped together in the collective terms "turistada" [bunch of tourists] (53) and "gringalhada" [load of gringos] (58). Sérgio jealously observes them enjoying their holidays and being served. His trip to Portugal has no fixed return date, however.

When he arrives in Lisbon, he does undergo a kind of transformation from indigenous, local-Brazilian, to migrant-, foreigner-Brazilian,[27] used and abused, like the brand new suitcase ("estalando de nova" [brand spanking new]) he bought for his trip which emerges, battered, on the luggage carousel: "rodando sozinha numa esteira, arranhada e amachucada [...] toda estropiada, achei uma desconsideração" [going round and round on the belt, scratched, battered ... all ruined, I thought it was really inconsiderate] (40). After a few false starts, he slots into a hierarchy of international migrants which uncannily mimics colonial society: Serginho fits in somewhere between the blond, blue-eyed Eastern Europeans and the dark-skinned Africans.[28] He is surprised to find out that in fact the Portuguese and Brazilians do not speak the same language after all, although his skill at adaptation to the new environment shows as his narrative starts to incorporate more and more European expressions. At one point, when he meets compatriot Rodolfo, he even has trouble understanding Brazilian Portuguese (47), a sign that his linguistic abilities are in flux.

Lisbon is not paved with gold, migrating there is not the answer to all his problems, as he was led to believe. Instead, from the very outset he encounters rudeness and xenophobia rather than the cordiality and *jeitinho* he is used to:

> Madragoa, um bairro antigo pra caramba [...] uma antiguidade tão grande que até as pessoas são passadas, velhas agasalhadas em **xailes** pretos, velhos de boinas de lã subindo-descendo devagar o ladeirame, sem ar, escorados nas paredes, gente extravagante que parece uma noite deitou jovem e acordou, dia seguinte, idosa [...] e, assustados, passaram a desconfiar de tudo, sempre enfezados, resmungando pra dentro, incompreensíveis [...].
>
> (39) (author's emphasis)

> Madragoa, is a super-old neighbourhood, such an antique that even the people here are past it, old women wrapped up in black **shawls**, old men in woollen berets going up and down the hill slowly, out of breath, leaning on the walls, extravagant people who it looks like they went to bed one night young and woke up the next day old ... and, terrified, started distrusting everything, always grumpy, grumbling to themselves, impossible to understand.

In this particular explorer's experience, the "Old World" is full of decrepit, bigoted elderly people, especially the men, who do not trust foreigners, and think Brazilians are all cheats or prostitutes.[29] Serginho is easily manipulated at home and abroad, and ends the novel in a much worse situation than which he began it, in a kind of limbo: without his passport, between cultures and languages, no fixed abode, no regular employment. His craving for status and recognition is thwarted, he no longer even has documents to prove he is a Brazilian citizen: already inescapably "outro" [other], he has become, as Rodolfo tells him "nada" [nothing].

Literature about the migrant experience, in very general terms, tends to be a way of documenting struggles and achievements against the odds, in triumph at surviving and thriving or frustration at failure; intended for the elucidation and admiration/commiseration of others. The narratives of illegal migration by Brazilians to Europe analysed here conform to the pattern common to migrant literature in their use of everyday language to describe daily routines, and the focus on verisimilitude, in the form of details like real place names, or facts about the host culture (Tosta 2005; see also Brandellero, 2017).They highlight key moments, such as getting a passport, purchasing an air ticket, passing through border control and lying about their plans, finding their first job, and felicitous encounters with compatriots, as well as problems encountered on a daily basis: the fear of discovery by the authorities, and, very likely, suspicion, mockery and prejudice from locals.

All three novels present characters who migrate in the awareness that they are taking a huge risk by working illegally, but who believe it is worth taking for the benefits they will reap in due course, either financial or cultural. The jocular, ironic tone that recurs in each text, and the embracing of the role of *malandro*, in order to outwit the authorities, appears to be a survival tactic to in some way counteract the trauma of rejection, prejudice, hardship and the challenge to one's very identity that are intrinsic to the migrant experience. Furthermore, they are all written in hindsight, enabling the narrators to exaggerate their feats. Indeed, Serginho's account is told willingly, even enthusiastically, in long, multi-claused sentences, with many wry asides and comments. Canto's diary is not just therapeutic for her, but elaborately composed, including poetry and critical commentary, and emphatically meant to be read by others.

To re-engage with Tonus's statement quoted at the beginning of this chapter: literary representations of illegal Brazilian migrants are few and far between, but when they *are* represented, the authors make sure their individual voices and experiences are recorded and heard. The examples discussed here are set before the global economic crisis of 2008, but in light of recent political and social change, there may be many more after 2018.

One element that helps console migrants struggling to integrate into a foreign culture, if we believe these narratives, is the act of sharing experiences with others, learning from others and offering advice, particularly about practical and legal problems. Projects such as "Strangers into Citizens", organisations like the *Casa do Brasil* in Lisbon, informal cultural hubs, like cafes,[30] and plentiful information online help today's migrants while warning of the dangers of breaking the law and trying to offset the "**glamourização exagerada**" [exaggerated glamourisation] (author's emphasis) of living and working abroad as being "uma grande ilusão" [a real fallacy] (Corrêa 2018). If narratives about Brazilian "clandestinos" are scarce, or published by small publishers, or even self-published, it must be because illegal migrants have more pressing priorities than writing fiction or memoir, such as working to survive, or because they do not wish to draw attention to their unlawful activities. Contemporary authors do not seem impelled to write about them perhaps because to be credible the stories will involve disappointment, humiliation and prejudice; although the topic of illegal migration can also intersect with discussions about class, gender and race in Brazil, as well, as we have seen, as the fraught relationship between Portugal and its largest former colony, and stereotyped ideas about Brazilians. The three narratives analysed above function as cautionary tales that despite their mock epic tone, grand aspirations and celebration of *malandragem* effectively disincentivise illegal migration.

Notes

1 All translations are by the author unless otherwise stated.

2 For example, Angela Torresan, Cathy McIlwaine, Yara Evans and Gustavo Dias are just some of the researchers who have published their work on Brazilian migrants in London; Torresan and Beatriz Padilla on Brazilians in Portugal, and Maxine Margolis on Brazilian migrant communities in the United States, particularly New York.

3 Apart from a previous report done in 2007 their only written source is Caetano Veloso's song 'London London' from 1971.

4 For examples of Brazilian-American literature, see Part 2 of *Luso-American Literature: Writings by Portuguese-Speaking Authors in North America* (Moser and Tosta 2011). I am grateful to Carmen Ramos Villar for bringing this book to my attention, and for her advice on migrant literature.

5 For example, to London in *Jean Charles* (dir. Henrique Goldman, 2009), Lisbon in *Terra Estrangeira* (dir. Walter Salles and Daniela Thomas, 1996), *Tudo Isto é Fado* (dir. Luís Galvão Teles, 2003) and *Um Tiro no Escuro* (dir. Leonel Vieira, 2005), and the United States in *A Fronteira* (dir. Roberto Carminati, 2003). See Arenas (2017) and Ferreira (2010).

6 My selection is by no means exhaustive. Other recent accounts of Brazilians' experiences in Europe include Cátia Morais's non-fiction work *Como é gostoso o meu inglês* (2010), which tells the story of the author's six-week trip to the United Kingdom to learn English at a language school in Oxford. In Ana Maria Machado's *O Mar Nunca Transborda* (2013), the protagonist is a Brazilian journalist living in London. Two contemporary British-Brazilian novels which analyse the bi-cultural experience are Luiza Sauma's *Fire and Blood and Water* (2017) and Yara Rodrigues Fowler's *Stubborn Archivist* (2019).

7 Rheda is a short story writer and novelist, based in the United States since 1999. Her debut collection, *Arca Sem Noé: Histórias do Edifício Copan* won a Jabuti prize in 1994. Her website is http://reginarhedawriter.blogspot.com (accessed August 14, 2019).

8 Canto is a journalist and writer born and based in the São Paulo suburb of Cidade Tiradentes. She writes a blog which can be seen at http://claudiacantonoscantosdomundo.blogspot.com (accessed August 14, 2019).

9 Ruffato is one of Brazil's best-known contemporary writers, whose experimental novel *Eles eram muitos cavalos* (2001) won two major literary prizes. Many of his works are set in the town of Cataguases, where he grew up, the son of poor Italian immigrants. He gave the inaugural speech at the Frankfurt International Book Fair in 2013, when Brazil was the featured country.

10 Kubal, Bakewell and de Haas are referring to a report by Evans et al for the 2007 'Strangers into Citizens' campaign which advocated an amnesty for undocumented migrants.

11 The United Kingdom is the European country with the third largest population of Brazilians, after Portugal and Spain.

12 See Fernandes and Castro (2013).

13 Brazil's Ministry of Foreign Affairs has a website (and publications, and a youtube channel) offering advice to Brazilians abroad, including "estimativas populacionais das comunidades brasileiras no mundo" [estimates of the numbers of Brazilian communities in the world], www.brasileirosnomundo.itamaraty.gov.br/a-comunidade/estimativas-populacionais-das-comunidades (consulted August 14, 2019). The latest available information dates from 2015 and shows that in 2013 there were 166,775 registered Brazilians living in Portugal and in 2015, 116,271 (two thirds in Lisbon); in the United Kingdom there were 120,000 in 2013 and 2016. The website "Eurodicas" quotes a report by the Portuguese *Serviço de Estrangeiros e Fronteiras* which says there are 85,426 living legally in Portugal, making up the largest population of foreigners: 20% (Discacciati 2019, wp).

14 This hierarchisation is a middle-class problem; she does not stop to consider those who do such jobs in her own country and the lack of social mobility available to them.

15 On her website, Rheda claims to be influenced by works such as Mário de Andrade's chaotic, comic epic *Macunaíma* (1928) and the irony of the nineteenth-century Portuguese writer Eça de Queirós.

16 The term also refers to an infamous and brutal means of torture used during the military dictatorship in Brazil (1964–1985), but this is not relevant to the text under analysis, which does not engage with criticism of the past political situation in the country.

17 Vestiges of colonial arrogance by Portuguese citizens towards Brazilians will be discussed later in this chapter, in relation to Ruffato's novel.

18 This fear of the Home Office official's unpleasant knock on the door is outlined in Dias (2017).

19 The film *Jean Charles* (dir. Henrique Goldman, 2009), about the last days of Jean Charles de Menezes and the aftermath of his shooting by British police in 2005, gives a convincing portrait of the day-to-day life of illegal immigrants among the Brazilian community in London. It starts, precisely, with the tense scene of an immigration interview, defused by Menezes telling a sob story to persuade the officials to grant his cousin a visa. As they leave the airport, he laughs at their victory over the gullible English ("burros" [idiots]), making it clear to the spectator that he is a *malandro*. His first lesson to his cousin on how to survive in London is how to lie convincingly.

20 "Zeca procurou explicar-lhe, não sem dificuldade, o jeito sinuoso e indireto que as brasileiras têm de dizer *não*, uma política forjada dentro do costume nacional do adiamento das decisões importantes, chamado, na gaiata linguagem popular, *empurrar com a barriga*" (51) [Zeca tried to explain, with some difficulty, the indirect and tortuous way Brazilian women say *no*, reflecting the local policy of postponing important decisions, cheerfully dubbed "pushing with the belly"] (118).

21 This denunciation of lack of cleanliness as a way of asserting moral superiority is studied by Mary Douglas in her classic *Purity and Danger: An Analysis of Concepts of Pollution and Taboo* (1961).

22 This example of face-to-face between fellow ex-pats exemplifies the relative lack of institutional support networks for Brazilian migrants. Such networks, set up by the first wave of immigrants who settled, have been helpful to later migrants (Kubal, Bakewell and de Haas 2011, 7).

23 See Pontes and Piscitelli on stereotypical ideas about Brazilian women.

24 *Malandragem* and *jeitinho* are described eloquently by Roberto DaMatta in his classic anthropological study *Carnavais, Malandros e Heróis* (1979), as "recursos de sobrevivência social" (140) [means of social survival] (1991, 138), survival strategies that flout the law. He calls the *malandro* "o personagem deslocado [que] vive nos [...] interstícios, entre a ordem e da desordem, utilizando ambas" (133) [the rogue who is almost always out of place. ... He ... lives in the interstices between order and disorder, using both] (131). For further discussion of *jeitinho*, see Georg Wink's "*Jeitinho* Revisited", Chapter 4 of this volume.

25 Gilberto Freyre nostalgically describes the domestic intimacy between slaves and young masters in *Casa Grande e Senzala* (2003, 367; orig. publ. 1933). In *Pau de Arara*, Monique, a polyglot, sexually-voracious Jungian psychologist on a student grant, confesses to having fantasies about "fazendo faxina e comendo o patrão" [doing the housework and screwing the boss] and encourages Rita to seduce her young charge because "Empregada que se preze *tem que* desvirginar o filho da patroa. Isso é arquetípico!" (108, 109) [Any self-respecting maid has to deflower the mistress's son. It's archetypal!] (159).

26 The novel was first published as *Estive em Lisboa e Lembrei de Você* in 2009, coming out in Portugal as *Estive em Lisboa e Lembrei-me de Ti* the following year.A film version, directed by José Barahona, was released in 2015. As well as the title, which reflects the difference in pronoun use in European and Brazilian Portuguese and also *mineiro*, the regional dialect from Minas Gerais (which explains the missing proclitic from '*me* lembrei'), words and phrases in the text are highlighted typographically. In the Brazilian version, italics are used to indicate *mineiro* expressions, slang or for emphasis, and Portuguese words not used in Brazil appear in a different font, in bold type. In the Portuguese version, both European terminology and slang or emphasised words are rendered in italics. The cover of the original features the iconic Barcelos cockerel in bright primary colours against a black background but the Portuguese edition shows a skewed, out of focus photo of houses in front of the Castelo de São Jorge in Lisbon, taken from far beneath, against a dark grey sky which fills two thirds of the image. It evokes the unwelcoming city the tourists do not see and the fairy tale castle out of the migrant's reach.

27 On seeing oneself as a Brazilian Foreigner, see Rezende (2010).

28 For more on Serginho's encounter with neo-colonial culture in Lisbon, see Rodrigues (2012).

29 The very few female characters in the novel are, in fact, exploitative gold-diggers or grumpy harridans.

30 *Flor de Linz* (2007) by Danielli Cavalcanti, a *paraibana* now living in Denmark, is named after the café Cavalcanti ran in the Austrian city of Linz for ten years, and which became a meeting point for immigrants of all nationalities, and a venue for cultural events. Each chapter tells the story of a regular female customer and her struggles, but there are as many happy outcomes as disappointments. I am grateful to Danielli for contacting me and sending me her book when she discovered I would be talking about migrant literature at the REBRAC conference in Copenhagen in October 2018.

References

Agência Lusa. "Há cada vez mais brasileiros a chegar a Portugal." *Expresso* online, April 19, 2019. https://expresso.pt/internacional/2019-04-09-Ha-cada-vez-mais-brasileiros-a-chegar-a-Portugal. Accessed on August 21, 2019.

Arenas, Fernando. "Lisbon Stories: Migration, Community and Intercultural Relations in Contemporary Cinema and Literature." *Journal of Lusophone Studies* 2, no. 1 (2017): 144–164.

Brandellero, Sara. "Táticas do cotidiano em *Estive em Lisboa e lembrei de você*, de Luiz Ruffato" *Veredas* 27 (2017): 12–23.

Canto, Cláudia. *Morte Às Vassouras*. São Paulo: Kazuá, 2002.

Cavalcanti, Danielli. *Flor de Linz*. Lisbon: Chiado, 2007.

Corrêa, Amanda. "Morar ilegalmente na Europa," Eurodicas, January 23, 2018. www.eurodicas.com.br/morar-ilegalmente-na-europa. Accessed on August 21, 2019.

DaMatta, Roberto. *Carnavais, Malandros e Heróis*. Rio de Janeiro: Zahar, 1981 [1979].

DaMatta, Roberto. *Carnivals, Rogues and Heroes: An Interpretation of the Brazilian Dilemma*. Translated by John Drury. Notre Dame, IN: University of Notre Dame Press, 1991.

Dias, Gustavo. "Dealing with the UK Inner Borders: A Study of Brazilians and Their Temporary Dwellings in London." *Mediações* 22, no. 1 (2017): 156–182.

Dias, Gustavo, and Angelo Martins Junior. "The Second Brazilian Migration Wave: The Impact of Brazil's Economic and Social Changes on Current Migration to the UK." *Século XXI, Revista de Ciências Sociais* 8, no. 1 (2018): 112–143.

Discacciati, Julia. "Brasileiros em Portugal: Veja quantos são, o que fazem e se são felizes," Eurodicas, February 13, 2019. www.eurodicas.com.br/brasileiros-em-portugal. Accessed on August 21, 2019.

Evans, Yara, Jane Wills, Kavita Datta, Joanna Herbert, Cathy McIlwaine, Jon May, Father José Osvaldo de Araújo, Ana Carla França, Ana Paula França. *Brazilians in London: a report for the Strangers into Citizens Campaign*. London: Queen Mary University of London, 2007. www.digaai.org/wp/relatorios/Brazilians%20in%20London.pdf. Acessed on October 23, 2019.

Evans, Yara, Tânia Tonhati, Gustavo Dias, Maria das Graças Brightwell, Olivia Sheringham. "Brazilians in London: A Report." *Canadian Journal of Latin American and Caribbean Studies* 36, no. 71 (2011): 235–248.

Fernandes, Duvaland Maria da Consolação G. de Castro. "Migração e crise: o retorno dos imigrantes brasileiros em Portugal." *REMHU – Revista Interdisciplinar de Mobilidade Humana* 21, no. 41 (2013): 99–116.

Ferreira, Carolin Overhoff. "Identities Adrift: Lusophony and Migration in National and Trans-National Lusophone Films." In *Polyglot cinema: migration and transcultural narration in France, Italy, Portugal and Spain*, edited by Verena Berger and Miya Komori, 173–192. Vienna and Berlin: LIT Verlag, 2010.

Freyre, Gilberto. *Casa Grande e Senzala: formação da família brasileira sob o regime da economia patriarcal*. São Paulo: Global, 2003 [1933].

Freyre, Gilberto, *The Masters and the Slaves: A Study in the Development of Brazilian Civilization*. Translated by Samuel Putnam. New York: Alfred A. Knopf, 1969.

Kubal, Agnieska, Oliver Bakewell, Hein de Haas. *The Evolution of Brazilian Migration to the UK*, Scoping Study Report, International Migration Institute, University of Oxford, 2011.

Machado, Ana Maria. *O Mar Nunca Transborda*. São Paulo: Companhia das Letras, 2013.

Maio, Alexandre de. "Cláudia Canto: Nada Deixei de Conseguir, Nem Tampouco Perdi." *Cultura Hiphop/Boletim do Kaos* 5 (2009): 6–7.

Margolis, Maxine. *An Invisible Minority: Brazilians in New York City*. 2nd edition, revised and expanded. Gainesville: University of Florida Press, 2009 [1998].

Ministério das Relações Exteriores. "Brasileiros no mundo." www.brasileirosnomundo.itamaraty.gov.br/a-comunidade/estimativas-populacionais-das-comunidades. Accessed on August 14, 2019.

Morais, Cátia. *Como é Gostoso o Meu Inglês*. Rio de Janeiro: Best Seller, 2010.

Moser, Robert Henry, and Antonio Luciano de Andrade Tosta (eds.). *Luso-American Literature: Writings by Portuguese-Speaking Authors in North America*. New Brunswick, NJ: Rutgers University Press, 2011.

Piscitelli, Adriana. "Looking for New Worlds: Brazilian Women as International Migrants." *Signs* 33, no. 4 (2008): 784–793.

Pontes, Luciana. "Mulheres brasileiras na mídia portuguesa." *Cadernos Pagu* 23 (2004): 229–256.

Rezende, Cláudia Barcellos. "Seeing Oneself Through the Eyes of the Other: Gender, Race and Brazilian Identity Abroad." In *Brazilian Subjectivity Today: Migration, Identity and Xenophobia*, edited by Szilvia Simai and Derek Hook, 109–124. Villa María: Eduvim, 2012.

Rheda, Regina. *Pau-de-Arara: Classe Turística*. Rio de Janeiro: Record, 1996.

Rheda, Regina. "First World, Third Class." Translated by David Coles and Charles A. Perrone. In *First World, Third Class and Other Tales of the Global Mix*, 87–236. Austin: University of Texas Press, 2005.

Rodrigues, Marco Antonio. "Mobilidade precária em *Terra Estrangeira* e em *Estive em Lisboa e lembrei de você*." *Estudos de Literatura Brasileira Contemporânea* 39 (2012): 181–192.

Rodrigues Fowler, Yara. *Stubborn Archivist*. London: Fleet, 2019.

Ruffato, Luiz. *Estive em Lisboa e Lembrei de Você*. São Paulo: Companhia das Letras, 2009.

Ruffato, Luiz. *Estive em Lisboa e Lembrei-me de Ti*. Lisbon: Quetzal, 2010.

Sauma, Luiza. *Fire and Blood and Water*. London: Penguin, 2017.

Scott, Paulo. *Habitante Irreal*. Lisbon: Tinta da China, 2012 [2011].

Tonus, Leonardo. "Espaços *na* e *da* clandestinidade." In *Espaços possíveis na literatura brasileira contemporânea*, edited by Regina Dalcastagnè and Luciene Azevedo, 139–55. Porto Alegre: Zouk, 2015.

Torresan, Angela. "Strange Bedfellows: Brazilian Immigrants Negotiating Friendship in Lisbon." *Ethnos* 76, no. 2 (2011): 233–253.

Torresan, Angela. "A Middle Class Besieged: Brazilians' Motives to Migrate." *Journal of Latin American and Caribbean Anthropology* 17, no. 1 (2012): 110–130.

Tosta, Antonio Luciano de Andrade. "Between Heaven and Hell: Perceptions of Brazil and the United States in *Brazuca* Literature." *Hispania* 88, no. 4 (2005): 713–25.

11 Painting racism

Protest art by contemporary Indigenous artists

Lúcia Sá and Felipe Milanez Pereira

Talk to almost everyone in Brazil about racism and they will tell you that it is "crime inafiançável". Indeed, the 1988 Constitution declared racism an unbailable and imprescriptible crime, punishable with detention. It is true that most people do not know that the law establishes a difference between "racial injury" (verbal racist attacks against a particular person) and racial discrimination (refusing services to someone based on her race or origin, for example or addressing offensive remarks against a whole group of people) – the first carrying a much lighter sentence, and being, in fact, bailable (Santos 2015, 186). There have been, however, remarkably few prosecutions for racial discrimination or injury since the adoption of the 1988 Constitution (Silva 2012, 108), a phenomenon that may be related to the lack of legal support for victims of racism (Barbosa 2011, 120), and, above all, to the fact that cases of racial injuries are often played down by prosecutors and judges, who treat them as simple (not racial) injuries (Santos 2015, 197; Silva 2012, 109). Moreover, when victims of racism have been asked why they did not pursue the legal prosecution of perpetrators, many responded that they did not believe they would be taken seriously (Santos 2015, 197). Of course, juridification and legal repression are not the only ways to fight racism: affirmative action, quotas, and other inclusionist policies may indeed be more effective anti-racist practices than criminal law. Nevertheless, the gap between the wide-spread knowledge, amongst Brazilians, that their country has strict laws against racism crimes, and the perception, on the part of the victims (and, probably, of the perpetrators), that judges would not take their claims seriously illustrates the (il)legality of racism in Brazil: it is *in theory* a serious crime, but *in practice* it is not taken seriously by the judicial system or potential perpetrators. This discrepancy could perhaps be traced back to the absence, in Brazil, of apartheid or segregationist laws similar to the ones that characterised countries like the United States, South Africa or Australia until the second half of the twentieth century: since racism in Brazil was not legally inscribed in state practices, it could more easily be denied or "not seen". It is, after all, a well-known fact that until the 1950s Brazil was often described as a "racial democracy", precisely because of such lack of official segregationist policies, as well as for its high rates of inter-racial marriages. Although the myth of "racial democracy" has been debunked by both Brazilian and foreign scholars since at least the 1960s, it still has great influence in Brazil's imaginary, including the judicial system (Barbosa 2011, 125; Silva 2012, 110). Thus, the refusal to treat racism as a serious crime can be linked, somewhat paradoxically, to an earlier absence of juridically inscribed segregationist practices.

Calling it the "inertia of the racial democracy myth", Kabengele Munanga (2018) referred to Brazilians refusal to recognise their own racism as a misidentification: "Instead of looking at themselves in their own mirrors, Brazilians look at themselves in the United States, South African and Nazi Germany mirrors and then conclude that they are not racist".[1] Even when recognising the existence of racism, Brazilians often see it in others, rarely in themselves. In an often-quoted poll by DataFolha from 1995, 89% of the interviewees recognised the existence of racism in Brazil, but only 10% admitted to ever having been racist themselves (Rodrigues 1995). The implementation of university quotas for descendants of African slaves and Indigenous peoples has recently brought the debate of whether or not Brazil is a racist country to the forefront of the national scene, with ever more polarised views being witnessed in the press and in social networks.[2]

Most discussion about racism in Brazil, however, has centred on Afro-descendants. Native populations are either seen as part of a more general category of non-whites (usually categorised as *pardos*, or brown),[3] or are completely ignored. In fact, in line with practices in other parts of Latin America, "race" and "racism" are categories rarely used to discuss violence against Brazil's original peoples. Instead, the oppression of Amerindians by European colonisers and their descendants tends to be discussed with reference to "ethnicity" and/or "culture", being therefore ignored in most academic and political debates on racism.[4] Yet, as Wade has argued, the tendency to separate "race" (to refer to Blacks and their descendants) from "ethnicity" or "culture" (to refer to Indigenous peoples) in Latin American studies have not been very productive. First, because as various scholars have argued, "race" and "culture" have a close and complex connection when it comes to racism, particularly from early 20th century onwards, with culture often being called to "do the work of race", in Fredrickson's famous formulation (Fredrickson 2002, 141). Second, because this separation not only ignores the fact that African slaves came, like Indigenous peoples from the Americas, from widely different cultures, but also that Amerindian peoples are, and have always been, victims of racism. In fact, as Walter Mignolo and Catherine Walsh (following Quijano, 2000) have argued, the modern concept of 'race' started with Europe's invasion of America:

> If modernity is a set of fictional narratives that justified and legitimised the actions of those who told the story and built institutions that made the story credible, then *race* is one of its conceptual fictions, effective fictions nonetheless.
>
> (2018, 299)

Racism, as Wade and others explain, is a complex phenomenon that often involves more than one element: phenotype, social class, culture, and ethnicity, as well as actors that identify themselves or others in more than one way, depending on context and circumstances. If, as Kabengele Munanga has said, Brazilian racism is "implicit" and characterised by the "silence of what is not said", racism against Indigenous populations is even more clearly marked by silence and invisibility: it is rarely "seen" or talked about, except, or course, when denounced by the victims of interpersonal acts of racism. It is still mostly ignored as a structural element in the country's inequality.

This invisibility has nothing to do with the lack of racist attacks against Amerindian peoples. On the contrary: if anything, Brazilian public figures seem to allow themselves, verbally, to be more candidly racist towards Indigenous persons than they would dare to be, publicly at least, towards Afro-descendants.[5] Early in 2019, for example Bolsonaro's Health Minister Luiz Henrique Mandetta classified Indigenous peoples as "anthropized, semi-anthropized and non-anthropized"[6] – "anthropized" being a technical term usually employed to describe landscapes or natural environments changed by human action. In other words, he resorted to a traditional colonial trope which equated Indigenous persons to nature, seeing them, basically, as non-human. In the same spirit, a very recent televised publicity campaign for a high-end furniture store in Manaus featured a decorator describing the firm's attempt to create a house inspired by Amazonia, but an Amazonia represented "not by Indians, but by persons" – clearly making the distinction between "persons" and "Indians".[7]

Thus, if racism against Indigenous populations remains invisible in Brazil it is not because of its inexistence or insignificance, but, on the contrary, because it has become so naturalised and institutionalised that it makes the very existence of Indigenous peoples invisible. This is what a recent movement of contemporary Indigenous artists, writers, film makers and musicians have been trying to point out in works that denounce violence against and oppression of Indigenous peoples, whilst attempting to make indigeneity visible in its multiple cultures, languages, and ways of relating with the non-Indigenous world.

This chapter will concentrate on the works of two visual artists from north Amazon: Denilson Baniwa and Jaider Esbell. Baniwa was born and grew up in a Baniwa village in the upper Rio Negro region, and currently lives in Rio de Janeiro, where he works as a visual artist and graphic designer. Esbell is Macuxi and grew up in area that has recently become part of the Raposa Serra do Sol reservation, in Roraima. He lives in Boa Vista, and works as visual artist and writer. Both artists have exhibited in galleries in Brazil and abroad and maintain a strong social media presence. They are also active participants in various Indigenous movements and use their work to support and promote Indigenous causes. Their work covers a myriad of topics, all related to Indigenous cultures or issues: from creation stories, traditional tales, and native graphisms, to analyses of colonisation past and present, denunciation of violence, deforestation, land invasion and, as we will argue, racism.

Neither Baniwa nor Esbell make direct use of the term racism in connection to their art. Yet, it is our contention that many of their works expose the racist logic of Brazilian society's treatment of Indigenous peoples. In order to support our analysis of how their art uncovers, maps, and helps us understand racism against Indigenous populations, we will refer mostly to descriptions and definitions of racism made by Indigenous persons. Our reason for this choice is two-fold: first, as we saw in the introduction to this chapter, there is very little scholarly work that deals with racism against Amerindian populations. Second, one of the most pervasive forms of racism against native peoples in settler-colonised countries in the Americas is the fact that their views, history, and protagonism are silenced, often by the same people who appropriate and make unrecognised use of their knowledge. The analyses of artwork will therefore be supported, when necessary, by talks and interviews given by Indigenous intellectuals, community leaders, activists and students during two meetings organised to discuss the topic of racism against Indigenous populations in Brazil.[8] The interviewees will be named and cited as sources, and their views will not be seen as words uttered by "informants", but as informed views of specialists – some trained in Western-style universities, others by shamans and elderly in their villages, and many of them by both.

In striking contrast to most academic literature on the topic, no Indigenous participant in the two meetings had any reservations to refer to the violence, ill-treatment and invisibilisation of Amerindians in Brazil as racism. In the opinion of artist and activist Daiara Tukano, it is important not only to recognise the existence of racism but also to analyse its inextricable connection, in the case of Amerindians, to colonisation, invasion of ancestral territories and denial of Indigenous identity (Tukano 2018). For historian Edson Kayapó, racism against Amerindians started immediately after the arrival of the Portuguese invaders, who saw the original inhabitants of the land as biologically and culturally inferior, giving rise to processes of cultural and physical violence that continue to this day (Kayapó 2018).

In a series of portraits from 2017, Baniwa celebrated Indigenous leaders who were assassinated. Of course, assassination does not strictly fit the category, studied in this volume, of a threshold between illegality and legality. But the specific targeting of Indigenous persons and the fact that the killings in question remain unpunished or were punished with extraordinarily light sentences point to the institutional and structural racism of Brazilian society. The acrylic painting "Galdino Pataxó" (Figure 11.1), for example is a portrait the Pataxó-hã-hã-hãe leader who in 1997 was burned alive in his sleep by a group of white upper-class teenagers in the capital of the country, Brasília, where he had gone to protest for the rights of his people to their traditional territory Caramuru-Paraguassu, invaded by powerful cocoa ranchers.

The teenagers who set him on fire later defended themselves saying "it was just a prank" [*foi só brincadeira*]. They were sentenced to 14 years in prison but because of their background, they were allowed privileges in jail, and were released after only two years, a fact that provoked outrage amongst Indigenous peoples. In Baniwa's portrait, Galdino's face is surrounded by the notorious words of the killers, written in white.

Figure 11.1 Denilson Baniwa, "Galdino Pataxó" (Acrylic on canvas, 33 cm × 32 cm, 2017). A colour version of the painting can be found on www.behance.net/gallery/57696187/Galdino-Pataxo. Copyright: Denilson Baniwa.

The other two acrylic paintings in the series portray, respectively, the leader Guarani-Nhandevá Marçal Tupã-y (Marçal de Souza),[9] who was assassinated in 1983, and the Xucuru leader Chicão Xucuru,[10] who was killed in 1998. Both Tupã-y and Xucuru were assassinated as a result of land conflict with surrounding ranchers, who refused to accept the Indigenous peoples' rights to their land. Tupã-y was shot in the mouth, a fact believed to be a symbolic attack on the power of his words. The suspects of his killing were taken to trial ten years after the crime, and were acquitted for lack of proofs. In the case of Xucuru, there has never been a trial and the assassin has never been identified. All three portraits are based on photographs that are widely available in the internet. Galdino's and Xucuru's are colour portraits, whilst Tupã-y is black-and-white. They all follow Western portraiture conventions: they either include the whole torso (in Tupã-y's case) or focus on the face and shoulders (Galdino and Xucuru). All three men gaze directly at the viewer. Tupã appears in a defiant position, speaking and holding a maraca, a sacred instrument for many Brazilian native cultures, and his black-and-white torso is surrounded by words written in red "I am a person marked for death" – a statement he made not long before his death. Xucuru's portrait follows the same style: the torso (adorned by a blue feather headdress and a large bead necklace) is surrounded by similar red writing stating "you must understand and be aware of the fact that I am being threatened". The writing in both portraits appears hurried and unfinished, resembling perhaps graffiti or, more appropriately, words written in blood on a wall or a mirror. Differently from the writing on Galdino's portrait (the words of the assassins, written in white), the red here could also indicate that the words were spoken by the Indigenous men themselves. Thus, adopting a conventional Western genre, Baniwa pays homage to historical leaders who have been ignored by Brazilian history. But the emphatic and loud presence of writing in all three cases (and the fact that the portraits are based on photographs that are widely available, anyway, in the internet) indicates that what is being portrayed is not just the leaders themselves, but the systematic violence against Indigenous peoples, a violence that is fed and perpetuated by a judicial system that ignores or downplays crimes when the victims are Indigenous – a judicial system, in other words, structured by racism.

Esbell similarly included denunciations of threats to Indigenous leaders in his work *Letter to the Old world* [Carta ao velho mundo], an artist's book that consists of a series of written, drawn and painted interventions on a volume of an *Enciclopèdia de Arte Universal* for an exhibition in France in 2019. Like Baniwa's portraits, these denunciations want to call attention to crimes that remain invisible in Brazilian society. In one of those interventions (Figure 11.2), for example Esbell interferes in Goya's painting "The Third of May" by adding a speech bubble to the central character being assassinated with the words "Chief Babau de Olivença is being threatened with death".

"The Third of May" is known for its unusual, for the time, depiction of violence on canvas, as it is centred on the killing of Spanish peasants by the French troops under Napoleon Bonaparte's invasion. By making the 1800s European peasant anachronistically denounce the threats against a contemporary Indigenous leader, Esbell links the current, land-based violence against Indigenous peoples in Brazil to a specifically European example of internal colonialism. In other words, according to the intervention, victims of colonialist invasions suffer the same type of violence, whether in the sixteenth-century Americas, nineteenth-century Europe, or contemporary Brazil. The use of writing in Baniwa's and Esbell's works (and of speech bubbles in the latter) attempts to un-silence words that are systematically silenced and ignored by the Brazilian judicial system and society as whole: the physical threats that Indigenous leaders suffer on a daily basis, many resulting in death.

But physical threats and abuse are not the only way in which interpersonal racism against Indigenous peoples manifests itself: it can also be found in everyday gestures and attitudes that are perfectly legal, and often invisible (except for the victims) – gestures that promote the systematic invisibilisation and denial of identity for Indigenous peoples. As activist and politician Sonia

Figure 11.2 Jaider Esbell, Carta ao velho mundo (2019), p. 343. Copyrights: Jaider Esbell. Photograph by Sam Devito-French.

Guajajara put it, Indigenous persons are often treated as if they are "in the wrong place", or "are not supposed to be there", even though there is no apartheid system in Brazil. Additionally, in her view, racism against Indigenous persons "has become so naturalised and is so much part of everyday life in Brazil that sometimes even when [non-Indigenous Brazilians] want to compliment us, they offend us"[11] (Guajajara 2018). This is the case of conventional "Dia do Índio" [Day of the Indian] celebrations in Brazilian Schools. Established by Getúlio Vargas in 1943, the "Day of the Indian" is supposed to be a celebration of Indigenous cultures and their legacy. In most cases, however, misinformed teachers and pupils end up promoting stereotypes of indigeneity that are profoundly offensive to Indigenous peoples. Baniwa's digital work "Dia do Índio"[12] plays humorously with such stereotypes. Two young Indigenous children, both wearing traditional decorations in their faces and school uniform shirts patterned with traditional native graphism appear to be praying. Next to them, we read a parody of the Lord's Prayer:

> Our Father, who art in heaven, / On this 19th of April / Deliver us from teachers who / decorate their students with coloured marker pens / Deliver us from schools who place paper "native" headdresses on the children / Our Father, who art in heaven / Don't let the teachers teach the children that the Day of the Indian is a celebration of the original people of this land / Keep away from us those who repeat the words: / Indian / Oca [Indigenous house], Tribe, Savage, Purity, and Exotic / Keep away from us the boo-boo-boo made with the hand around the mouth/ Our Lord, forgive those who, for lack of knowledge, turn us into a stereotyped image / But deliver them from the lack of knowledge and the prejudice who make them still believe that we are Indigenous men and women from 1500. / Amen.[13]

The children's praying position stands in clear contrast to the parodic tone of the Lord's Prayer on the right, in the same way that their conservative school uniform shirts contrast with the Indigenous graphisms that adorn them (and whose flatness and the fact that it matches the background makes it clear that it was added later, in the artwork, and was not part of the original shirts), and with the face paintings. Both the mixture of (non-Indigenous) uniform and graphisms, and the parodic tone of the Lord's Prayer reinforce the point being made by the parody itself: that indigeneneity defies the stereotypes about it widely held by Brazilian society.

This defiance of stereotypes is also the topic of a series of large oil paintings in which Baniwa portrays Indigenous youth making use of technology. In one of them (Figure 11.3) a young girl listens to music on an iPod or mobile phone.

From her profile, we can see that she is naked, wearing only an Indigenous bracelet and face painting. The background of the painting is made up of geometric Indigenous graphisms. A second painting[14] shows a young boy facing the camera. He is wearing traditional genital covering, and holding a computer – the gesture and the shape of the computer are a reference to the iconic photo of Steve Jobs holding the first Apple computer. Next to him, we can see a basket and a maraca. The third portrait[15] shows two Indigenous young men wearing shorts or trousers, with bead decorations on their naked torsos and arms. Each of them holds a filming device which they point to the viewer: a small film camera in one case, and a smartphone on the other.

Together, the three portraits are an obvious celebration of Indigenous use of technology, as well as homage to contemporary Indigenous arts: the

Figure 11.3 Denilson Baniwa, "Cunhantain" (Acrylic on canvas, 2.50 m × 1.60 m, 2018). A colour version of this painting can be found on www.instagram.com/p/BzX9ss_HIiT. Accessed on February 17, 2020. Copyright: Denilson Baniwa.

filmmakers, for example are a reference to Indigenous directors, such as the Kuikuro filmmaker Takumã Kuikuro. This celebration of Indigenous use of technology contradicts one of the most pervasive forms of racism against Indigenous peoples in Brazilian society: the belief that any Indigenous person who engages with tools, clothing, or habits from non-Indigenous modernity stops being Indigenous. As the Guarani chief and activist Eunice Keruxu Yxapyry (2018) said in a recent interview:

> When we want to have some structure, some tools, some vehicles from this society, [things that] come with this evolution we are living through today, the denial of rights comes like this: if we have these things, we stop being Indigenous, we are not recognised as Indigenous anymore. And [on the other hand], when we demand that things be in accordance with our customs, beliefs, our ways of organisation, the system doesn't accept it, it doesn't allow it because it doesn't recognise it, and so I ask: does it not recognise it or does it in fact not want to and wants to exclude Indigenous peoples more and more?[16]

A similar point is made by historian Edson Kayapó (2018):

> So this girl said to me: "oh, you're not Indigenous because you wear trainers, you wear trousers, you wear a shirt", and I responded that it's a very violent type of racism, I responded calmly, saying: "look, I think the colonisers need to have a congress, an international conference, to decide whether Indigenous people can wear clothes or not, because when you arrived here in the 18th Century you enforced strict laws against the nudity of the native population, laws that criminalised nudity, and now you want to demand that we Indigenous people walk around naked."[17]

Indeed, the belief that Indigenous peoples cannot dress in Western clothes, consume Western products or engage in Western technology is based on a racist paradox: Indigenous peoples are constantly pressurised to "modernise", for if they refuse to do it they are labelled as backward or savages, and at the same time they are accused of being "non-indians" when they do adopt some facilities from the Western way of life. Indigeneity, according to this view, is a fossilised, unchangeable attribute, defined according to ideas held by the non-Indigenous of what "Indigenous" should be – in other words, "primitive", tied to the past, and unable to deal with modern tools. It is also something that can only be lost, never changed or re-gained. If, as both Yxapyry and Kayapó said, following Indigenous traditions is not acceptable by Brazilian society, and adopting certain non-Western ways of life is also not acceptable (non-Indigenous), the only possible future for any Indigenous person, according to this view, would to stop being Indigenous altogether. Innocent as they may appear to those who make it, these comments are actually extremely violent in their denial of the possibility of Indigenous identity. Even more so because, besides being used every day on the streets, these comments are also made by politicians or the media. Very recently, for example in a response to the Amazon fires that have gathered international attention, right-wing congresswoman and supporter of president Jair Bolsonaro, Joyce Hasselmann alerted to the need to "distinguish the real Indigenous communities from the Indians driving Hilux and wearing Nikes and Rolex watches"[18] – clearly insinuating that any Indigenous person driving such cars or wearing such objects were not "real Indians". But such prejudices are not exclusive to the right: in 2014, when Indigenous peoples were protesting against the World Cup in Rio, the well-known leftist actor José de Abreu made ironic comments on Twitter about "Indians wearing Nikes", followed by laughing expletives – the clear implication being that if they were wearing Nike shoes they were not "Indians".[19]

Through their large size (2 m × 1.60 m), their vivid colours, and the striking beauty and youth of the men and woman portrayed – all of them characterised by traits traditionally associated with indigeneity (reddish skin, straight dark hair, traditional Indigenous attire, body painting and decoration) – and by the ease and natural way in which they manipulate the technological devices,

Baniwa's paintings celebrate indigeneity in the present, contradicting the much-repeated – and racist – belief that indigeneity and modern contraptions are mutually exclusive.

Another expression of racism against Indigenous peoples that is touched upon by both Esbell and Baniwa is religious conversion. Christian conversion was one of the pillars of colonisation of the Americas, and continues to play a major factor in the destruction of Indigenous cultures in Brazil.[20] Defenders of religious conversion will say that conversion itself is not illegal, although the presence of missionaries in Indigenous reservations has been subject to rules, which have been relaxed under recent governments. Conversion has often been accompanied by violent methods of persuasion, such as the forced burning of sacred artefacts and changes in ways of living.[21] Conversion is usually governed, in any case, by power imbalance between well-financed missionaries with goods to give in exchange for changes in habits, and it always implies, necessarily, a disrespect for the other's religion, and the idea that only one form of religion is true. As Eunice Kerexu Yxapyry (2018) says:

> Of all the colonisers that came here, the only ones that we didn't resist were the Jesuits, because they came in the name of "God", but they told the Europeans who arrived here that the Indigenous people didn't have a king, didn't have souls, didn't have law, that is to say: "they are nobody".[22]

For Ruivaldo Valdenilson Neizinho Gavião (2018), conversion is a major expression of racism from settlers against Amerindian populations, and one of the most efficient vectors of cultural destruction in current times:

> So, how is it that a shaman, who brought us our existence, who shared all the cures, primarily the spiritual cures, who also elevated us to arrive at this point we are in this society, could be discarded in this way by a pastor saying that he is evil? If he were evil, we wouldn't be here and he would have killed everyone. In truth, there is a paradox between religion and our culture. Religion is killing our culture through preaching, permeation, coercion. I'm sad because our society is a society of struggle, of dispute, of battle and of strengthening, but above all of resistance. And this isn't a resistance. Everyone is succumbing to this question of religious principles.[23]

In his exhibition of black-and-white drawings titled in English "It was Amazon" Esbell presents a list of problems facing the Amazon today. The list has a didactic purpose: as the English title indicates, it was put together in order to educate foreign audiences about the problems faced by the Amazon forest. Each work focuses on a specific problem: deforestation, alcoholism, land grabbing, killing of animals, mercury-poisoning, etc. One of the issues included is religious conversion, which is depicted through two stick-like human figures that characterise many of Esbell's works.[24] One of them bears a cross around his neck and holds a bible (titled "Bible", in English) in one hand and a maraca in the other. The position of his arms seem to indicate that he is removing the maraca whilst brandishing the bible onto the other figure, who appears knelt or cowed into a position of submission. The process being depicted is the familiar discrediting of shamans and of Indigenous spirituality more generally.

Baniwa's "Fede In dio" (Figure 11.4) is a visual poem about the history of religious conversion and colonisation.

On the middle of the page/screen a cross bears the expression "in dio" written from top to bottom. The upper part of the cross is black, with the word "in" written in red. The bottom of the cross is red, with the word "dio" written in black. Below the cross, a wide band, also red, serves as a base for the cross. Although "fede" is not written on the cross itself, it appears clearly as a title that identifies the piece in the internet (not reproduced here), and on

Figure 11.4 Denilson Baniwa, "Fede In dio" (Digital art, 2019). A colour version of this artwork can be found on www.behance.net/gallery/77246215/Fede-In-Dio. Accessed on February 17. Copyright: Denilson Baniwa.

an extra text that accompanies the piece. "Fede in dio" is Italian for "Faith in God", but it includes, as we can see on the cross, the homophone "índio" [Indian in Portuguese]. So, the expression could also be heard as "fé de índio" [Indian faith]. In addition, "fede" is homonym for some conjugations of the verb "feder" [stink in Portuguese: he/she/it stinks]. Thus, the expression "faith in god" is playfully transformed into "Indian faith" as well as "you, Indian, stink", or "Indian stinks".

Visually, the cross' transformation from black to red, with the red continuing onto the base and forming a thick layer at the bottom, strongly suggests the idea of bleeding – an idea also linked, of course, to Christian doctrine and iconography. In this case, however, the word "índio" links the bleeding cross to the sacrifice of Indigenous people: that is, the cross (Christian faith) causes the bleeding of the Indigenous peoples. This reading is supported by the text that accompanies the poem in the internet: "Fede in Dio / and for your sins they took us (to) the cross".[25] The use of "a/à" ("the/to the") equates conversion ("levar a cruz" or "bring the cross to") to crucifixion ("levar à cruz", or "crucify"). The text also creates a dichotomy between "your sins" and "us", that is, between Christ (and/or Christians) and the Indigenous peoples, from whose position the text is enunciated. Thus, instead of the cross representing, as in the Christian doctrine, Christ's sacrifice for the sins of humanity, it is the Indigenous peoples who are sacrificed (crucified) for the sake of Christ/Christian's sins. It is important to note, as well, that the Italian language provides the pun that serves as the base for the poem, but it was also an important language of conversion, as many Catholic orders that were active in the Amazon in the 1800s and throughout the 1900s were Italian, including the Salesians, whose devastating effects for the Baniwa people was well documented by Wright (1981).

The piece's poetics is based on various degrees of mis-understandings: mis-hearings, mis-interpreting, mis-translations. These misunderstandings give the poem its humorous tone whilst replicating common experiences of colonisation – the misunderstanding, mishearing and misinterpreting of concepts, languages, and ways of living that happen during colonial encounters, as well as the violent imposition of certain meanings over others (the imposition, for example of "fede in dio" over Indigenous beliefs, or "fé de índio"). At the centre of the poem is the unpicking or uncovering of those meanings that have been hidden by the process of (on-going) colonisation: for the original inhabitants of Brazil, "faith in god" actually means "fede índio", that is, the racist disparaging of Indigenous peoples' own faith. As we can see, the poem is a remarkably condensed analysis of the links between Christian conversion and colonialism/coloniality, and their effect on Indigenous cultures.

Finally, another expression of racism that is described by the artists is the objectification of Indigenous peoples, a practice with a long trajectory that traces back to the exhibition of Indigenous persons in Europe in the sixteenth century, and which by the early twentieth century had become scientific norm, with the exhibition of Indigenous objects and sometimes even human mummies

Figure 11.5 Denilson Baniwa, "Voyeurs" (Digital collage, 2019). A colour version of this artwork can be found on www.instagram.com/p/Bu6xeeKgq0Z/. Accessed on February 17, 2020. Copyright: Denilson Baniwa.

in museums. Baniwa's digital collage "Voyeurs" (Figure 11.5) is based on an illustration titled "Puri shacks" [*As Cabanas dos Puris*], from Prince Maximilian of Wied-Neuwied's volume *Journey to Brazil in the years 1815–1817*.

On the original illustration we can see an Indigenous man lying on a hammock, observing a woman playing with a child on the floor. Baniwa modified the image by adding, on the foreground, a group of contemporary non-Indigenous onlookers who are photographing the family as if they were a tourist attraction. All the onlookers have their backs to the viewers, except for a woman on the lower left who faces the viewers with a finger on her lip. The bright colours of the current onlookers contrast with the faded monochrome of the Indigenous peoples, in an obvious, humorous anachronism that points to a common (still popular) Western belief, supported by nineteenth-century science, that Indigenous peoples "live in the past", or represent the "infancy of civilisation". Our view of the Indigenous family is thus mediated by the non-Indigenous observers, or voyeurs, as the title of the collage describes them. Moreover, the finger-on-the lip gesture targeted at the viewers brings them into the picture as participants in voyeuristic experience. If nineteenth-century travel illustrations objectified Indigenous peoples (paving the way to their destruction), Baniwa's collage links the practice with today's ongoing exoticisation of their bodies and cultures. In a private conversation that happened during the event "Racism and anti-Racism in Brazil", in Salvador, Bahia, in October 2018, activist and educator Célia Xakriabá told me that racism against Indigenous peoples happens in unexpected ways, for example when people stopped her on the streets in Brazilian cities (particularly when she was wearing body paint and traditional attire) to ask her if "she was a real Indian". "They often stroke me, touch me, it is really violent, but they do not see it as such" (Xakriabá 2018), she said. Sure enough, as we left the restaurant she was approached by a woman asking her is she was an "índia de verdade" (real Indigenous person) whilst touching her in the arm.

Baniwa's and Esbell's art also criticises the objectification of Indigenous culture by museums and knowledge institutions. In the video art performance called "Etnografia",[26] exhibited online as part of the project "At the time of the huacas" [No tempo das huacas],[27] Baniwa, dressed in loin cloth and naked torso, sits in a shamanic position slowly shaking a maraca in his hand. But soon he gradually stops playing the maraca, appearing disturbed as a box-like transparent structure is placed around him. An un-identified woman covers him in red liquid resembling blood, which makes him appear cold and profoundly uncomfortable, and finally, red-stained pages (resembling the folios of an academic thesis) are thrown over him. The video installation is an allegory of the "mummification" of Indigenous knowledge and Indigenous bodies by museums and universities. The deposition of thesis pages at the end the of performance links current institutional methods to prior colonial and early nineteenth-century practices of actually capturing and/or exhibiting human beings. In other words, for Baniwa, the act of capturing and exhibiting Indigenous persons finds continuity in the academic practice of appropriating and re-categorising (boxing in) Indigenous knowledge, a knowledge which is then returned to the Indigenous peoples in the form of (in their view) dead or useless theses or dissertations. The red stains on the pages of the dissertations highlights the violence of imbedded in this process.[28]

Esbell's contribution to the same project is a video installation that focuses on his hand holding an archaeological Indigenous stone axe from a museum window.[29] The hand massages and feels the axe, showing it to the camera. Then, slowly, drops of blood (presumably coming from the hand) start staining the axe and fall onto the window. The video installation is a critique of Western museum practices regarding Indigenous objects and, we would suggest, it is made more powerful by the fact that it is authored by a contemporary Indigenous artist. In other words, the drops of blood that stain the axe and the window serve as an allegory for the Indigenous persons who died and whose cultures were destroyed so that the West could appropriate their territories, collect their artefacts and take their knowledge. But they also represent the suffering of present Amerindians, caused by the destruction and appropriation of their ancestors and their memories.

Perhaps more than any other type of criminal offence in Brazil, racism lies in the threshold between legality and illegality: it has become illegal and supposedly subject to heavy punishment, but is rarely taken seriously; it is experienced and discussed everyday by countless victims, yet denied by perpetrators and by a judicial system that for the most part, refuses to see it. In the case of Amerindians, racism has been made even more invisible, partly because specialised literature has traditionally avoided to discuss violence against Indigenous peoples as racism, and partly because, thanks to the strength of structural racism against them, the Indigenous peoples themselves are made invisible and have their very existence denied by official powers and society at large. Repeating Paul Klee's famous dictum, Baniwa's and Esbell's art make the invisible visible, by showing us how racism permeates Brazilian society's treatment of Indigenous peoples in different ways. Not only is racism seen in the violent way that land grabbers and farmers threaten and kill Indigenous persons with increasing violence, treating them as non-human, but also in the way that Indigenous persons are exoticised through stereotypes, objectified, robbed of their knowledge and beliefs, and, ultimately denied even the right to identify and exist as Indigenous persons.

Notes

1 "(…) os brasileiros se olham nos espelhos americanos, sul-africanos e nazistas e se percebem sem nenhuma mácula ao invés de se olharem em seu próprio espelho". Talk given at Universidade Federal do Recôncavo da Bahia on May 14, 2018. The talk was part of the events related to the AHRC/GCRF Network "Racism and anti-racism in Brazil: the case of indigenous peoples". The talks are currently being prepared for publication. All translations are by the authors unless otherwise stated.

2 For an in-depth study on how opponents of racial quotas built on the "master narrative" of "racial democracy", see Wink (2018).

3 Including official classifications in census and by children registration officials. Gamella (2018), for instance, relates cases of officials refusing to register Amerindian children as "indigenous" (indígena), and registering them, instead, as "pardas".

4 A recent exception is the dossier "Racismo no Plural", edited by McCallum, Restrepo and Reesink (2017). Anibal Quijano (2000), as well as Mignolo and Walsh (2018), amongst other theorists of "decoloniality", have also elaborated on the importance of the concept of "race" for the establishment of the colonial enterprise and subsequent "coloniality of power" in Latin America.

5 Needless to say, we are referring here only to racist verbal tirades. The brutally racist treatment of Afro-descendants by Rio de Janeiro's militarised police under current governor Wilson Witzel is but one example of open racism against the black populations in Brazil, a topic that falls beyond the remit of this chapter.

6 "Índio antropizado, semi antropizado e não antropizado" https://racismoambiental.net.br/2019/03/29/apos-semanas-de-protestos-crescentes-por-todo-o-pais-movimento-indigena-vence-e-ministro-da-saude-mantem-sesai. Accessed on November 2, 2019.

7 This publicity campaign appeared in a video intervention by artist Denilson Baniwa on his Facebook page: www.facebook.com/dbaniwa/videos/vb.100001521988438/2384303654963677/?type=2&video_source=user_video_tab. Accessed on November 2, 2019.

8 The AHRC/GCRF Network "Racism and anti-racism in Brazil: the case of indigenous peoples" organised two meetings in Bahia. The first meeting happened in May 2018 in Cachoeira, Bahia, and the second in October 2018 in Salvador, Bahia. For more information on the project, the events, and the complete interviews, see http://projects.alc.manchester.ac.uk/racism-indigenous-brazil/pt/pagina-inicial. Accessed on November 2, 2019.

9 An image of the painting, titled Marçal Tupã, can be found on www.behance.net/gallery/ 57544877/Marcal-Tupay. Accessed on November 2, 2019.

10 An image of the painting, titled Xicão Xucuru, can be found on www.behance.net/gallery/ 57544687/Xicao-Xucuru. Accessed on November 2, 2019.

11 "O racismo hoje em dia se expressa de forma muito naturalizada, como se já fizesse parte do dia-a-dia das pessoas, que mesmo quando querem elogiar, às vezes ofendem".

12 A reproduction of this work can be found on the following article: https://g1.globo.com/sp/sao-paulo/noticia/2019/04/19/indigenas-lancam-campanha-contra-estereotipos-para-o-dia-do-indio-nao-precisamos-de-outras-pessoas-para-nos-definirem.ghtml. Accessed on November 2, 2019.

13

> Pai Nosso que estás nos céus / Neste dia 19 de abril / Nos livre das professores e professores que pintam seus alunos com canetinhas hidrocor / Nos livre das escolas que colocam cocares de papel nas crianças / Pai Nosso, que estás nos céus / Não deixe as professoras ensinarem para as crianças que o Dia do Índio é uma homenagem aos povos originários / Mantenha longe de Nós aqueles que repetem as palavras: / Índio, Oca, Tribo, Selvagem, Pureza e Exótico / Afaste de Nós os bu-bu-bu feito com a mão na boca / Senhor, perdõem aqueles que por desconhecimento nos fazem uma imagem estereotipada / Mas livre-os do desconhecimento e do preconceito que os fazem acreditar que ainda somos os indígenas de 1500 / Amém!

14 A reproduction of this work can be found on www.instagram.com/p/B2D1elmHWT4. Accessed on November 2, 2019.

15 A reproduction of this work can be found on www.instagram.com/p/B13KqD-H7UV. Accessed on November 2, 2019.

16

> Primeiro quando você quer ter algumas estruturas, alguns instrumentos, alguns veículos que são dessa sociedade nessa evolução que a gente está vivendo hoje, a negação do direito vem que se a gente tem isso, a gente deixa de ser indígena, a gente não é reconhecido como indígena. E quando a gente exige que isso seja então de acordo com nossos costumes, crenças, nosso modos de ser, o sistema não aceita, não permite porque não conhece isso. E aí eu pergunto, não conhece ou não quer de fato executar e quer cada vez mais excluir os povos indígenas?

17

> Uma moça me falou assim "olha você não é indígena, porque você usa tênis, você usa calça, você usa camis", e eu respondi para ela (um racismo muito violento), e eu respondi tranquilamente para ela: "moça, eu acho que os colonizadores têm que fazer um congresso, uma conferência internacional para decidir se o indígena pode ou não usar roupa. Porque quando vocês chegaram aqui, no século XVIII, vocês impuseram leis severas contra a nudez dos povos originários, e criaram leis que criminalizam a nudez, e agora estão querendo cobrar que nós indígenas andemos nus".

18 www.acritica.com/channels/manaus/news/amazonia-nao-esta-em-chamas-diz-joice-hasselmann-apos-sobrevoo-a-680-km-de-focos-de-incendio-no-am. Accessed on November 2, 2019.
19 See article: http://imediata.org/margem/quem-e-indio. Accessed on November 2, 2019.
20 For an excellent study of Christian presence in the Amazon, see Villaça (2016).
21 See, for example, Wright (1981).
22

> De todos que chegaram, os colonizadores que chegaram aqui, os únicos que a gente não teve essa resistência foram os jesuítas, porque eles vieram em nome de "Deus". Mas, eles falaram para europeus que chegaram aqui que os indígenas não tinham rei, não tinham alma, não tinham lei, isso quer dizer, não são ninguém.

23

> (...) Como, se um pajé que trouxe a nossa vivência, que compartilhou de todas as curas, pincipalmente a espiritual, que nos elevou a chegar a essa sociedade também, ele pode ser descartado dessa forma por um pastor dizendo que ele é uma pessoa do mal? Se fosse do mal nós não estariamos aqui: ele teria matado todo mundo. Na verdade é um paradoxo entre a religião e a nossa cultura. Mas a religião está matando a nossa cultura através da pregação, da impregnação, da coerção. E eu fico triste porque a nossa sociedade é uma sociedade de luta, de briga, de batalha e de fortalecimento, mas acima de tudo de resistência. E isso não está sendo uma resistência. Todos estão sucumbindo a essa questão de princípios religiosos, de doutrinas religiosas.

24 The image can be seen at www.jaideresbell.com.br/site/2016/07/01/it-was-amazon. Accessed on November 2, 2019.
25 "Fede In Dio: e por teus pecados nos levaram a/à cruz."
26 The performance can be seen on www.behance.net/gallery/77655767/Etnografia. Accessed on November 2, 2019.
27 "No tempo das huacas" is a joint project led by Filipa Cordeiro and Ruy Mourão at the Archaeologic Museum of Carmo, in Lisbon, to debate the Museum's exhibition of two Chankay mummies. The project brings together several artists, many of them indigenous. https://sites.google.com/view/otempodashuacas. Accessed on November 2, 2019.
28 The discussions with indigenous university students that took place during the second event of the project "Racism and Anti-Racism in Brazil: The Case of Indigenous Peoples", on October 31, 2018, at the Federal University of Bahia in Salvador, repeatedly highlighted this point. For the indigenous students and scholars that were present at the event, the appropriation of indigenous knowledge by universities in the form of theses and dissertations that do not properly credit or recognise indigenous knowledge is profoundly racist.
29 See https://sites.google.com/view/otempodashuacas/sobre/videos. Accessed on November 2, 2019.

References

Barbosa, Fabio Feliciano. "O caso Simone A. Diniz: A falta de acesso à justiça para as vítimas dos crimes raciais da Lei Caó." *Revista de Estudos Jurídicos* 15, no. 22 (2011): 119–146.

Fredrickson, George. *Racism: A Short History.* Princeton: Princeton University Press, 2002.

Gamella, Kum Tum Akroa. Untitled talk at event "Racism and Anti-Racism in Brazil: The Case of Indigenous Peoples" in Cachoeira, BA, on May 14, 2018. The talk is currently being prepared for publication.

Gavião, Ruivaldo Valdenilson Neizinho. Interview with Alexandre Pankararu and Graciela Guarani on May 14, 2018. http://projects.alc.manchester.ac.uk/racism-indigenous-brazil/outputs. Accessed on November 2, 2019.

Guajajara, Sonia. Interview with Alexandre Pankararu and Graciela Guarani on October 30, 2018. http://projects.alc.manchester.ac.uk/racism-indigenous-brazil/outputs. Accessed on November 2, 2019.

Kayapó, Edson. Interview with Alexandre Pankararu and Graciela Guarani on October 30, 2018. http://projects.alc.manchester.ac.uk/racism-indigenous-brazil/outputs. Accessed on November 2, 2019.

McCallum, Cecilia, Eduardo Restrepo, and Edwin B. Reesink. "Racismo no Plural nas Américas: Povos Indígenas e Afro-Indígenas." *Revista Anthropológicas* 21, vol. 28 (2), 2017: 1–139.

Mignolo, Walter D., and Catherine E. Walsh. *On Decoloniality: Concepts, Analytics, Praxis.* Durham, NC: Duke University Press, 2018.

Munanga, Kabengele. Untitled talk at event "Racism and Anti-Racism in Brazil: The Case of Indigenous Peoples" in Cachoeira, BA, on May 14, 2018. The talk is currently being prepared for publication.

Quijano, Anibal. "Coloniality of Power, Eurocentrism, and Latin America." *Nepantla: Views from South* 1, no. 3 (2000): 533–580.

Rodrigues, Fernando. "Racismo cordial." In *Racismo cordial – a mais completa análise sobre o preconceito de cor no Brasil, Folha de São Paulo/Datafolha*, edited by Cleusa Turra and Gustavo Venturi, 11–55. São Paulo: Ática, 1995.

Santos, Gislene Aparecida dos. "Nem crime, nem castigo: o racismo na percepção do judiciário e das vítimas de atos de discriminação." *Revista do Instituto de Estudos Brasileiros* 62 (December 2015): 184–207.

Silva, Cesar Augusto. "O Estado brasileiro e o racismo contra os afrodescendentes: Questões jurídicas." *Revista Videre* 7, no. 4 (January–June 2012): 96–114.

Tukano, Daiara Figueroa. Interview with Alexandre Pankararu and Graciela Guarani on May 14, 2018. http://projects.alc.manchester.ac.uk/racism-indigenous-brazil/outputs. Accessed on November 2, 2019.

Villaça, Aparecida. *Praying and Preying: Christianity in Indigenous Amazonia.* Oakland: University of California Press, 2016.

Wade, Peter. *Race and Ethnicity in Latin America.* London: Pluto Press, 1997.

Wink, Georg. "'Looking for More Brazilian solutions': Rhetorical Strategies against Racial Quotas in Brazilian Higher Education." *Brasiliana – Journal for Brazilian Studies* 6, no. 2 (2018): 3–41.

Wright, Robin. "History and Religion of the Baniwa Peoples of the Upper Rio Negro Valley", PhD diss., Stanford University, 1981.

Xakriabá, Celia. Personal conversation with Lúcia Sá on October 31, 2018 in Salvador, Bahia.

Yxapyry, Eunice Keruxu. Interview with Alexandre Pankararu and Graciela Guarani on October 30, 2018. http://projects.alc.manchester.ac.uk/racism-indigenous-brazil/outputs. Accessed on November 2, 2019.

Index

Note: Page numbers in *italics* indicate figures on the corresponding pages.